Critical Essays on Günter Grass

Critical Essays on
World Literature

Robert Lecker, General Editor
McGill University

Critical Essays on Günter Grass

Patrick O'Neill

G. K. Hall & Co. • Boston, Massachusetts

Library of Congress Cataloging in Publication Data

Critical essays on Günter Grass.

  (Critical essays on world literature)
  Includes index.
  1. Grass, Günter, 1927- — Criticism and interpretation.
I. O'Neill, Patrick, 1945-
II. Series.
PT2613.R338Z597 1987   838'.91409   86-19411
ISBN 0-8161-8830-0

This publication is printed on permanent/durable acid-free paper
MANUFACTURED IN THE UNITED STATES OF AMERICA

CONTENTS

INTRODUCTION

The year 1959 was something of an annus mirabilis in modern German literary history. After nearly a decade and a half of gloomy prognostications that German literature might still take further decades or even centuries to recover from the near-fatal frost of the Third Reich, a single year saw the appearance of what were quite clearly three major novels, Heinrich Böll's *Billiards at Half Past Nine*, Uwe Johnson's *Speculations about Jacob*, and Günter Grass's *The Tin Drum*. All three raised uncomfortable questions about the very comfortable West German present in the light of a recent history many readers would have preferred to forget — Johnson about the sensitive relationship between East and West, Böll and Grass about the even more sensitive relationship between a rapidly increasing postwar prosperity and the horrors of the Nazi past. All three novels were marked by formal intricacy, but while Böll's and Johnson's texts seemed to most readers to operate on a level of sobriety appropriate to the serious task of questioning the national system of values, Grass's Oskar, the tin-drumming, glass-shattering, blasphemous, apparently lunatic midget who served as the first-person narrator of *Die Blechtrommel* (*The Tin Drum*), seemed to many to be an outrageous, calculated insult to common decency, Christianity, and the German heritage, all of which were held up to the basest ridicule in a tour de force of perverted comedy. Günter Grass, in his manifestation as enfant terrible of German letters, had well and truly arrived.

With the clarity of vision afforded by more than a quarter century of hindsight, the uproar that accompanied Grass's first book now seems merely quaint. Much water has flowed under many bridges since then, our susceptibility to literary shock techniques has markedly decreased, and the enfant terrible of the very early sixties has become the international literary celebrity of the mid-eighties. In an age lavish with superlatives, Grass continues to attract a lavish share. As long ago as 1970 *Time* magazine featured Grass in a cover story as probably Germany's and possibly the world's greatest living novelist.[1] Twelve years later John Irving, writing in *Saturday Review*, felt justified in declaring *The Tin Drum* to be still unsurpassed as the greatest novel by a living author: "In

1

whatever category of reader you see yourself, you can't be called well-read today if you haven't read him. Günter Grass is simply the most original and versatile writer alive."[2] He is routinely seen as filling shoes left empty by Thomas Mann and/or Bertolt Brecht, and references are routinely dropped as to the inevitability of an eventual Nobel Prize. Not surprisingly, he is also the center of a bustling literary and critical industry, his work the subject of dozens of books and hundreds of papers and articles, reviews and interviews, news stories and gossip columns.

The object of this flood of attention — who, as well as being a novelist, is, almost incidentally, also a poet, painter, sculptor, stage designer, script writer, dramatist, gourmet cook, one-time jazz musician, and, when necessary, a practicing political orator and commentator — was born on 16 October, 1927, in the Free City of Danzig, now the Polish city of Gdańsk. His father was a grocer; his mother was of Slavic, Kashubian origins. "At fourteen I was a Hitler Youth; at sixteen a soldier; and at seventeen an American prisoner of war. These dates mean a great deal in an era that purposefully slaughtered one year's crop of young men, branded the next year's crop with guilt, and spared another. You can tell by my date of birth that I was too young to have been a Nazi, but old enough to have been moulded by a system, that, from 1933 to 1945, at first surprised, then horrified the world."[3] He left Danzig in 1944 as a German soldier, and after his release in 1946 from an American prisoner-of-war camp in Bavaria he worked in what had now become West Germany first as a farm laborer, then as a potash miner, an apprentice gravestone carver, a jazz musician in a Düsseldorf nightclub. By 1949 he was studying painting and sculpture at the Düsseldorf Academy of Art and writing his first poems. By 1953, after travels in Italy and France, he was enrolled in the Berlin School of Fine Arts; by 1954, he was married to Anna Schwarz, a Swiss ballet dancer, and writing his first plays. His public literary career was launched when he won third prize with a selection of his poems in a radio competition in 1955 and with it the right to attend meetings of what was by then the dominant literary circle of the country, the powerful Group 47, named after the year of its foundation. To quote *Time:* "It was a monumental encounter that must rank in literary legend with the day Hemingway first visited Gertrude Stein for tea."[4] Between 1956 and 1958 he held his first exhibitions of plastic and graphic art (in Stuttgart and Berlin), moved to Paris, fathered twins, traveled to Poland, saw the publication of his first book, a collection of poems called *Die Vorzüge der Windhühner* (1956; The Merits of Windfowl), and the first performances of his play *Hochwasser* (*Flood*), his ballet *Stoffreste* (Remnants), and a second play, *Onkel Onkel* (*Mister, Mister*).

Several further ballets, art exhibitions, another collection of poetry (*Gleisdreieck*, 1960; Triangle of Tracks), and two plays, *Noch zehn Minuten bis Buffalo* (1959, *Only Ten Minutes to Buffalo*) and *Die bösen Köche* (1961; *The Wicked Cooks*) followed over the next few years and were duly admired by the same small circle of connoisseurs as had applauded his earlier work. For the multitude in Germany for whom Grass's name would become a household word after 1959, however, these achievements were scarcely known; rather, Grass was the author of the sensational bestseller *Die Blechtrommel* (*The Tin Drum*), written during the years in Paris while he was ostensibly devoting his main efforts to painting and sculpture. In 1960 he moved back to Berlin, and the following year delighted, scandalized, and amazed the public a second time with another runaway bestseller, *Katz und Maus* (*Cat and Mouse*). And after another two-year pause he did it all over again, completing what has since come to be known as the "Danzig Trilogy" with yet another tour de force, the long and intricate novel *Hundejahre* (*Dog Years*).

If the years before 1959 can be seen as Grass's apprenticeship years, filled with formal experimentation in an impressive variety of media, the years between 1959 and 1963 are certainly his first great creative period. The early work had been detailed work, miniatures poised on a single stylistic or thematic point or cluster of points. The Danzig Trilogy exploded onto a huge panoramic canvas, analyzing German history over the past half century, exploring the social symptoms that heralded the massive sickness of National Socialism, reviewing the bestiality of the war years, probing the self-contented apathy of postwar affluence and finding the same symptoms all over again. The stunning cumulative effect of the trilogy, however, is and was less due to the epic sweep of its satiric undertaking than to the wholly unaccustomed raw power of the language, the imagery, and the narrative presentation. In a word, Grass's style seemed completely and startlingly *inappropriate* to the task of uncovering the hypocrisy and cant involved in the "ordinary" German's total rejection of any complicity in or responsibility for the horrors of the Third Reich. By no means all of his readers agreed that the task should have been undertaken in the first place, for surely some things were better forgotten altogether, and the gratuitous muck-raking of a publicity-hungry smut-monger was simply a contemptible exercise in making money out of the after all probably unavoidable mistakes of the war years. But even if the man did have less despicable intentions, what was one supposed to make of a narrator who was allegedly clairaudient at birth, claimed to be the son of two fathers at once (one German, one Polish), deliberately arrested his own further growth by flinging himself down the cellar stairs at the age of three, could smash glass at will with his piercing voice, and allegedly drummed the entire story on a tin drum while the inmate of a lunatic asylum? Or Mahlke, the hero of *Cat and Mouse*, attempting to compensate for his "monstrously" large Adam's apple by wearing screwdrivers around his neck and the Knight's Cross around his genitals, winning transient fame by his devotion to the Blessed Virgin, his invincibility in competitive masturbating, and his skill as a swimmer and destroyer of Russian tanks; and apparently drowned at the end by his greatest admirer, the narrator, who seemed surprisingly vague on a number of key points? Or *Dog Years,* where the hero (whose name is either Amsel or Brauksel or Brauchsel or Brauxel or Brooks — or possibly Goldmouth) constructs brigades of Nazi scarecrows, where one thin little girl decides she is a dog and goes to live in a kennel, and another fat little girl is beaten up and left to thaw inside a snowman, whence she emerges as a slim and talented ballet dancer, where a postwar crusader against Nazi war criminals wreaks terrible vengeance by (pleasurably) infecting their daughters with gonorrhea? Was any of this to be taken seriously, and, if so, what should be done about it? Opinions differed. In 1958 Grass was awarded a prepublication literary prize by Group 47. In 1959 he was awarded another major literary prize by a panel of critics in the north German city of Bremen, only to have the Bremen city government promptly refuse to present him with the award. He received the Berlin Critics' Prize in 1960, the French *Prix pour le meilleur livre étranger* in 1962, and was elected a member of the German Academy of Arts in 1963. In 1965 he received the prestigious Georg Büchner Prize, and in the same year *The Tin Drum* was publicly burned in Düsseldorf by a religious youth organization. By that time he was also the defendant in some forty legal actions which had been launched against *The Tin Drum* and *Cat and Mouse* — none of them was successful. Sales in Germany were in the hundreds of thousands, and sales in translation were booming. *The Tin Drum,* for example, had been translated into Norwegian in 1960, into English, Danish, Finnish, French, and Swedish in 1961, into Serbo-Croatian and Spanish in 1963, into Dutch and Portuguese in 1964, into Italian in 1965. It would later be translated into Japanese (1967), Slovenian (1968), Czech, and Roumanian (1969) as well.[5]

The year 1965 also brought a transatlantic distinction for the thirty-eight-year-old Grass: an honorary doctorate from Kenyon College in Gambier, Ohio. The trilogy reached North American readers in Ralph Manheim's translations over a more concentrated period of time than had been the case in Germany, *The Tin Drum* appearing in the United States in February 1963 (though carrying a 1961 copyright date), *Cat and Mouse* only six months later in August 1963, and *Dog Years* in May 1965. They arrived preceded by their European reputation, and *The Tin Drum* in particular unleashed a flood of reviews. Though opinions were by no means undivided, North American readers were obviously less likely to be upset by the historical and political implications of the three books than their German counterparts had been, and the general reaction of the reviewers was that it was a very good thing that at long last a German author was forcing German readers to come to grips, however uncomfortably, with the still unresolved national past. As to the style, *The Tin Drum* was variously declared to be fantastic, romantic, expressionist, surreal, grotesque, absurd, realistic, and/or naturalistic, and to have more or less marked affinities with the work of Dante, Rabelais, Grimmelshausen, Bunyan, Swift, Sterne, Voltaire, Goethe, Melville, Proust, Thomas Mann, Joyce, Beckett, Faulkner, Camus, Dos Passos, Kafka, Döblin, Brecht, Böll, Johnson, Ionesco, Nabokov, and/or Heller.[6] *The Tin Drum* was on the *New York Times* list of bestsellers for three months and sold some 400,000 copies in its first year, thus largely guaranteeing the instant success of *Cat and Mouse* and *Dog Years* as well. There was some disappointment expressed that *Cat and Mouse* was such a slim volume; this deficiency was more than made up for by the imposing bulk of *Dog Years*, which was praised as taking up the Danzig saga again along the lines laid down in *The Tin Drum*. This reaction was to become a recurrent one both in Germany and in North America over the next decade or so, each novel in turn, for all the praise that might also be lavished on it, being greeted with faint disappointment that Grass had not chosen to rewrite *The Tin Drum* all over again.

Grass, meanwhile, was showing no signs of resting on his drummer's laurels, and was already well into what the critics call his third period, the period of overt political activity. As early as 1961 he had spoken out publicly on behalf of the SPD, the Social Democratic Party of Germany led by his friend Willy Brandt, which was campaigning against the CDU/CSU, the Christian Democratic Union and Christian Social Union of Konrad Adenauer, now Chancellor since 1949. Brandt's 1961 campaign was unsuccessful, the small Free Democratic Party (FDP) swinging the balance of power towards the CDU/CSU. Adenauer resigned and was succeeded as Chancellor by Ludwig Erhard in 1963. Under Adenauer's fourteen-year chancellorship the country had made an astonishing economic recovery after the devastation of German cities and industries during the war. The so-called *Wirtschaftswunder* or 'economic miracle,' however, had gone hand in hand with a cold war policy of confrontation towards the Warsaw Pact bloc and a determined refusal to recognize the legitimacy of the East German regime. Brandt's SPD, a party of moderate reform, advocated recognition of the de facto existence of East Germany as a separate state, the abandoning of the notion of German reunification, the improvement of relations with communist countries, and the strengthening of the European Economic Community. Grass campaigned vigorously on behalf of Brandt and the SPD during the next electoral campaign, in 1965, traveling throughout the country and holding speeches on more than fifty separate occasions. The campaign was again unsuccessful, but the following year saw the withdrawal of the FDP from their coalition with the CDU/CSU, the resignation of Ludwig Erhard, and the formation of the so-called Great Coalition between the CDU/CSU and the SPD, with Kurt Kiesinger as Chancellor. Three years later another electoral campaign saw Grass on the road again, driving thousands of miles through West Germany in a Volkswagen bus over the seven months of his campaign activity, giving campaign speeches on more than ninety separate occasions. This time the SPD was at last successful and was able to take power in coalition with the FDP, Willy Brandt succeeding Kiesinger as Chancellor. One of his earliest symbolic gestures of reconciliation towards Eastern Europe was his historic trip to Poland in 1970, in the course of which he laid a commemorative wreath on the site of the Warsaw ghetto. Grass, appropriately, accompanied Brandt on this journey of reconciliation.

One might justifiably expect his literary output to have slackened off somewhat during these years. The data speak for themselves, however. *Goldmäulchen* (Goldmouth), a ballet based on an episode in *Dog Years*, was first performed in Munich in 1964. A revised version of the play *Onkel, Onkel* (*Mister, Mister*) appeared in 1965. His fifth and most ambitious play, *Die Plebejer proben den Aufstand* (*The Plebeians Rehearse the Uprising*) was produced at the Schillertheater in Berlin in 1966 and appeared in book form the same year. A third volume of poems, *Ausgefragt* (Interrogated), followed in 1967, three volumes of political speeches and writings and one volume of literary essays in 1968. The play *Davor* (*Max*) appeared on stage and in print in 1969, which year also saw the publication of his fourth novel, *Örtlich betäubt* (*Local Anaesthetic*). Another ballet, *Die Vogelscheuchen* (The Scarecrows), based on another episode in *Dog Years*, was first performed at the Deutsche Oper in Berlin in 1970. The year 1970 also saw the publication of his collected plays (*Theaterspiele*), and the following year that of his collected poems (*Gesammelte Gedichte*). All of these, with the exception of *The Plebeians*, *Davor*, and *Local Anaesthetic*, however, are relatively slight pieces of work, and *Davor* is essentially a dramatized version of the central conflict of *Local Anaesthetic*. All three of these latter pieces reflect Grass's political activism of these years in being overtly political in theme. Unlike the Danzig trilogy, they move away from both the Nazi past and the Danzig locale which had served as Grass's trademark, and are centered firmly on the here-and-now of contemporary West German reality. More specifically, *The Plebeians* is set in East Berlin, on 17 June 1953, in Bertolt Brecht's theater. While outside the theater the East German workers rise (as they in fact did on that day) in revolt against oppressive government labor norms, inside the famous dramatist rehearses his adaptation of Shakespeare's *Coriolanus*. When the workers send a delegation to ask Brecht to support their cause he fails to respond—and in so failing becomes guilty of betraying both the workers and himself. *Davor* and *Local Anaesthetic* both focus on the threatened sacrificial burning of a dachshund by an idealistic student in Berlin (West), who hopes in doing so to force the apathetic into appreciating the reality of the American napalming of Vietnam and the fact that they can, if they wish, speak out against it. The center of attention, however, is less the radicalized student than his harried, middle-aged, middle-of-the-road teacher, a martyr to toothache, who musters what liberal thought he can to persuade the student that radical action is never as useful in the long run as reasoned, legal, democratic action.

Even on the basis of such skeletal plot summaries as these it is immediately apparent that the Grass of the later sixties is a very different writer from the Grass of the early sixties. There is little of the old Rabelaisian gusto here, the grotesque characters, the absurd detail, the expansive delight in language. There are no drumming midgets or thirty-two-legged dogs (the latter example of Grassean fauna inhabiting the final pages of *Dog Years*). Rather, in both *The Plebeians* and *Local Anaesthetic* there is a severe clarity, an overall discipline and economy of expression that is something quite new — Grass had already shown in *Cat and Mouse* that he could write a masterly piece of short fiction, but there the diction and expression still had the flamboyance, what reviewers liked to call the baroque luxuriance of *The Tin Drum*. *The Plebeians* is composed in dignified, restrained, quasi-Shakespearean verse; *Local Anaesthetic*, though it retains enough of the early Grass to inspire the blurb writers of the American paperback edition to call it sprawling, rowdy, wildly imaginative, and the like, was greeted in Germany with general disappointment. Critics suggested none too kindly that Grass had written a political tract praising the merits of an SPD-inspired moderate reformism within the rule of law, the resignation of the anaesthetized middle-aged pedagogue carrying the day over the selfless commitment of the radical schoolboy. It was, in fact, especially the radical young, who had seen Oskar as an emblem of anarchic disruption, who now turned away disgustedly from what they perceived as the neorationalist dogmatic moralism of *Local Anaesthetic*. Both *The Plebeians* and *Local Anaesthetic* dealt with the central problem of how one should behave responsibly in a world filled with pain. The apparent solution proffered, that we should anaesthetize ourselves against the pain we cannot alter in order to devote ourselves more efficiently to combating the pain we may have some control over, was too downbeat, too depressive, too little "wildly imaginative" to generate enthusiastic applause in the Germany of the late sixties.

Ralph Manheim's translation of *The Plebeians Rehearse the Uprising* appeared in English in 1966, but was not staged in North America until 1968. In both forms it met with only a lukewarm response, and for many reviewers it was flattened into a personal attack on Brecht by his ungrateful pupil Grass. The play fared better in Britain, but not until 1970, when it was presented to critical acclaim by the Royal Shakespeare Company and declared by the *Observer* to be "the richest, most complex and sardonic play to come out of Germany in the past decade."[7] *Local Anaesthetic*, on the other hand, fared very well indeed in the USA, and in a sense set the capstone on Grass's North American reputation. Its appearance in early 1970 was greeted enthusiastically in the major reviewing organs, the seal of approval being publicly conferred and confirmed when, as already mentioned, *Time* ran a cover story on

Grass (the only German author so far ever to appear on *Time*'s cover), saluting the forty-two-year-old author as possibly the world's greatest living novelist.

Grass continued his political involvement throughout the seventies, campaigned for Brandt and the SPD again in 1972, and continued speaking out for the Social Democrats long after Brandt's resignation over a spy scandal in 1974. Brandt was succeeded as Chancellor by Helmut Schmidt, on whose behalf Grass took up the cudgels yet again in the electoral campaigns of 1976 and 1980. After Brandt's last campaign in 1972, however, Grass's involvement in front-line politics was considerably less visible and less time-consuming than it had been in the sixties. His artistic output between 1972 and 1977 was also somewhat low-key. *Aus dem Tagebuch einer Schnecke (From the Diary of a Snail)* appeared in 1972, combining the diarylike treatment of Grass's involvement during the 1969 electoral campaign with a narrative concerning the fate of Danzig Jews during the war, snapshot reflections on the role of a German father of four in the seventies, an essay on Dürer's engraving *Melancholia*, and a wealth of information on gastropods — the snail of the title symbolizing the slow, unexciting, melancholy, highly vulnerable, but steady evolutionary reformism of the SPD. In one sense the *Diary* looks back towards the political involvement of *Local Anaesthetic*; in another sense, experimenting as it does with fictional and nonfictional forms of narrative, with the juxtaposition of novel and diary, history, autobiography, and political tract, it points forward towards the complicated narrative structuration of *Der Butt (The Flounder)* five years later. It has been pointed out that the period 1972–1977 can be seen as a fourth phase in Grass's career, a reflective, preparatory period issuing in *The Flounder*, much as his first, experimental phase in the fifties had resulted in *The Tin Drum*.[8] The first period had produced a number of minor works in the course of writing *The Tin Drum*; similarly, after the *Diary of a Snail*, a number of secondary works prepare the way for *The Flounder*. In 1973 a volume of drawings and photographs illustrating a poem, *Mariazuehren (Inmarypraise)* appeared. In 1974 the collection of political commentaries *Der Bürger and seine Stimme* (The Citizen and his Voice) was published, as was a new edition of the Danzig trilogy, now for the first time officially so entitled, *Danziger Trilogie*. An expensive bibliophile edition of seven etchings accompanied by poems, *Liebe geprüft (Love Tested)*, appeared in the same year. In 1976, together with Heinrich Böll and Carola Stern, he founded the journal of political criticism *L. 76*. Throughout these years his etchings and drawings were exhibited, from Berlin to New York, London, Paris, Zurich, Munich, and at least a dozen other cities. In 1976 he received an honorary doctorate from Harvard.

Though his drawings and etchings began to receive more attention and praise during these years, the only one of his literary texts that attracted any real attention, either in Germany or abroad, was *From the*

Diary of a Snail. In Germany it was greeted with a mixture of irritation, polite interest, and occasional cautious words of praise for the narrative experiments. In North America, where the translation appeared in 1973, the reaction was not, in general, much different: the attention, on the whole, was more respectful, as befitted an author so recently apotheosized in *Time,* but the excitement of the old days of the trilogy had wholly evaporated, and there seemed little likelihood that it would ever return. That was before *The Flounder,* however.

Heralded by a well-coordinated advance publicity campaign, *Der Butt* (*The Flounder*) saw the light of day in July 1977, sold 450,000 copies within two years, and realized a profit for Grass on its first edition alone of some three million marks — with part of which Grass established a literary prize named for the writer whom he had long claimed as his model, Alfred Döblin. The reaction was highly enthusiastic on the part of the critics as well, almost every major journal and newspaper with pretensions to literary interests devoting the new novel generous space and generous praise — and with almost every reviewer noting that *The Flounder* was far closer to the style of *The Tin Drum* and *Dog Years* than to that of the later novels. Critical and popular reaction in North America, where *The Flounder* arrived in translation in 1978, was, if anything, even more enthusiastic. The scale was epic, the story covering a generous four millennia of European history, centered on two male characters: one the first-person narrator, variously named, who claims to have been the lover of each of the nine (or eleven) female cooks whose stories form the bulk of the book; the other a talking fish, the flounder of the title, who doubles as the patriarchal spirit throughout history. Also included are considerable amounts of historical documentation, a modern extrapolation of the Grimms' fairytale of the fisherman and his wife, a respectably sized collection of forty-six lyrics, a generous selection of recipes for outlandish dishes, and a quasiautobiographical, quasifictional account of the author's comings and goings as public figure over the preceding five years or so. In terms of narrative technique, in short, *The Flounder* emerges as a synthesis of the Danzig trilogy and the *Diary of a Snail.* Reactions ranged from delight to fury — the latter mainly, and very largely undeservedly, on the part of readers oversimplistically espousing feminism — but one thing was quite clear: the tin drummer was back.

The following year saw another major success for Grass, and another confirmation of the tin drummer image. Volker Schlöndorff's film version of *The Tin Drum* was released in 1979 to both popular and critical applause, winning the German *Goldene Schale,* the Golden Palm at the Cannes Film Festival, and an American Oscar for the best foreign film of the year. Nineteen seventy-nine also saw the publication of *Das Treffen in Telgte,* translated two years later as *The Meeting at Telgte.* An elaboration of a chapter in *The Flounder* in much the same way that *Cat and Mouse* had drawn on the original *Dog Years* complex, *The Meeting at Telgte* is a fictionalized meeting of Group 47, the literary circle where Grass had first made his name, but transported three hundred years back in time to the chaotic Germany of the Thirty Years' War, the time of Grimmelshausen's famous picaresque novel *Simplicissimus*. There is much rambunctiousness and wenching in the straw, but the central issue is clearly whether writing is worthwhile in a world in which the writer is totally impotent. The answer is a resounding Yes: only in its best writing do we find the true nation, be it called Germany or whatever. The book, riding on the coat-tails of *The Flounder*, to be sure, was well received in both Germany and North America. Hard on its heels, in 1980, there followed two further publications, one of them a collection of his major literary essays (*Aufsätze zur Literatur*), the earliest dating back to 1957, the latest written in 1979. More flamboyantly, however, the narrative *Kopfgeburten oder Die Deutschen sterben aus* also appeared in 1980, the English translation of it, *Headbirths or The Germans Are Dying Out*, appearing in North America in 1982. In 1978 and 1979 Grass had visited Indonesia, Japan, China, and India; in 1979 his friend and fellow writer Nicolas Born died; in 1980 the next German electoral campaign was about to take place; in Asia the population was exploding; in Germany right-wing politicians were forecasting a complete takeover by foreigners if the German birthrate continued to decline; nuclear weaponry was piling up, apparently uncontrollably, on German soil — all of this, and much more besides, finds hospitable lodgings in the pages of *Headbirths*. Pushing further still the narrative techniques first employed in the *Diary of a Snail*, then in *The Flounder*, Grass weaves fact and fiction, East and West, past, present, and future, comedy and melancholy, into a complex literary web. The central characters, whose fictional doings constitute the main narrative thread, a couple of German high school teachers vacationing in Asia, are products of the generation of 1968, but older now, wiser and sadder perhaps, like the narrator, who is also called Günter Grass and continually visualizes the book he is writing as a possible script for another film by his friend Schlöndorff. *Headbirths* aroused the by now not unusual reaction to Grass's books in Germany, outraged indignation on the one hand, from those who saw only SPD-electioneering in the very thin disguise of narrative fiction, enthusiastic praise on the other, from those who saw another demonstration of Grass's consummate mastery of the art of narrative. American reaction, as in the case of most of Grass's books, tended to substitute at one end of the scale boredom for outrage, and at the other extreme even more lavish plaudits.

Over the twenty-odd years of Grass's public literary career since *The Tin Drum*, the North American reaction to his work has for most of the time largely parallelled the German reaction, even if the reasons for that reaction are in two major ways at least quite different. The first major difference is that of politics, the second that of language. Günter Grass is a German writer, writing for Germans, as far as his German readership is concerned; for his English-language readers, however, and this more particularly in North America, Grass was quite quickly elevated to the somewhat ethereal status of a "world author" — a status also achieved, for example, by Pasternak, Solzhenitsyn, Borges, and García Márquez. The implications of this on the level of politics are obvious enough: German readers of Grass might react immediately, for example, to the criticism of the West German past and present in the Danzig trilogy, while North American readers, though no doubt well aware of the likelihood of such a reaction on the part of German readers, could afford to distance themselves from these "private" dynamics of the work's German reception. The North American reaction, in this sense, has consequently always been more the reaction to a conversation overheard than the response of a participant in that conversation. We are talking primarily (though not exclusively) about the more immediately political implications of the work here, of course; clearly, there were other thematic areas where readers from either culture would be more or less equally disposed to perceive blasphemy, sacrilege, pornography, hope, resignation, and the like. It should be remembered, however, that Grass's German readers as a group became increasingly politicized, especially during the years immediately preceding and following the student protest movement of 1968, to a much greater degree than did their North American counterparts. It was during these years that Grass, once seen by the radical young as a tin-drumming, glass-smashing mascot of the extreme left, was suddenly discovered to have gone over to the enemy in supporting the wishy-washy, hypocritical reformism of the SPD, itself seen as a major part of the problem rather than the solution. For the conservatives who had been mortally offended by the early books, however, Grass continued to be the long-haired, foul-mouthed, evil-minded atheist and enemy of law and order. Grass thus found himself effectively marooned in the middle, reviled by both ends of the political spectrum. Most of this was of little or no importance to North American readers and critics, as can be seen particularly in the case of *Local Anaesthetic.* In Germany the reaction to this novel's apparently defeatist political attitude was generally very negative; in North America the political content could easily be defused into an acceptably generalized, nonspecific, threnodic satire on Western Liberalism and its perceived impotence.

The second major differentiator between the German and the North American responses is that of language. Obviously, most American readers deal with Grass in translation; once again the conversation is, to a degree, overheard. Almost all of Grass's work to reach North American readers, including all of the fiction, has been translated by Ralph Manheim, and from the beginning Manheim has been roundly condemned and simultaneously given the highest praise for his translations. John Simon, in his review of *The Tin Drum* reprinted in the present collection, was among the first and most vigorous of Manheim's critics, assessing his translation as "persistently inept" and deploring the introduction of the novel to English-speaking readers in such a guise. The following year, however, Manheim was the recipient of the P.E.N. Translation Prize for the same piece of work. This has been the model for the response to each of the translations since then, each one in turn finding violent detractors and enthusiastic supporters. For every critic who gives a long list of unpardonable blunders, there is another who would agree, more or less, that "when the gnomes of Stockholm get around to giving [Grass] his Nobel Prize, they should give one as well to his admirable translator, Ralph Manheim."[9] The demands of translating Grass's German must be considered almost insuperable over large stretches of the fiction: the stonecutting terminology of *The Tin Drum*, the potash mining jargon and the parody of Heideggerean discourse in *Dog Years*, the intricacies of dentistry in *Local Anaesthetic*, the gastropodic lore of *From the Diary of a Snail*, the mycological and culinary excursions in *The Flounder*. No translator can ever hope to win all the battles; the most he can hope for is to emerge with some dignity at the end of the war, and this Manheim has certainly done. Moreover, as a recent critic has pointed out, if it were not for Manheim's translations Grass's American career might well have been quite different: "The degree of simplification which Grass's style has undergone in Manheim's translations," Sigrid Mayer argues, "has been precisely the amount necessary to make his writings, particularly the prose fiction, appealing to the English-speaking reader." Her conclusion, after an analysis of Manheim's translations up to the *Diary of a Snail*, is a fair one: "Ralph Manheim's loyalty to Grass's work and the steadily improving quality of his translations, in spite of the increasing difficulty of the texts at hand, have done much to bring about the unusual esteem in which Grass is held in this country."[10]

Though Günter Grass the engaged citizen invariably comes down on the side of moderation, his work, as we have seen, tends to polarize reactions. Each new text elicits its complement of enthusiastic and hostile, expert and not-so-expert reviews, as well as a flurry of scholarly articles in a variety of natural and critical languages, and although Grass criticism has not yet reached the overwhelming dimensions of the industries devoted to Joyce or Kafka, it still represents a formidable conglomeration of disputing voices. The present collection singles out some score of these voices, presenting just one review of each of the major works so far and a dozen articles on various aspects of these works, individually and as they affect each other, by professional critics. All of the pieces that follow this introduction have already appeared in print before, and all of them first appeared in English-language publications. One of the major aims of this particular collection has been to place Grass in a broad Anglo-American rather than a German context, to convey a sense specifically of the English-speaking world's reception of Grass's work, both in terms of reviewers' initial reactions to the appearance of each work and academic critics' more leisurely consideration of each work's implications. The overall arrangement of the pieces is therefore broadly chronological in each of the two sections (the first containing reviews, the second critical articles), in order to suggest also a sense of the relationship between output and critical response. It will be obvious, of course, that the result is only *one* of the hundreds of possible collections that could have been made, unavoidably stamped, as any one of them would also be, by the collector's individual biases and beliefs as to what makes Grass's work worth reading.

In view of this inevitable element of the arbitrary, this collection, like any "critical" anthology, must cheerfully renounce all claim to be an authoritative summing up of the critical state-of-play, and acknowledge that as a collection of interpretations it is also itself an interpretation. In other words, the collection is partly a documentation, partly another statement in the continuing critical conversation. Like the work of Kafka, or Joyce, Grass's work encourages extreme explanatory positions — psychological, mythological, numerological, sociological — and even though such exclusive positions often produce lucid and startling insights, in the end they work against the predominantly anti-ideological thrust of all of Grass's work. The essays collected here, individually and collectively, resist this impulse to close off the discussion, to decide finally what the text "really means," to curtail and define its richness. These are in no sense the "definitive" essays on Grass's work — rather they are a demonstration of something of the scope and nature of Grass's impact on a collection of arguably representative critics in a collection of representative critical and popular English-language publications. As a collection, they demonstrate internal contradictions and frictions, differences in perception and method and evaluation. Individual interpretations, however, not to mention the rise and fall of Günter Grass as a commodity on the international literary stock exchange, are matters of relatively superficial interest. The arguments and counter arguments supporting and contesting such bullish and bearish positions and behaviors, however, are of more engaging interest, and their overheard exchanges can provide us with challenging materials for the construction of our own "headbirth": not *the correct*, but *a richer* and more complex and more satisfying reading of the artist Günter Grass.

"It is one of Grass's several geniuses to ask the appropriate question at the appropriate time. 'My God, what did we do?' was the simple right question to ask when *The Tin Drum* was written. 'My God, what do we do now?' is the complicated right question to ask today," wrote the anonymous *Time* reviewer of *Local Anaesthetic* in 1970.[11] From the beginning, Günter Grass has been a poser of questions and a rejector of easy answers. From the beginning too, Grass has been *excessive* in his questioning, an excessiveness which J. P. Stern, writing of the Danzig trilogy, characterizes as an attempt "to match an almost unbelievable, inexplicable past with almost unbelievable and inexplicable metaphors, and thus to make it believable and explain it without reducing its tragic pathos and without explaining it away," without succumbing either "to that ghastly tendency (so characteristic of post-Nietzschean Germany) to justify and vindicate everything by adverting to a 'tragic view of life,' " or to the opposite tendency to accept whatever horrors may befall mankind with the cynical triviality of " 'all's grist to the human mill.' "[12] Balancing between these two rejected extremes, a demonization of evil such as Thomas Mann had undertaken in *Doctor Faustus* on the one hand and a trivialization of human suffering in an absurd world on the other, Grass emphatically subscribes to the dictum of Brecht (and before Brecht the Russian Formalist critics) that the cardinal function of art is to *shock* the reader (or viewer or listener) into a new and astonished awareness of the world he or she inhabits. Brecht called this the *Verfremdungseffekt*, the effect of making perceived reality *strange*, and Grass's central means of achieving this same end is a massive, pervasive, and uniquely effective use of *humor* as a literary device. It need hardly be said that we are not talking here about the carefree laughter of happy children or the Sunday after- noon chuckling of a well-fed Pickwick, in a world where God's in his heaven and all's right here below. Flashes of such humor may very occasionally occur, but the dominant mode throughout Grass's work is the comic treatment of material which massively resists comedy. This rou- tinely involves the risk of prosecution for blasphemy, sacrilege, pornogra- phy, and the various forms there are of lèse-majesté. It also provides an extremely effective scalpel for dissecting the hypocrisies of the present and the dissimulations of history.

The essential factor in Grass's comic treatment of the monstrousness of humankind is an ostentatious flaunting of incongruity as a device: it is plainly "wrong" that Oskar's mother should gorge herself to death on fish, that the greengrocer Greff should commit suicide on a whimsical machine counterweighted with potatoes, that Christ should be called the world's champion hanger on the Cross by regulation nails, that the deaths of 4000 children should be presented in terms of a merry-go-round, or indeed that *The Tin Drum* as a whole should be narrated by such a simultaneously ridiculous, touching, and monstrous figure as Oskar. It is plainly prepos- terous that the black dog of *Dog Years* should apparently represent both Nazism *and* the pangs of conscience, that Matern should choose his particular method of punishing ex-Nazis, or that the whole of *Dog Years* should be so obviously laden down with obvious "symbols." Grass's work as a whole is ostentatiously cluttered with a junkshop collection of tin drums, cats, mice, nuns, seagulls, horses' heads, screwdrivers, dogs, dolls, nurses, dentists' chairs, snails, flounders, mushrooms, teachers, cooks, and liver sausages. Ann L. Mason several years ago drew attention to this parodic use of overinflated "absurd symbols,"[13] pseudosymbols whose primary function is self-advertisement and the consequent alerting of the critical reader to the processes by which "truth," be it social or historical or narrative, is constructed.

Grass, as we have seen, is very much the socially engaged artist, and as such he has repeatedly shown himself to be a satirist of brilliance. In the Danzig trilogy he is merciless in his attack on those who would pretend that the twelve years of the Third Reich had never happened or at any rate were best forgotten as quickly as possible in the name of progress and the future. One can still speak of satire in *Local Anaesthetic* and *From the Diary of a Snail,* but the target of the satire has become more diffuse as the focus shifts from the burdens of the past to the responsibilities of the present. The target now becomes human impotence in the first place rather than an organized conspiracy of silence. There is a guarded movement towards a cautiously optimistic pragmatism, though never without what John Reddick has called "a penetrating sense of ambivalence."[14] *The Flounder* reverts to one of the major themes of the Danzig trilogy in its scrutiny of the processes of writing history and thus manufacturing not only what passes for Truth in Our Time but also the Historical Past that underwrites that current perspective. In the process *The Flounder* becomes, in Morris Dickstein's phrase, "an encyclopedic satire."[15] The diffracted historical articulation via culinary and sexual history questions the whole undertaking of historiography in suggesting that historiography (rather than history) is all we can ever hope to have. The same theme is developed in *The Meeting at Telgte,* while in *Headbirths* the focus shifts to the future whose history is yet to be written. The overt target of satire here is Grass's political foe Franz Josef Strauss, whose alleged fear that the Germans are dying out is ridiculed by the equally fanciful hypothesis that one day there might be as many Germans as there now are Chinese. Judith Ryan suggests also a less overt target in seeing *Headbirths* as a rewriting of Orwell's *Nineteen Eighty-Four,* but as an attack not so much against a dehumanized bureaucratization as against "the creeping invasion of uncertainty, triviality, and banality,"[16] not so much against nightmare as against boredom and sameness, indecision and stasis.

Though Günter Grass as a good citizen of the Federal Republic leaves no doubt as to his willingness to act and speak out against indecision and stasis, there exists throughout his work a strong undertow of the absurd. As early as 1966, W. G. Cunliffe, in an article reprinted in this volume, could claim that Grass was not a satirist at all, but rather an absurdist: "Grass is no satirist; he has none of the satirist's absurd hope that the world can be improved. Rather, he is doubting whether progress is possible at all in human affairs, whether there are any goals to aim at."[17] Part of what makes Grass's work fascinating, however, is precisely that he is *both* an absurdist *and* a satirist — for the boundary separating the two is by no means watertight. I have argued elsewhere, in another context, that while there is indeed a self-confident mode of satire which assumes that the world can be improved by the application of caustic humor, there is also a mode of entropic satire which abandons that "absurd hope," becomes unfocused, nonspecific, diffuse, and shades over into the absurd.[18] But while hope of any improvement in the wider scheme of things may indeed be abandoned, there is still always the Sisyphean *choice* to attempt the improvement at least of one's own back garden, whether or not this may "mean" anything. The choice is a painful one, and, as *Local Anaesthetic* has it, there will always be new pains. Or, as Grass, quoting Camus, puts it in *Headbirths*: "The absurd man says yes, and his labor will know no end."[19] Grass's central characters are all absurd men — and absurd women too, as *The Flounder* adequately demonstrates. But absurdity does not necessarily translate into despair. Grass is fond of quoting Camus, who observes in *The Myth of Sisyphus* that "the struggle itself towards the heights is enough to fill a man's heart. One must imagine Sisyphus happy."[20]

John Reddick was the first to examine in detail just how bleakly the world of the Danzig trilogy, against which we must imagine Sisyphus happy, is portrayed. He finds *The Tin Drum* in particular marked by a vicious existential circularity: "a cycle of existence so desolate that little value and absolutely no uniqueness can be ascribed to any of its separate elements, indeed these elements may be said to have no existence of their own at all but to be merely functions of what precedes and causes of what follows."[21] The episode where Jan Bronski, Oskar's Polish father, builds a house of cards while awaiting the German stormtroopers and his execution is characterized by Reddick as "an unforgettable instance of that kind of irony . . . through which a reality, too gross to be meaningfully evoked by direct means, is indirectly mirrored through an almost caricatural rendering of its periphery" and as illustrating "the paramount principle of existence: the inception of anything at all of an integrated nature is at once the omen of its disintegration."[22] The repeated destruction of Danzig, the sailors who eat the eels grown fat on drowned sailors, the ants who refuse to be diverted from their affairs by the corpse of Oskar's German father, Matzerath: these are individual examples of the vast and total impassivity of nature in which any individual life or death is silently drowned. "A phrase from Goethe passed through my mind," relates Oskar. "The ants found themselves facing a new situation but, undismayed by the detour, soon built a new highway round the doubled-up Matzerath; for the sugar that trickled out of the burst sack had lost none of its sweetness while Marshal Rokossovski was occupying the city of Danzig."[23] Reddick characterizes the trilogy overall as a great threnody, a poetic lament of great intensity bewailing its characters' lostness in a world which in both the natural and the social spheres is hostile and monstrous. The narrative, in spite of this, avoids any false pathos or sentimentality, privileges indirection and peripherality over direct statement, questions over answers, comedy over tears. The comedy, however, takes the form of "that compelling irony whereby clownish caricature may serve to communicate sorrow more poignantly than tears might do."[24]

This is certainly true, but it would be hasty to assume that it constituted the whole truth, to assume that the *point* of Grass's use of indirection, incongruity, and excess was to communicate more efficiently sorrow or anger or hope for a better future. It is worth restating the contention that what is of most importance throughout Grass's work is less the answers it appears to provide than the questions it invites us to carry on exploring. From the beginning, Grass's texts are marked by a narrative complexity which we, as readers, ignore at our own risk. "Granted: I am an inmate of a mental hospital," the first sentence of Oskar's narration reads, a very fair warning that we must guard against accepting at face value *any* statement Oskar may make — including the one he has just made. "Even if we were both invented, I should have to write," writes Pilenz, the narrator of *Cat and Mouse*. "You tell. No, you. Or you. Should the actor begin? . . . One of us has to begin: You or he or you or I," begins the first page of *Dog Years*. "I told my dentist all this. Mouth blocked and face to face with the television screen which, soundless like myself, told a story of publicity," reads the beginning of *Local Anaesthetic*. Over and over again — the examples could be multiplied indefinitely — our attention is drawn to the self-aware fictionality of these ostentatiously fictive, and yet so beguilingly realistic narrative worlds. Oskar relates with all the signs of remorse how he deliberately led Jan Bronski to his death; fifty pages or so later he acknowledges that this account was a fiction and provides us with a new version. Which is the truth? The second version? The first? Neither (but a possible third version which Oskar still conceals)? Neither (for Jan Bronski never existed anyway, being only a character in a story)? Both (for as fictional accounts each is completely valid within its own fictional universe)? Opting for one of the first three alternatives (i.e., accepting Oskar as a realistic narrator of a realistic narrative) is probably what most of us would instinctively do as readers, at least on the occasion of our first reading of the novel — but in doing so we put ourselves in the power of a narrator who cheerfully demonstrates throughout his complete lack of reliability. Answering that Jan Bronski never existed anyway, though true, is completely unproductive in that it disqualifies us as readers. Answering that both versions, though mutually exclusive, are true is the beginning of an adequate reading of Grass — while accepting *all* of the suggested possibilities at once, in spite of their completely irreconcilable contradictions, as true, but maintaining that acceptance with the utmost provisionality, would be the ideal response.

This is by no means to suggest that Günter Grass as a man is by nature somehow incapable of unambiguous utterances — his election speeches are sufficient proof of the firmness of his political views, after all, if such proof is needed. In his literary texts, however, questions are always more important than their answers, the search always more important than the

quarry, the game more important than the decision. There are readers
who count it as a fault of such a massive work as *The Flounder* that they
find themselves unable to distill its narrative complexity into a single,
unambiguous message and consequently resort to berating the author for
the "confusion" which causes his "message" to "fail." Less hostile readers
will suggest helpfully that while his motives and intentions are indeed
praiseworthy, he really should be more careful in presenting them, since
some readers (other readers, that is) might easily miss the points which he
is trying to make. But, as W. G. Cunliffe aptly put it in 1966, "Grass does
not preach, he arranges his materials in such a way as to make certain
thoughts possible."[25] Perhaps the most productive trend in Grass criticism
over the last decade or so has been just this growing awareness of Grass's
art, though there are, of course, individual critics who have been pointing
it out from the very beginning. Several of the essays in this collection are
good examples: Ann L. Mason's study of the relationship of art and
politics, fiction and nonfiction in *From the Diary of a Snail*; Scott Abbott's
demonstration of the reflexivity of Grass's style in *Dog Years*; J. W. Rohlf's
demonstration of just how much artifice informs the apparent artless
simplicity of *Headbirths*.

Günter Grass is certainly a likely candidate for the next German
Nobel Prize — but is he really a Great Writer? Is he really a Goethe For Our
Times? Less trivially, perhaps, is he a profound moral humanist, a cynical
mocker, or, in J. P. Stern's phrase, a man without ideology? To what extent
is his voice, like Oskar's, an amalgam of Goethe and Rasputin, Apollo and
Dionysos, Jesus and Satan, harmonizing chaos and intoxicating reason?
Happily, introductions do not (and should not) have to provide answers
any more than poets do. "The problem," as Robert Maurer writes, "is to
locate the boundaries between the circumstantial and the meaningful, the
laughable and the sublime. Failure to solve that problem leaves only one
remaining tone, irony, and one mood, the interrogative."[26] But that failure
can be more useful than any victory, for it is precisely the richness and
ambiguity of Grass's texts that ensures the placing of the onus of decisions
and answers exactly where Brecht said it should be, that is on the
shoulders not of the author but of the reader. Grass the artist, as opposed
to Grass the citizen and politician, is not to be pinned down to single
meanings. The narrators who share the experiences of the empirical
Günter Grass in such works as *From the Diary of a Snail*, *The Flounder*, or
Headbirths, who attend the same conferences, undertake the same journeys, write the same books, are just as much characters in an ongoing
fiction as are Mahlke or Starusch or Oskar or Vasco da Gama. Questions
and answers, parody and politics, impotence and action, imagination and
history, fiction and what we agree to call facts happily sleep many to a bed
in promiscuous innocence. What Stephen Spender says of *The Meeting at
Telgte* can be applied to the work as a whole: it is "a brilliant entertainment, and there is much to be grateful for," and even if we are constantly

reminded that "poetry makes nothing happen" we are also constantly shown that "it survives" as "a way of happening, a mouth."[27] As a tireless teller of very tall tales, Grass is essentially a humorist — but humor and despair may differ only in name[28] — a juggler of words and worlds, a confidence trickster like those other, archetypal humorists, Scheherazade, who opposed brute force with fragile fictions, or Sisyphus, who finding no meaning in a universe gone silent was obliged to invent his own. "The rock is still rolling," writes Camus,[29] and as long as it continues to roll the game is not over. To quote *Dog Years*: "As long as we're telling stories, we're alive. As long as stories keep coming, with or without a point, dog stories, eel stories, scarecrow stories, rat stories, flood stories, recipe stories, stories full of lies and schoolbook stories, as long as stories have power to entertain us, no hell can divert us."[30] To rephrase: as long as the questions prevent us from settling down with the answers, the answers will not succeed in blinding us to the questions.[31]

* * *

Many of the articles reprinted in this volume originally included quotations in German from Grass's works and from other sources. For the purposes of this collection translations into English have been substituted (in square brackets) in all cases — in one or two individual cases it seemed desirable for one reason or another to give the original as well as the translation. In a few articles these translations are the work of the respective authors; in most the translations from Grass are taken from Ralph Manheim's standard English versions. Due acknowledgment is made in the footnotes in all cases, and page references are provided to both the German and the standard English versions. Translations not otherwise identified are the work of the editor. Titles of Grass's works are cited in German or English as in the original articles; appropriate references are provided to English titles where this is necessary.

PATRICK O'NEILL
University of British Columbia

Notes

1. Anonymous, "The Dentist's Chair as an Allegory of Life," *Time*, 13 April 1970, 68–70; reprinted in the present collection.

2. John Irving, "Günter Grass: King of the Toy Merchants," *Saturday Review*, March 1982, 57–60, here 60; reprinted in the present collection.

3. *Speak Out! Speeches, Open Letters, Commentaries*, trans. Ralph Manheim (New York: Harcourt, Brace and World, 1969), 89–90.

4. *Time*, 13 April 1970.

5. For details on translations see Patrick O'Neill, *Günter Grass: A Bibliography, 1955–1975* (Toronto: University of Toronto Press, 1976), 16–21.

6. My account here is indebted to two studies of the North American reception of

Grass: Sigrid Mayer's "Grüne Jahre für Grass: Die Rezeption in den Vereinigten Staaten," in *Text + Kritik* 1 / 1a (1978): 151–61, and R. L. White's *Günter Grass in America: The Early Years* (Hildesheim: Olms, 1981).

7. Ronald Bryden, "Germany's Tragedy," the *Observer* (London), 26 July 1970, 24; reprinted in the present collection.

8. Volker Neuhaus, "Günter Grass," in *Kritisches Lexikon zur deutschsprachigen Gegenwartsliteratur*, ed. Heinz Ludwig Arnold (Munich: edition text + kritik, 1978 and continuing).

9. John Leonard, "Consider a Billion Germans," *New York Times Book Review*, 14 March 1982, 21.

10. Sigrid Mayer, "Growing Grass in English," *Yearbook of Comparative and General Literature* 25 (1976): 69.

11. *Time*, 13 April 1970.

12. J. P. Stern, "Günter Grass's Uniqueness," *London Review of Books*, 5–18 February 1981, 11–14; reprinted in the present collection.

13. Ann L. Mason, *The Skeptical Muse: A Study of Günter Grass' Conception of the Artist* (Bern: Lang, 1974).

14. John Reddick, "Action and Impotence: Günter Grass's *Örtlich betäubt*," *Modern Language Review* 67 (1972): 578.

15. Morris Dickstein, "An Epic, Ribald Miscellany," *New York Times Book Review*, 12 November 1978, 12; reprinted in the present collection.

16. Judith Ryan, " 'Into the Orwell Decade': Günter Grass's Dystopian Trilogy," *World Literature Today* 55 (1981): 567; reprinted in the present collection.

17. W. G. Cunliffe, "Aspects of the Absurd in Günter Grass," *Wisconsin Studies in Contemporary Literature* 7 (1966): 320.

18. Patrick O'Neill, "The Comedy of Entropy: The Contexts of Black Humour," *Canadian Review of Comparative Literature* 10 (1983): 145–66.

19. Ralph Manheim, trans., *Headbirths* (New York: Fawcett Crest, 1983), 140. Cf. Albert Camus, *The Myth of Sisyphus*, trans. Justin O'Brien (Harmondsworth: Penguin, 1979), 110.

20. Ibid., 111.

21. John Reddick, *"The Danzig Trilogy" of Günter Grass* (London: Secker & Warburg, 1975), 9.

22. Ibid., 22, 25.

23. *The Tin Drum*, trans. Ralph Manhiem (New York: Vintage, 1964), 395.

24. Reddick, *The "Danzig Trilogy" of Günter Grass*, 16, 17.

25. W. G. Cunliffe, "Günter Grass, *Katz und Maus*," *Studies in Short Fiction* 3 (1966): 183.

26. Robert Maurer, "The End of Innocence: Günter Grass's *The Tin Drum*," *Bucknell Review* 16, no. 2 (1968): 57; reprinted in the present collection.

27. Stephen Spender, "Elbe Swans and Other Poets," *New York Review of Books*, 11 June 1981, 36; reprinted in the present collection.

28. Cf. Nicole Casanova's volume of interviews with Grass, *Atelier des métamorphoses* (Paris: Belfond, 1979), 180: "Humor is for me another name for despair."

29. *The Myth of Sisyphus*, 111.

30. *Dog Years*, trans. Ralph Manheim (New York: Fawcett Crest, 1966), 536 (translation slightly amended for emphasis).

31. For a discussion of Grass's latest narrative, *Die Rättin* (1986), see the "Postscript" below.

REVIEWS

The Drummer of Danzig
[*The Tin Drum*]

John Simon*

From time to time we must re-examine the meaning of the concepts "classical" and "romantic," which, like the works of Homer or Dante, need to be retranslated or, in this case, redefined for every age. As we look at twentieth-century fiction, we see one kind of writing whose ideal is omission, whose unit is the vignette which yearns to compress itself into an aphorism. This is our classicism. And there is another writing whose aim is inclusion, whose basic form is the catalogue striving to heighten itself into a prose poem. This is our romanticism. To draw examples from France, where they have a way of being more exemplary, there is the classicism of Gide, Radiguet, Camus confronting the romanticism of, say, Proust, Montherlant, and Genet. The greater writers try to bridge the gap: Gide had to write *The Counterfeiters*; the work of Proust is shot through with maxims.

In *The Tin Drum*, Günter Grass has written a novel without equal so far in post-war Germany—let no one mention in the same breath the lucubrations of an Uwe Johnson. Grass's book is a major romantic novel which, in its carefully designed structure and economical use of a welter of incidents, approaches classicism.

Duality runs through the book. Even the provenance of *The Tin Drum* is dual, just as its hero, Oskar Matzerath, has two putative fathers. For the novel derives, first, from a French tradition—Grass lived for a long time in Paris—represented by writers like Jarry, Apollinaire (particularly the Apollinaire of *Les Onze mille verges*), and Céline, writers in whom furibund sexuality and Rabelaisian humor, sadism and stylistic experimentation and innovation, proceeded *pari passu*. There is in Günter Grass a great, metaphysical anger. But the anger comes at us in trappings of humor, eroticism, absurdity, poker-facedness—it is, in short, a Mardi-Gras anger—and is not readily recognizable for what it is. But its impact on sensitive readers is all the greater for that.

While adopting this French orientation, *The Tin Drum* manages to

*Reprinted from *Partisan Review* 30 (Fall 1963): 446–53, by permission of *Partisan Review* and the author.

improve on its models. Explaining German romanticism to French readers, Heine wrote: "A French madness is nowhere near so mad as a German one; for in the latter there is, as Polonius would say, method. With unrivaled pedantry, with terrifying conscientiousness, with thoroughness such as a French lunatic cannot even conceive of, this German frenzy was practiced." *The Tin Drum* is also nourished by German romanticism. Oskar is the obverse of E. T. A. Hoffmann's Klein Zaches, another mischievous dwarf. Zaches has the magic gift of receiving the reward due any great action performed by anyone in his presence; conversely, Oskar has genuine talents of sorts, but they are sinister, and, directly or indirectly, lead those around him to disaster. The stealing of the Good complements the palming off of Evil. But whereas in *Klein Zaches* justice triumphs, in *The Tin Drum* injustice goes its merry way. It does not exactly triumph — there are no more triumphs in our day, not even triumphs of injustice — but it does go on.

The Tin Drum is the story of Oskar Matzerath, born in the Twenties, whose mother was a Danzig woman, and whose father was either her German husband or her Polish lover. The infant is gifted with an adult brain at birth, and resolves not to grow up to be a shopkeeper like the elder Matzerath. Aged three, Oskar throws himself down some stairs and arrests his growth; he refuses to go to school or talk properly but becomes a fiendish artist on the toy drums his mother keeps him supplied with. When a new drum is not forthcoming, he discovers that he can shout glass to pieces even at great distances, which proves a useful method of petty blackmail and, later, of other mischief-making. As Oskar grows older, he becomes the cause of the deaths of his mother and both presumptive fathers, and of several other people to boot. Not so much the cause of death as its catalyst, and who can assess the responsibility of a catalyst? So Oskar gets away with murder.

The story covers the rise of Nazism, the war, the collapse of Germany, but all only as reflected in Oskar's existence. He has many picaresque and demonic adventures: he becomes an "artiste" entertaining troops in Normandy, a "reincarnation" of Jesus who leads a gang of likable JD's into destruction, his brother's father if not his keeper (by having a child by his stepmother), and so forth. After the war, he sees fit to grow a little, but in so doing develops a hump. He is relocated to Düsseldorf, where he becomes by turns carver of funeral monuments, nude model for crazy artists, drummer in a jazz trio, and, finally, a famous and rich concert-drummer who, in solo recitals throughout Germany, drums elderly people back into their youth — a kind of faith healer, in short. Accused, at last, of the one crime he did not commit, he is found guilty of murder but reprieved to a mental institution. Though he finds happiness there, it looks as if he will soon be released. And then what? He is thirty, and he is afraid.

Such an outline does no justice whatever to the plot, let alone to the work of art. Günter Grass is also a poet, painter, sculptor, stage designer, dramatist, literary critic, and genuine eccentric; all these occupations have helped him fill his long novel with a splendid *mélange adultère de tout*. Grass calls himself a realist, but this is true only to the extent that he can describe with equal verisimilitude plain things like the contents of a grocery, more abstruse things such as the work of a stone-carver or waiter in a ferocious harbor canteen, and fantastic things like minor miracles. Always, however, the romantic poet is eager to take over. Thus we read of the child Oskar, in a garret, disturbed in his drumming by noises from the courtyard: "A hundred carpet-beating females can storm the very heavens, can blunt the wing tips of young swallows; with a few strokes, they tumbled the tiny temple that Oskar had drummed into the April air." The world is too much with Oskar, but the expression is not that of the worldly realist. Consider Oskar's words about how his mother, after four days' painful vomiting and dying, gave up "that bit of breath which everyone must cough up in order to obtain his death certificate." Whereupon, Oskar goes on, "we all breathed easy again . . ."[1]

The novel is distinguished by its blend of dreary reality and spectacular fantasy, of wit and toughness, of lyricism and amorality. If Grass's vision is realistic, it is the realism of someone who does not allow for optical illusions, who does not know or does not care to know the laws of causality, who has no visual or moral perspective: a sharp observer, but an observer from Mars. Thus Oskar watches a neighbor woman carrying a carpet rolled up and slung across her shoulder "exactly as she might have carried a drunken man; but her man was no longer living." And thus Oskar wonders upon seeing the toy soldiers abandoned in Danzig by a little Polish escapee, "Perhaps he had stuffed a few uhlans into his trouser pocket that they might later, during the battle for the fortress of Modlin, reinforce the Polish cavalry." Thus, too, Oskar notes that at his father's funeral "it decidedly smelled of dead Matzerath."

The salient feature is irony, but an irony which, for all that it is immense, is not savage. It is indifferent rather than angry, and the reader's own indignation must rush in to fill the moral vacuum left by the protagonist's nonchalance. Grass is a master of all ironies: simple, complex, multilateral. Simple: ". . . films in which Maria Schell, as a nurse, wept, and Borsche, as a chief surgeon close upon a most difficult operation, played Beethoven sonatas through the French windows and displayed his sense of responsibility." Complex — because it can do double duty, as when it not only lets the absurdity of a situation dawn on us slowly, but also affords a gruesome insight into Oskar's non-human reaction to a severed ring finger which he picks up with a collector's zeal: "Oskar . . . realized that the inside of the finger was marked high up to the third joint with lines attesting to its diligence, determination, and ambitious perseverance." (The translation completely misses the horrible, matter-of-fact disregard of reality, couched in a syntactical construction that treats the dead finger as a living being; Manheim translates: "this had been a hard-working finger with a relentless sense of duty.") And multilateral irony—when Oskar's tiny son, already somewhat taller than his father, strikes Oskar down and makes him muse: "Could he, too, express childlike affection such as is supposedly worth striving for between fathers and sons, only in homicide?" Note that the homicidal scene takes place at Matzerath Senior's funeral, caused by Oskar, hence the "too," i.e., filial hatred as something basic and inherited, viewed by Oskar as "affection" but of a "childlike" sort, a term suited to "sons" but here, as a zeugma, referring also to the feelings of "fathers." Yet in the face of all this, love is still supposed to be "worth striving for."

In a perceptive essay, Hans Magnus Enzensberger has examined Grass's style and found in it everything from syntactic ballets to imitations of the Litany, from rondos and fugatos to the language of case histories, from legal jargon to underworld slang, from dialect to gibberish.[2] To this list should be added the technique of film montage, with all kinds of superimposition and cross-cutting, and certain devices of parody (e.g., the history of Danzig told as a cabaret monologue) also such strategems as describing something that, it turns out, did not happen, then blithely going on to what did; or enumerating several possibilities of how something might have been; or getting at an important point only by way of the longest verbal retards. Add to this anticlimaxes and non sequiturs, and you begin to have an image of Grass's style. But then, out of nowhere, a whole prose poem, or a mere lyrical cadenza: "Stillness, maybe a fly, the clock as usual, very softly the radio." (Which Manheim prosifies into: "It was quiet, maybe the buzzing of a fly, the clock as usual, the radio turned very low.")

What makes The Tin Drum spellbinding, however, is something beyond story and style; it is the hauntedness of its author, and the personal myths he creates, full of urgency and driving power. There are a number of continually recurring motifs in Grass's work. Thus the play Ten Minutes to Buffalo deals with a fantastic trip to Buffalo, in which the destination is not reached. In The Tin Drum, Oskar's arsonist grandfather may or may not have escaped to Buffalo; Oskar himself tries to escape there, but never makes it. Another play, The Wicked Cooks, displays a horde of viciously intriguing ladle-wielders. These same cooks with their ladles recur in a poem in Triangle of Rails (Gleisdreieck), Grass's volume of verse. In The Tin Drum, the unloved and killed father is a passionate cook, and Oskar's final bogey, the only fear he cannot shake, is "die Schwarze Köchin," a black female cook, whom Manheim foolishly turns into "the Black Witch," just so as to rhyme with "pitch"!

From the garb of cooks it is not far to that of nurses and nuns. Grass has publicly stated that nuns fascinate him; his private obsession with them is manifest in his fantasy world. As a painter, he has exhibited whole series of paintings of nuns, which is exactly what the painter Lankes does in *The Tin Drum*. Compulsively, almost all of Oskar's passions are for nuns—or nurses. The nurse is the secular replica of the nun, and her uniform is the photographic positive of the nun's negative. She, too, wears a cross, albeit a red one, and, in German, she, too, is called "Schwester." Nuns are the subject of a poem sequence in *Triangle of Rails* that reiterates, almost verbatim, certain passages of *The Tin Drum*. In the novel, nuns and nurses are repeatedly adored, longed for, made love to unsuccessfully, assaulted, raped, shot, deferred to, exalted.

Other obsessive motifs include the firebug, doves and seagulls, physical malformation. Now various commentators—including the blurb writer—have perceived Oskar as a symbol of the alienated artist, of guilty Germany, of corrupt mankind, to say nothing of diverse religious allegories. Some of these identifications may be in order, but they beg the underlying issue: Grass's unrelenting need to write the biography of his unconscious. Which is, of course, both the most and the least respectable reason for writing: it accounts for the best of Goethe, and for all of Sade.

This is not the time or place for an analysis of Grass's personal mythology, even if I were competent to undertake it. But something can be cautiously hinted at, something to which the polarity nun-nurse points, and which brings us back to the problem of duality with which we began. For *The Tin Drum* is fundamentally about duality. Its very narration shuttles, at the drop of a comma, between present and past, even as the narrator, sometimes within the same sentence, shifts from "I" to "he, Oskar." Oskar has two presumptive fathers: the solid burgher and amateur cook, Matzerath, who could "express sentiments only in soups," and the dreamy, dandified, sentimental Bronski—Germany and Poland, West and East, action and idea. Oskar's mother is hopelessly partitioned between two men; Matzerath is caught in the cross fire of scowls exchanged by the two pictures in his bedroom: Beethoven and Hitler, genius and madman. Oskar's two favorite books—almost his only ones—are the Dionysianly orgiastic memoirs of Rasputin, and Goethe's Apollonianly transfigured *Elective Affinities*. And, above all, the plot thrashes about between two poles. There is Oskar's insistent striving backward into the womb: as a boy, he keeps trying to hide under his grandmother's skirts; as a young adult, he still shuts himself into the clothes cupboard of the nurse he covets; at thirty, he finds the insane asylum's bed insufficiently crib-like. But there is also life moving forward and pushing Oskar before it: out of every asylum, lunatic or otherwise, and, ultimately, into death.

It is here that the couple, Nurse and Nun, becomes relevant. The Nurse stands for the return to the womb: Oskar cherishes a youthful picture of his mother as an auxiliary nurse; throughout the various maladies of his later life, nurses take care of him; often they hover over him while he enters a coma that is like the dark of the womb. At the other extreme stands the Nun, the black sister who succors the dying and prays for the dead. Oskar, significantly, craves both the Nurse who stands for earthiness (she is presumed to be of loose morality), and the Nun, immaculate Bride of Christ who points to the Beyond.

Our tragedy is that we fail in both directions: life can neither retreat into the embryo nor pass on through death. The main nurse in the novel cannot be possessed by an Oskar suddenly struck with impotence; the principal nun is, with Oskar's help, raped by someone else. The nurse is subsequently murdered; the nun, apparently, commits suicide. Fulfillment is not to be had. Oskar's friend, Herbert Truczinski, tries to copulate with a wooden figurehead in the shape of a naked girl, which would bridge the gap between transient flesh and enduring wood. He dies in the attempt. Oskar interfoliates his Rasputin with his Goethe, but the resulting mixture is a trick and delusion: life knows no idyll in which "Ottilie docilely strolls on Rasputin's arm through the gardens of Central Germany, while Goethe sits in a sleigh by the side of some dissolutely aristocratic Olga, as they glide along through wintry St. Petersburg." Indeed, in the end, even Goethe becomes a bogey for Oskar and merges with "the Black Cook": in death, to be sure, there is fusion, but what avails fusion then?

It is to be deplored that *The Tin Drum* comes to English readers diminished by Ralph Manheim's translation: in length, by well over a hundred pages; in quality, inestimably. Much that was either too difficult, or seemed too elaborate or obscene, has been flattened out, abridged, or omitted. On almost every page constructions, jokes, meanings are weakened, disregarded, or missed. None of which, however, has kept the translation from being extolled by literary and academic reviewers alike.

This is profoundly regrettable, because *The Tin Drum*, with its linguistic superabundance, its mythopoeic nature, its uncannily loving and palpable evocation of a city as it was but never again will be, its exploration of sex both bitter and humorous, its scatology, its dwelling on the father-son relationship while doing true obeisance to the eternal feminine, its religious coloring, its esoteric lore, its inextricable blend of reality and hallucination, its split between sensuality and spirituality, its wealth of magnificently grotesque invention is a German approximation of — you guessed it — *Ulysses*. Approximation only, not equivalent; but a spectacular achievement all the same. *The Tin Drum* pursues, dazzles, sinks its claws into the mind. Whether it can also ambush the future remains to be seen.

Notes

1. Ralph Manheim, the translator, renders this as "the bit of breath which each of us must give up if he is to be honored with a death certificate. We all sighed with relief . . ." This loses not only Oskar's tone of almost innocent callousness, but also the terrible yet pregnant

play on "bit of breath" and "breathed." Since Mr. Manheim's translation is persistently inept, I am obliged to make up my own versions.

2. [Ed. note: H. M. Enzensberger, "Wilhelm Meister auf Blech getrommelt," *Frankfurter Hefte* 14 (1959): 833–36.]

An Inept Symbolist
[*Cat and Mouse*]   Stanley Edgar Hyman*

I missed Guenter Grass' *The Tin Drum* when it was published in this country in a translation by Ralph Manheim. The chorus of praise for it, some from people whose judgment I respect, convinced me that I had been mistaken to pass it by. When Grass' second novel, *Cat and Mouse*, appeared, also translated by Ralph Manheim, I took advantage of the event to read both books.

My original impulse appears to have been right. I found *The Tin Drum*, despite some virtues, quite disappointing; much of it is repellent and, fatally, repellent in a boring fashion. As everyone must know by now, *The Tin Drum* is the story of Oskar Matzerath, a Danzig dwarf born in 1924, who narrates the first 30 years of his life while incarcerated in a mental hospital following his conviction for a murder he did not commit. Oskar resembles a three-year-old and often plays a child's tin drum; he had the power of shattering glass with his voice, but lost it and grew a hump instead; he believes himself to be the son of his mother's lover, and the father of his half-brother Kurt. Oskar has worked as a tombstone carver and a life model; most recently he has been a commercial success as a concert drummer, enormously popular with the elderly for the regressive fantasies that his drumming produces in them.

The book has a great deal of raw power, and many scenes are quite upsetting. These include: an encounter with an eel fisherman, lovingly shown pulling his catch out of the horse's head he uses for bait; the consequent suicide of Oskar's pregnant mother, by forcing herself to eat eels and other fish and them vomit them up; a neighbor's killing of his four tomcats with a poker when he could not stand their smell; a card game in which a dying man is forced to participate, with a poke in the ribs every time he sags; the blithe machinegunning of five nuns gathering crabs on a Normandy beach in front of a German pillbox; the mercy shooting of young sailors stuck in the portholes of a burning submarine.

Some of Grass' language is eloquent and effective. Oskar does fantasias on words; he will create an eel prayer, or a loving dialogue between two radishes. Here is Oskar meditating on his love for his

*Reprinted from the *New Leader*, 19 August 1963, 16–17, by permission of *The New Leader*. © the American Labor Conference on International Affairs, Inc.

stepmother Maria: "I might have my eyes vaccinated and find tears again. At the nearest butcher shop Oskar would put his heart through the meat-grinder if you would do the same with your soul. We might buy a stuffed animal to have something quiet between us." Grass' language is sometimes a little forced and spurious, as German jazz is: Oskar coughs in church, and the cough climbs into the choir and organizes a Bach society; when Oskar feels an impulse, "hedgehogs mated under the soles of my feet."

The other great strength of the book is its mockery of German hypocrisy. When a dwarf friend of Oskar's becomes Goebbels' jester, the friend describes himself as the "inward emigration." After the war, little Kurt becomes a black market businessman, specializing in lighter flints. The most successful nightclub in Duesseldorf is the Onion Cellar, serving nothing but onions, which the patrons cut up to have a good public cry. In two mad postwar vignettes, the lieutenant who ordered the machinegun-ning of the nuns in 1945 reappears a decade later for a military inspection of the ruined pillbox, and two German soldiers ordered to execute a Polish partisan in 1939 are seen as civilian businessmen in 1954, still obediently trying to execute him.

Some of the book is authentically funny, although the humor is always on the edge of the macabre. Oskar says of a friend that he lay in bed for days, urinating into beer bottles, when "with a little spirit of enterprise he might have urinated in the washbasin." There is an uproari-ous love affair between a sadist and a masochist, rising to passion each time he tramples her big toes and turns the nails black, ending sadly when new nails will no longer grow.

Having dutifully listed all the things that I can find to praise, I must now confess that they do not seem to me to add up to anything. The meaninglessness of the symbols is the major defect. Oskar's tin drum, marked as central by the book's title, at first seems to have a clear significance, when Oskar hides under rostrums and breaks up Nazi meetings by turning the marches into waltzes and Charlestons. Ah, the reader thinks, Oskar is Thoreau's different drummer, a symbol for the Other Germans. But Oskar denies this, and says that he similarly broke up meetings of Boy Scouts and Vegetarians. The reader soon discovers that the important feature of the drumming is hiding under the stand, as Oskar similarly hides under the family table and under his grandmother's skirts. Eventually the drum comes to symbolize so many things that it symbolizes nothing.

So with the other symbols. A great deal is made of an identification with Jesus. At one point a plaster statue of the boy Jesus miraculously drums for Oskar, and at another point Oskar calls himself "Jesus." It is all hokum, however, and Oskar is more nearly Judas: he betrays his legal father and his true father to their deaths, the former in a genuinely horrifying scene. Similarly, Oskar's ability to shatter glass with his voice seems at first as though it will turn out to be a meaningful symbol, perhaps for the power of art. By the time Oskar sings a heart-shaped opening in a water glass, with an engraved inscription under it, as a souvenir for a girl midget, this too is hokum.

The Tin Drum's vision of sex is not as distasteful as Naked Lunch's only because it is less sadistic. Oskar's mother and her lover play a kind of footsie under the card table, in which his sock-clad foot gropes between her thighs. A married woman who tries to take her pleasure with a live eel is bitten and maimed. Oskar is seduced by Maria after they make a fizz drink, from fruit-flavored powder and his saliva, in her navel; later he fights with her and punches and bites her genitals. And so on, and so on.

Much of Grass' style is pointless mannerism. He switches at random from the first person to the third; he retells one chapter endlessly, beginning it again and again with slight changes. He describes Oskar's conquest of one lady in a military metaphor, then switches to metaphors from poetry and music; other coy metaphors add salacity to other sexual adventures. Sometimes a nasty detail becomes a political metaphor: the ghastly disintegration of an exhumed female corpse is a comment on the dismantling of industrial plants in the Ruhr and Rhineland; the inability of two drunken lesbians to copulate makes Oskar despair of the reunification of Germany.

It is all shapeless and random. Oskar meets a girl named Ulla at a party and helps her throw up by putting a finger down her throat; she soon joins him as a life model, and they are painted surrealistically, with Ulla cut open in the middle and Oskar sitting reading between her spleen and liver. What is the relationship of these details to each other? None, except that they are equally disgusting. But Swift, in Gulliver's Travels, ordered the disgusting and nauseating to produce a meaningful work of art. The comparable details in The Tin Drum seem chosen only to produce their individual frissons. In one scene, Oskar and his employer Korneff stand in a cemetery during a funeral, and Oskar squeezes the boils on Korneff's neck; the squeezing is described between lines of the Lord's Prayer. Why? Why not? If the eel-fishing scene is revolting, as it truly is, why not repeat it later in the book? And so Grass does. The reviews announced him as the German Joyce or Faulkner, but I am afraid that he is only the German Gregory Corso.

Grass' second novel, Cat and Mouse, is even more disappointing than The Tin Drum. Cat and Mouse is about the fixation that the adolescent narrator, Pilenz, has on a schoolfellow, Joachim Mahlke. Mahlke is a loner with a protuberant Adam's apple, a wizard at diving for salvage. In the course of the novel Mahlke outgrows his anti-war sentiments to become a heroic tank commander. When he is not allowed to make a speech at his old school, which had expelled him for stealing a veteran's Iron Cross, Mahlke kills himself. The "mouse" of the title is Mahlke's Adam's apple — I do not know why, and I do not know what the "cat" stands for — and everything Mahlke does is to distract attention from it or to conceal it.

Cat and Mouse suggests Alain-Fournier's *The Wanderer* rescored for a German brass band. It is as obsessed with the bladder as is *The Tin Drum*, and merely adds an obsession with the Adams' apple. Grass' style is even more self-conscious than it is in his first novel. Pilenz refers to Grass as "the fellow who invented us because it's his business to invent people." He starts to tell a story and breaks off with the remark: "a dismal, complicated story, which deserves to be written, but somewhere else, not by me." He wonders "who is writing this in the first place," and asks at the conclusion, "Who will supply me with a good ending?"

A little fellow pounding on a tin drum wanders through *Cat and Mouse*, and seagulls emit "glass-cutting screams." The narrator switches pointlessly from the first person to a second-person address to Mahlke. The symbols — cat, mouse, Adam's apple, Iron Cross, the absurd salvaging — are again meaningless. A kind of foreshadowing that we might call "shotgun foreshadowing" is used to foretell Mahlke's eventual suicide: the boys predict "Someday he's going to hang himself, or he'll get to be something real big, or invent something terrific."

One perfect detail in *The Tin Drum* convinces me that Grass has talent. A band of SA men wreck the toystore of a Jew named Markus; they then go after Markus and find him slumped over his desk, a suicide. "One of the SA men with puppets on his fingers poked him with Kasperl's wooden grandmother." I do not think that this gem of bitter irony justifies almost 800 pages, but it shows that if Grass ever learns his craft, he might be quite a writer.

The Nerve of Günter Grass
[*Dog Years*]

George Steiner*

Günter Grass is an industry: 300,000 copies of *The Tin Drum* sold in Germany; more than 60,000 in France; the American edition passed 90,000 in hardcover, well over 100,000 in paperback. In England, the vignette of the little man with the daemonic drum has become a publisher's symbol. Now there is hardly a bookstore window in Europe from which the black dog of Grass's second major novel, *Hundejahre*, does not stick out his red, phallic tongue. But it is not Grass's enormous success that matters most, nor the fact that he has put German literature back on the market. It is the power of that bawling voice to drown the siren-song of

*Reprinted from *Commentary* 37 (May 1964): 77–80, by permission of *Commentary*; and from George Steiner, "A Note on Günter Grass," in *Language and Silence* (New York: Atheneum, 1967). © 1963, 1967 George Steiner. Reprinted with the permission of Atheneum Publishers, Inc.

smooth oblivion, to make the Germans—as no writer did before—face up to their monstrous past.

A grim fantasy lurks at the heart of *Hundejahre*. The fable turns on the love-hate and blood brotherhood of Nazi and Jew. Walter Matern, the S.A. man—Eduard Amsel, the Jew; brothers under skin and soul, twin shadows in a weird, ferocious parable of how Germany turned to night.

The neurotic conjecture of some secret, foredoomed relationship between Nazi and Jew, of a hidden fraternity or mutual fascination deeper than the outward show of loathing and destruction, crops up tenaciously. We find it in the suspicion, argued with varying degrees of historical finesse, that Nazism derived from Judaism its own dogma of a "chosen race" and of a millennial, messianic nationalism. It emerges in Hannah Arendt's macabre reading of Eichmann's "Zionism," and in the persistent belief or allegation that certain eminent Nazis—Heydrich, Rosenberg, Hitler himself—had traces of Jewish descent.

This intimation feeds on two deep-buried sources. Jewish masochism at times inclines to the notion that there was an occult rationale for the catastrophe, a savage yet somehow natural rebuke to the proud hopes fostered by Jewish assimilation into German culture. The German or the outsider, on the other hand, yields to the obscure imagining that German Jewry in some way brought the whirlwind on itself, that the temptations it offered to bestiality were too subtle, too intimate to be resisted. So utter a process of recognition and extermination must have involved some hidden complicity between torturer and victim. For all men kill the Jew they love.

Two boys play and dream by the sedge and mud-banks of the Vistula, in the flat marshes on the Polish frontier and around Danzig which Grass has made uniquely his own. Matern, the teeth-gnasher and miller's son; Amsel, the half-Jew (or is it more, who knows?). The schoolboy pack yelps at Amsel; he is a butterball with a jackdaw tongue, and their fists hammer at him. Matern becomes his strong shield. When he's about, no one clobbers Amsel or screams *kike!* Butterball gives Matern a penknife. But the river has a strange drag, and one day, finding no stone at hand, Matern throws in the knife. So what? It was only a dime-store penknife, and Edi Amsel is a smart kid. Give him a bundle or rags, a few wood-shavings and scraps of wire. Before you know it, there's a scarecrow (in German, *Vogelscheuche* has lewd undertones). These are no ordinary scarecrows. They look like people in the neighborhood, and the birds spin above them in affrighted swarms. Put a few gears in their straw gut, and they start moving.

Matern isn't so dumb either. He tries the Communists and finds the beer thin. Down at the club, all the boys are turning brown. And they're nice about it: "We'd rather have one repentant Red than a dozen farting bourgeois." Matern joins. What the hell. And there's that screwball Amsel begging for all the cast-off S.A. uniforms Matern can scrounge, for the greasy caps and brown shirts torn in the latest street brawl. He drapes them on his scarecrows, and the hollow men, the stuffed men, start strutting. Goose-strutting, eyes right, arms outflung. As if they were legion.

There's snow in Amsel's yard. One day something queer happens. A covey of S.A. boys, their faces masked, comes soft over the fence. The kike is pounded to bloody shreds. Then they roll him in the snow; Amsel the snowman with no teeth left in his mouth. Not one. Who were the hooligans? Jochen Sawatzki, Paul Hoppe, Willy Eggers . . . Names that stretch from Pomerania to the Rhineland and Bavaria. Alfons Bublitz, Otto Warnke . . . Keep counting. Eight names. But there were nine men. It's all so complicated and long ago. Like in a foul dream or attack of nausea. You can't expect a man to remember everything. The snow lay deep and there were thirty-two teeth in it. And eighteen fists pounding Amsel into a bloody pulp. Eight fine German names. There's one missing. Still.

So Matern decides to find out. War is over and the thousand-year Reich lies in a stinking heap. But amid the graffiti in the men's urinal at the Cologne railway station, Matern sees the name and address of friend Sawatzki. He finds other names. Roaming north and south through the moon landscape of rubble and defeat, he tracks them down one by one. He asks for truth and justice. Where were you when the mad carpet-eater led us into the great brown sea? Where were you when they rolled my friend Edi Amsel into a bloody snowball and cleaned their boots on his face?

Matern is not alone. He travels with a large German shepherd. Prinz is Hitler's dog. He has escaped from the Führer's last redoubt, in the Berlin death-bunker. Straying westward, he meets Matern coming out of a P.O.W. camp. Now they're inseparable. While Matern infects the wives and daughters of his old cronies with venereal disease — it's odd how little things get into the German bloodstream and make it all hot and wild — Prinz fattens. But he's now called Pluto. *Nice* dog; have a biscuit; be a Disney dog.

Matern becomes a radio idol. One day he consents to be interviewed by a chorus of eager, well-scrubbed young folk. But some lunatic firm has been selling them glasses. Put them on and you see mom and dad in a queer brown light. You see them doing all sorts of surprising things — smashing shopwindows, yelling like apes in heat, making old, frightened men wipe latrines with their beards. Is that you, dad? So the bright young things ask Matern: who are those nine masked thugs climbing over the garden fence? Herr Walter Matern, friend of the Jews, anti-Nazi first class, will broadcast their names to the repentant nation. Eight names.

Then he starts running. Eastward. To the other Germany beyond the silent wall. He leaves Pluto safely tied up at the Cologne station. The train is smooth and swift. The Germans are expert at making trains race across

Europe. But there's a dog bounding along the track, quicker than a diesel. And just at the border, a shadow steps out of the shadows. An old friend. He has a pen-knife. And when Matern throws it into the Berlin canal, he doesn't even mind. Canals can be dredged. But certain things can never be lost, never thrown away. Knives, for instance.

The tale ends in a grotesque *Walpurgisnacht*, a descent into a potash mine which is also the forecourt of damnation. Now we know what we have known all along. That Walter Matern loved Eduard Amsel so well that he had to get his hands on the very heart of him, and see his thirty-two teeth in the snow. That when the right man whistles, German shepherds are the hounds of hell.

Such a summary is not only inadequate (there are half a dozen novels crowded into this one baggy monster), but it makes the book sound tighter, more persuasive than it is. Before reaching the *Materniade* — the mock-epic of Matern's vengeful wanderings — the reader has to slog through a morass of allegory and digression. The middle section, some three hundred pages, is cast in the form of letters (at moments a parody of Goethe's *Wahlverwandschaften*). Through them, we glimpse the chaotic destinies of Matern, of Amsel, who survives the Nazi period under a false name, and numerous minor characters.

There are various welds. Prinz-Pluto is descended from a long pedigree beginning with Perkum the wolfhound. The story of his forebears interweaves with that of the Materns. The two boys played with the dog Senta on the low banks of the river. The birch copse in which the children moiled and listened for owls seems to melt and darken into other groves (*Birken-Buchen* — put an extra syllable on a German tree and what do you have?). But although Grass plots and ravels with crazy gusto, the book tends to fall apart. What sticks in one's mind is the general statement of chaos and the brilliance of discrete episodes.

The early chapters of boyhood and river, with their meandering, heavy cadence, are an extraordinary feat. Grass wraps himself inside the visceral totality of children. He sees as they do, in slow wakings and abrupt flashes. Like *The Tin Drum, Hundejahre* conveys the impression that there is in Grass's power a deliberate streak of infantilism, a child's uninhibited, brutal directness of feeling.

The narrative of an S.A. gang-up in a beer hall is unforgettable. Grass brings to light the banal roots of Nazi bestiality. We see the steamy, cozy vulgarity of German lower-middle-class manners, the wet cigar ash, and the slap on the buttocks, twist, by a sudden jerk of hysteria, into the sweating fury of the killers. One comes to understand how the sheer grossness of German pleasures — the bursting sausages and the flowered chamber-pots, the beer-warmers and the fat men in tight leather shorts — was the ideal terrain for the sadistic-sentimental brew of Nazism. Again, one feels that Grass has allowed a certain freedom of vulgarity in himself, in his own talent. That is what gives his plunge into the mind and voice of Sawatzki and his boys its nauseating truth. Only in Rudolf Nassauer's neglected novel, *The Hooligan*, is there anything that cuts as deep.

Grass is merciless on post-war Germany, on the miracle of amnesia and cunning whereby the West Germans shuffled off the past and drove their Volkswagens into the new dawn. He reproduces, with murderous exactitude, the turns of phrase and gesture, the private silences and the public clichés through which Adenauer Germany persuaded itself, its children, and much of the outside world, that all those frightful things hadn't really happened, that "figures are grossly exaggerated," or that no one in red-roofed Bad Pumpleheim really knew *anything* of what was going on in the woods three miles away. Quite a few fine houses and villas *did* come on the market in those years (Lieschen and I and little Wolfram are living in one right now, as a matter of fact). But you know how Jews are — always off to Sorrento or South America. The Führer? Now that you mention it, I never saw him. But I did see his dog once. *Nice* dog. Biscuit, please.

Grass singles out the moment of untruth. In the three years of desolation from 1945 to 1948, there was a real chance that the Germans might come to grips with what they had wrought. "Germany had never been as beautiful. Never as healthy. There had never been more expressive human faces in Germany than in the time of the thousand and thirty-two calories. But as the little Mulheim ferry accosted, Inge Sawatzki said: 'Now we'll soon be getting our new money.' "

With the currency reform of 1948, and the brilliant recovery of German economic strength (in the very combines and steel mills where slave labor had been ground to death only a little while earlier), the past was declared irrelevant. Prosperity is an irresistible detergent: it scours the old darkness and the old smells out of the house. Grass has captured the whole ambience: the evasions and the outright lies, the cynicism of the little men grown fat on the manure of the dead, and the nervous queries of the young. The shadow of Amsel (or is it the man himself?) is full of genuine admiration for the German genius. Look at all these good folk "cooking their little pea-soup over a blue gas-flame and thinking nothing of it." Why should they? What's wrong with gas ovens?

On May 8, 1945, Prinz comes to the banks of the Elbe. Should he head east or west? After mature sniffing, Hitler's dog decides that the West is the right place for him. In that central fable, Adenauer Germany has its mocking epitaph.

Hundejahre confirms what was already apparent in *The Tin Drum* and *Cat and Mouse*. Grass is the strongest, most inventive writer to have emerged in Germany since 1945. He stomps like a boisterous giant through a literature often marked by slim volumes of whispered lyricism. The energy of his devices, the scale on which he works, are fantastic. He suggests an action painter wrestling, dancing across a huge canvas, then rolling himself in the paint in a final logic of design.

The specific source of energy lies in the language. *Hundejahre* will prove formidably difficult to translate (even the title has no just equivalent). In these seven hundred pages, Grass plays on a verbal instrument of uncanny virtuosity. Long stretches of Baltic dialect alternate with parodies of Hitlerite jargon. Grass piles words into solemn gibberish or splinters them into unsuspected innuendo and obscenity. He has a compulsive taste for word-lists, for catalogues of rare or technical terms (it is here that he most resembles Rabelais). There are whole pages out of dictionaries of geology, agriculture, mechanical engineering, ballet. The language itself, with its powers of hysteria and secrecy, with its private parts and official countenance, becomes the main presence, the living core of this black fairy tale.

In 1958 I wrote an essay, much misquoted and denounced since, asking whether the German language had survived the Hitler era, whether words poisoned by Goebbels and used to regulate and justify Belsen could ever again serve the needs of moral truth and poetic perception. *The Tin Drum* appeared in 1959, and there are many to proclaim that German literature has risen from the ashes, that the language is intact. I am not so sure.

Grass has understood that no German writer after the holocaust could take the language at face value. It had been the parlance of hell. So he began tearing and melting; he poured words, dialects, phrases, clichés, slogans, puns, quotations, into the crucible. They came out in a hot lava. Grass's prose has a torrential, viscous energy; it is full of rubble and acrid shards. It scars and bruises the landscape into bizarre, eloquent forms. Often the language itself is the subject of his abrasive fantasy.

Thus one of the most astounding sections in *Hundejahre* is a deadly pastiche of the metaphysical jargon of Heidegger. Grass knows how much damage the arrogant obscurities of German philosophic speech have done to the German mind, to its ability to think or speak clearly. It is as if Grass had taken the German dictionary by the throat and was trying to throttle the falsehood and cant out of the old words, trying to cleanse them with laughter and impropriety so as to make them new. Often, therefore, his uncontrolled prolixity, his leviathan sentences and word inventories, do not convey confidence in the medium; they speak of anger and disgust, of a mason hewing stone that is treacherous or veined with grit. In the end, moreover, his obsessed exuberance undermines the shape and reality of the work. Grass is nearly always too long; nearly always too loud. The raucous brutalities which he satirizes infect his own art.

That art is, itself, curiously old-fashioned. The formal design of the book, its constant reliance on *montage*, on fade-outs, and on simultaneities of public and private events, are closely modeled on *U.S.A.* The case of

Grass is one of many to suggest that it is not Hemingway, but Dos Passos who has been the principal American literary influence of the twentieth century. *Hundejahre* is also Joycean. One can hardly imagine the continuous interior monologue and the use of verbal association to keep the narrative moving, without the pattern of *Ulysses*. Finally, there is the near voice of Thomas Wolfe. Grass's novels have Wolfe's bulky and disordered vehemence. *Of Time and the River* prefigures, by its title and resort to the flow of lyric remembrance, the whole opening section of *Hundejahre*.

Where Grass knits on to the tradition of German fiction, it is not the modernism and originality of Broch and Musil that count, but the "Dos Passos-expressionism" of the late 1920's. Technically, *Hundejahre* and *The Tin Drum* take up where Döblin's *Berlin Alexanderplatz* (1929) left off.

This is, in part, because Grass is resolutely "non-literary," because he handles literary conventions with the unworried naïveté of an artisan. He came to language from painting and sculpture. He is indifferent to the fine-spun arguments and expectations of modern literary theory. His whole approach is essentially manual. But there is a second reason. Totalitarianism makes provincial. The Nazis cut the German sensibility off from nearly all that was alive and radical in modern art. Grass takes up where German literature fell silent in the 1930's (even as young Soviet poets are now "discovering" surrealism or Cocteau). His ponderous gait, the outmoded flavor of his audacities, are part of the price German literature has to pay for its years in isolation.

But no matter. In his two major novels Grass has had the nerve, the indispensable tactlessness to evoke the past. By force of his macabre, often obscene wit, he has rubbed the noses of his readers in the great filth, in the vomit of their time. Like no other writer, he has mocked and subverted the bland oblivion, the self-acquittal which underlie Germany's material resurgence. Much of what is active conscience in the Germany of Krupp and the Munich beer halls lies in this man's ribald keeping.

Germany's Tragedy [*The Plebeians Rehearse the Uprising*]

Ronald Bryden*

Günter Grass called *The Plebeians Rehearse the Uprising* "a German tragedy." His subtitle should have given pause to the young German leftists who took it as a betrayal, a posthumous slander of Bertolt Brecht. They received it with much the same outcry that Hochhuth's *Soldiers* provoked here among the older generation of Churchillian Tories; which may be one

*Reprinted from *The Observer* (London), 26 July 1970, 24, by permission of *The Observer*.

of the reasons why Grass's superb play has taken four years to achieve its first professional production in London, staged by David Jones at the Aldwych for the RSC.

Had the German student Left paused, it might have occurred to them that the man who wrote *The Tin Drum* and *Dog Years* was unlikely to perpetrate anything so simple. *The Plebeians* is the richest, most complex and sardonic play to come out of Germany in the past decade. We'll be lucky if we see a finer this year.

A tragedy is a situation with no satisfactory outcome, no right solution. That, as Grass sees it, is how things were on 17 June 1953, when the workers of East Berlin rose in revolt against the norms imposed on them by the Ulbricht regime and their Soviet masters. For 24 hours the future of Communism and Europe hung in the balance. It seemed possible that Russia's strongest satellite would break for freedom, establishing a truly democratic socialism, the nucleus of a genuine third force in the world, across the ruins of the Iron Curtain. All that was needed was a leader: one great man who could give the incoherent forces swirling down the Stalinallee a voice and focus.

Unfortunately, the one German great enough to give the rising a voice was the one who had spent his life trying to teach his countrymen that a nation's first need is to live without heroes. Bertolt Brecht had spent his whole career watching the German people destroy themselves in the quest for leaders, pleading with them to stand on their own feet, without the aid of colossi. He had always refused to be a hero, and he did so now.

Cagy as his favourite common man, Schweik, he went on rehearsing his company, while rain dampened the ardour of the marchers outside and the first Russian tanks rumbled in from the east. Too late, he sent a cautious letter to the party leadership endorsing the workers' claims. Only its final paragraph, a formal statement of loyalty to the party, was allowed to be published.

To underline the tragic irony of this, Grass chooses to imagine a strikers' delegation bursting into the theatre while Brecht is rehearsing his version of *Coriolanus*; the reworking of Shakespeare's chronicle, which engaged him sporadically in 1952–53, to show the plebeians of Rome shaking off their dependence on their arrogant generalissimo. Mistrustfully, he delays writing the manifesto they ask for, taunting their confusion, contrasting their docile muddle with the fierce lucidity of Shakespearean passions. Too late, he sees that he has missed his one chance to behave like a common man, has behaved like Coriolanus. "We are colossi," he cries, "we deserve to be demolished."

Grass clearly means to attack the puritan aloofness of left-wing intellectuals who would rather plan ideal models of revolution than soil their hands with actual political means; who enact mini-dramas of symbolic revolt, but dismiss the masses as brainwashed and alienated. This may have stung the German student Left more than his portrayal of

Brecht, trapped by his greatness. "What can I do?" he appeals to his dramaturge. "I can't stand revolutionaries who won't walk on the grass."

In other words, the play is less about Brecht than about Germany and Grass himself. The Aldwych production brings this out wordlessly by giving its Brecht, Emrys James, a drooping moustache which makes him look more like Grass than his reluctant hero. He hasn't the authority the part needs, but it's an ingenious performance: sly, driven and biting. Peggy Ashcroft is commanding and fatalistic in a role standing for Brecht's wife, Helene Weigel, and Morgan Shepherd stands out as the most militant striker. They do justice to the power of an immensely imposing play.

The Dentist's Chair as an Allegory of Life [*Local Anaesthetic*]

Anonymous*

Mann and Camus: dead. Sartre: silent. Malraux: Minister of Culture. The old mullers and brooders, the old definers of crisis, are heard no more in the European novel. For a long time it seemed that there might be no successors. A surprise candidate has now emerged from the wings, an odd figure with a loser's accent and a bizarre past. His earlier books had astonishing power, using dwarfs and drums and scarecrows to explore the nightmare dominion of Nazi Germany and the guilt that followed. To many readers, particularly in the U.S., all this was fascinating. It also seemed very long ago and far away.

Now, with a small new novel, *Local Anaesthetic*, West Germany's Günter Wilhelm Grass has reached into the pressing present. The book's setting is Germany today. Its grim narrative device, characteristic of Grass's grotesque humor, offers society as a patient in a dentist's chair. The plot, if it can be called that, involves the threatened sacrificial burning of a dachshund. But Grass's real concern, which currently throbs like a sick tooth through the mind and conscience of the Western world, is the Generation Gap, the morality of revolutionary protest, the apparently helpless and surely tragic bankruptcy of liberalism.

At 42, Grass certainly does not look like the world's, or Germany's, greatest living novelist, through he may well be both. He has a gruff manner and a Dutch-comic soup-strainer mustache. There is a manic-gypsy look at the corners of his eyes, like that of an elf on a high. His face

*Reprinted from *Time*, 13 April 1970, 68–70, by permission of *Time*. © 1970 Time Inc. All rights reserved.

has been described as the sort that nervous mothers warn children against before they skip off to play in the Black Forest. At charades, he couldn't miss as one of those ambivalent wood cutters that lurk in the background of Grimm fairy tales.

For a German, Grass is a nonconformist in more important ways. His country reveres specialization. Grass has exuberantly sprawled out as minor poet, polemical dramatist, artist, sculptor and jazz musician. He has persistently made fun of the Establishment and the past. In the matter of language, he is a total revolutionary. Too often in Germany, culture has suggested lofty abstractions and an aristocratic style. Grass has always liked to stand the German language on its head and shake it. The result is Rabelaisian horselaughs, horrifying images and earthy sights, smells and sounds that make his visions of yesterday as immediate as a stubbed toe — or, yes, a toothache.

Lately, he has also crossed the most sacred boundary of all: the one that separates the German literary artist from politics. By custom, Germans expect a soulful aloofness from intellectuals. Art is enduring, a thing apart, not to be contaminated by the daily, dirty round of politics. Naturally, the last thing that Germans expect of a writer is that he will paint a rooster crowing "Es-Pe-De" (for Social Democratic Party) on the side of a secondhand Volkswagen bus and vulgarly, vulgarly bounce thousands of miles through West Germany campaigning for Willy Brandt. Last summer Grass did just that.

Distrustful Man

In a country still prone to convulsions of superhuman idealism, Grass remains a man thoroughly distrustful of the soaring and the abstract. "I have no ideology, no weltanschauung," he recently wrote to a friend. "The last one I had fell apart when I was 17 years old."

The principal personification of his distrust, his key corrective agent, as well as Grass's most famous character, is Oskar the dwarf, the protagonist of his first novel, *The Tin Drum*. The book sold more than 1,500,000 copies around the world (about 600,000 in the U.S.), as appalled and fascinated readers in 16 languages absorbed the dwarf's devastating, knee-high view of the rise and fall of the Third Reich. Oskar's "sing-scream" could shatter glass. His magic drum carried him back and forth in time. One of his best tricks was breaking up Nazi rallies by hiding beneath the speakers' platforms and beating out counter-rhythms on the tin drum. In his writing, in his life, Grass has played his own version of Oskar. He too has done his demonic best to break up all the going German rhythms, from the marching-to-destiny beat of *Deutschland über Alles* to the amnesiac waltz of postwar prosperity. In three war novels he has drummed: Remember! Remember! REMEMBER!

In articles and speeches, Grass has consistently attacked former members of the Nazi Party, including ex-Chancellor Kurt Georg Kiesinger and ex-Defense Minister Franz-Josef Strauss. In *Cat and Mouse* (1961), a nearly flawless small novel about German teenagers during World War II, Grass openly made fun of the Iron Cross—by having his hero dangle it in front of his genitals. Mad dreams of superstates, militarism and the kind of procrustean idealism that makes preposterous demands and holds out impossible hopes for society are inevitable Grassian targets. But Grass has also cleverly spun the coin of guilt to show that the Nazi nightmare was built upon Everyman's petty greed, with its corresponding indifference to the fate of others. In dealing with this, Grass's critical contrivances are customarily subtle.

The typically grim, fairy-tale props in *Dog Years* (1963), for instance, were magic spectacles that allowed postwar German children to see exactly what their innocent parents were actually doing between 1939 and 1945. The cruelest metaphor for greedy indifference occurs toward the end of *The Tin Drum* when Oskar's father is killed in his grocery cellar by occupying Russian forces. His body falls across the path of some ants that have set up supply lines to a smashed sack of sugar. "The ants found themselves facing a new situation," Grass wrote, "but, undismayed by the detour, soon built a new highway round the doubled-up Matzerath, for the sugar that trickled out of the burst sack had lost none of its sweetness while Marshal Rokossovski was occupying the city of Danzig."

Such imagery, put to the service of moral passion, has won Grass renown outside Germany as his country's most committed writer. "Much of what is the active conscience in the Germany of Krupp and the Munich beer halls," Critic George Steiner once put it, "lies in this man's ribald keeping." Characteristically impatient with grandiose claims of any sort, Grass rejects this sort of praise out of hand. For other reasons, a great many of his fellow countrymen reject the judgment too, particularly former Nazis, the middle class and petty shopkeepers of the older generation from whom Grass himself sprang. Such folk like to refer to him as "Pornograss," or contemptuously as *der Schnauzbart* (the mustache).

A Melancholy Awareness

Local Anaesthetic (Longmans; $7.25) is Grass's fourth novel. It still contains labyrinthine tunnels into the Nazi past. But the book is more obsessed with the affluent society, student revolt and the moral wound of the Viet Nam War. Is it a mark of German progress or American decline that Grass's anguished study of a contemporary German student, his teacher and a threatened antiwar demonstration seems as American, and as unsettling, as the latest homemade-bomb scare? It is one of Grass's several geniuses to ask the appropriate question at the appropriate time. "My God, what did we do?" was the simple right question to ask when

The Tin Drum was written. "My God, what do we do now?" is the complicated right question to ask today.

How sick was the middle class in Nazi Germany? Grass knew, and for three novels would not let anyone forget it. How sick is the middle class today throughout the Western world? In *Local Anaesthetic* the ex-tin drummer is testing, testing.

Give him a crisis. Can Middle-Class Man, 1970, make a decision?

Give him a duty. Can he perform it?

Give him a son. Can he play father?

Grass's principal character is a 40-year-old high school teacher and bachelor named Eberhard Starusch. Stretched between past and future, he preaches reason to an age now raging toward an absolutism as extreme as that held by the Nazis. Starusch appeared fleetingly in earlier books as Störtebeker, the teen-age leader of the Dusters Gang of Grass's hometown of Danzig, pillager of churches and wartime delinquent extraordinary.

Now it is 25 years later in West Berlin. Störtebeker has been ground down into a rueful academic mediocrity. A notably unsuccessful lover, he leads an unswinging life. It consists of books, records, a collection of Celtic shards, a new Berber rug, bottles of Moselle wine that generally fail to seduce and a profoundly melancholy awareness that there is no dramatic cure — and perhaps no cure at all — for the pain of the world.

Starusch is stirred to action by Philipp Scherbaum, one of his students. The boy threatens a public immolation, partly to protest violence in general but mainly to lament the use of napalm in the Viet Nam War. He does not plan to burn himself — not from any cowardice, Grass makes clear, but because of a probably correct belief that jaded and cynical Berliners would hardly stop yawning if a 17-year-old made himself a human torch. But, the boy reasons, Berliners love dogs. Accordingly, in front of the pastry-gobbling matrons on the terrace of a Kurfürstendamm café, Philipp plans to burn Max, his own much-loved dachshund, and hold up a sign that reads: "This is gasoline, not napalm."

Even a few years ago, such a situation would have seemed pure farce conjured up by someone peculiarly given to the grotesque — Grass himself, perhaps, or the late Lenny Bruce. Not today. Starusch knows that Philipp means it, and he cares deeply. The boy is his most gifted and likable student. The real thrust of Grass's book concerns the teacher's attempts to save his pupil, casting about in his mind for such shreds of love, logic and learning as Western civilization can provide.

Rummaging urgently through the storehouse of history, Starusch shows his class that revolution inevitably devours its children and ends in reformism. "With a little patience," he points out, "they could have had the same thing at less cost." Says Scherbaum, gently: "You oughtn't to take this business about history so tragically. Spring has no meaning, either, or has it?"

Morality and metaphysics are marshaled. "Public burnings are no deterrent," Starusch thinks, "they only satisfy base instincts. (I'll tell Scherbaum that.)" To show the absurdity and ineffectuality of any action, Starusch ponders assigning a paper on "What are acts?" Democracy, that most inefficient if most provocative form of government, is also invoked. Scherbaum is not impressed. "Freedom of choice and second helpings," he says, summing up the café ladies, "that's what they mean by democracy."

Growing desperate, Starusch even offers to burn another dog with Scherbaum. He hopes to confuse the issue and thinks that, at the very least, he will be able to protect the boy from the angry crowd. Scherbaum refuses sadly. "You're over thirty," he observes. "All you care about is limiting the damage." "Watch yourself, Flip," advises Scherbaum's politicized girl friend Vero, who wants to see her lions eat her Christians, or vice versa. "Mao warns us against the motley intellectuals."

Meandering into Love

The crucial third party in the tug of war over Scherbaum's soul, however, is an unnamed man in tennis shoes: Starusch's dentist. Starusch has an overshot underjaw. Pain and multiple appointments are involved. Along with other local anaesthetics, the dentist maintains a diversionary TV set on his wall. As a modern opiate it is not far behind Novocain and the ultra-high-speed drill.

Much of what Starusch thinks, feels and seems to dredge up from his memories and fantasies occurs in the form of a surrealist TV show glimpsed past his tormentor's ear. Meanderings into Starusch's early love life, barely suppressed feelings of violence and real or imagined career in reinforced concrete multiply, not always fruitfully for the reader. Grass, who has long admired Herman Melville, sometimes seems bound to do lightly for dentistry what the author of *Moby Dick* did for whaling. Symbols clang. Tartar on the teeth, one gathers, is Evil — "calcified hate." Parallels are drawn — and stretched — between pumice (for cleansing) and pumice (for building), and between middle-aged teeth and the decayed pillboxes on the Normandy beaches.

Grass's intention is broader than one at first suspects. *Local Anaesthetic*, in fact, may go down in history as the first novel to turn the dentist's chair into an allegory of life. Absolutist revolutions, religions and moralities have all foundered on the problems of pain and how to cure it. Now Grass's dentist steps forward, an apostle of technology as priest of the "relative." He reduces philosophy to Seneca plus hygiene. He is the exact fulfillment of Spengler's prophecy that absolute engineering is man's historical destiny.

"One man held the patient's left arm," he complacently lectures Starusch, comparing the painless extractions of today with the dental horrors of a century ago. "The second wedged his knee into the pit of his stomach, the third held the poor devil's right hand over a candle flame so as to divide the pain." True, too true. Few benefactors of humanity can more easily prove relative progress in the conquest of pain than dentists. Few are less lovable. The dentist takes an interest in Scherbaum's case. He even offers the boy a free examination. Mercilessly, Grass shows how close in some ways the dentist's liberal views are to the muddled humanism of Starusch. "I can counsel moderation," says the proud dentist. "I refuse to demand the abolition of Kirsch Torte and hard candy." Then comes the *coup de grâce.* "How do you feel about napalm?" Starusch asks between rinsings. The reply: "Well, measured against the nuclear weapons known to us, napalm must be termed relatively harmless."

Local Anaesthetic is thinner and more schematic than Grass's earlier books. The positions taken by Starusch, Scherbaum and the dentist are not new. How could they be? But they have more nuances of feeling and rueful perceptions than can be imagined or explained easily, or than the elements of a Socratic trialogue have any right to demonstrate.

The Sadness of Knowledge

Grass is Starusch, essentially. Yet Starusch is the least effectual spokesman present. Student Scherbaum, whose feelings Grass also largely shares, is a more plausible, a purer personality. What lends the story its inner force is the relationship between student and teacher — a compound of affection, melancholy, slight understanding and profound gap. The truths of middle age are usually enunciated with the smugness of Spiro Agnew speaking of effete snobs. But Humanist-Fumbler Starusch possesses charity, or what he calls "the sadness of my better knowledge."

Like Grass, Starusch is aware of how depressing it is to know that all actions, even the purest, are likely to be compromised, and that society, possessed of enormous power to harm itself, has only small power to improve. Like Grass, he mourns the fall of valor and of hope that occurs each time his kind of knowledge prevails, catching up a youthful spirit in the toils of conventional wisdom.

Childless Starusch comes very close to a father's love. What can man learn? What can man teach? Grass asks these questions while confronting a world where conventional wisdom seems to find itself hopelessly compromised and often outflanked by impatient rage. But his book's debate also seems to accept the classic definitions — though not the romantic solutions — of Nietzsche, whom Starusch quotes both seriously and ironically.

Man, Nietzsche thought, tugs himself in two opposite directions. The Greek god of wine, Dionysus, represents the feeling part of man: vital, creative, inspired but, if carried to excess, also deranged and destructive. Apollo, the sun god, stands for the reasoning part of man, drawn toward order, systems, and justice — with the risk, of course, of deadening over-organization.

Totally Reasonable

Looking at Scherbaum, Starusch, in effect, asks: Can life be passionate, *alive*, Dionysian, without spinning off into chaos? Looking at his stoic dentist, spouting Seneca, Starusch asks: Can life be orderly, totally reasonable, Apollonian, without becoming as sterile as a dentist's office?

Here is the dilemma of the middle class, and here is Grass flapping wildly to maintain balance, while looking despairingly at the record of bourgeois society, 1939–1970. The patient, especially in Germany, keeps going on awful binges — between which he snores away in a complacent stupor. Bloodlust or Novocain-tingle: Are there no alternatives? Grass has been haunted by this question all his life.

In a remarkable passage in *The Tin Drum*, he dreams of the perfect Nietzschean synthesis: "Oskar was a little demigod whose business it was to harmonize chaos and intoxicate reason." This may also be as close to a definition of the artist's job as Grass has come. The bloodletting material, the tindrumming style of the war novels, has partly disguised what *Local Anaesthetic* makes apparent: Grass is a fanatic for moderation. He is a moderate the way other men are extremists. He is a man almost crazy for sanity.

Balance is Grass's game. He is in love with the firm, the tangible. He has a peasant's instinct for the solid ground, an artisan's feeling for materials. His West Berlin home — described by one visitor as "a god-awful Wilhelmian house" — is solid as a fort. The furniture is reassuringly thick-legged. The floors are bare. There are no curtains.

In clean, wrinkled, absolutely undistinguished clothes — open-necked shirts are the rule — Grass walks from room to room with workmanlike purpose. He looks like the visiting plumber who has a job to do and knows quite well that he can do it. He is a man who rolls his own cigarettes, from black, earthy, wonderfully vile-looking tobacco (Schwarzer Krauser No. 1). His notion of vacation is to rent a cottage in Brittany and dig all day for clams.

He loves West Berlin, including its *Kneipen* (corner pubs). With his Swiss wife Anna, a former ballet dancer, and the children — twins, Franz and Raoul 12, Laura, 8, and four-year-old Bruno — he still goes on long investigatory walks. Whatever puts him at one remove from the physical, Grass hates, including the automobile (he refuses to learn to drive) and the telephone (he used to hide his in a cupboard and beg his friends not to call).

On Sundays and other special occasions, he cooks for the family and friends. His speciality: roast mutton à la Grass (recipe, secret), which he has used occasionally as the lure to political gatherings in his home.

"Cooking is like sculpture," he says. "It's working with real material. Writing, just words on a page; it's too abstract to satisfy."

Still, Grass makes writing as corporal and kinetic as he can. He composes standing up, as Hemingway and Thomas Wolfe did before him, planting himself before a tailored-to-order desk like a craftsman at his workbench. And when he works, he works: up to seven hours a day. He makes notes in a large scrawl with a felt pen but does his actual writing on a typewriter. A good day he will usually produce six pages, double-spaced, that eventually go through two, maybe three, rewrites. Even so, *The Tin Drum* took more than five years to complete.

From his very beginning, Grass was born to be one of nature's liveliest balancing acts. German grocer father. Mother a volatile product of the Kashubians, a Slavonic tribe with its own language that figures, right down to its recipes, in all of Grass's novels. A good, sturdy mongrel strain for an artist who would have to carry out (literally) Joyce's advice to the writers' guild: silence, exile and cunning.

What his native city of Danzig (now the Polish city of Gdańsk) meant to young Grass is laid bare in his novels in passages as close to lyricism as this anti-sentimental man can come. The boyhood scenes along the Vistula in *Dog Years* bear a universal-urchin resemblance to Mark Twain's recollections of his own lost Eden, the Mississippi. "For me," Grass recalls, "Danzig was a modern port and a medieval town, a marvelous mixture."

Grass's Danzig comes through the pores: the swoop of gulls, the rainbow oil slicks on harbor water, those unique greens and maroons that encrust the sides of tramp steamers, the look of rusty iron against snow. Then there is the city itself: a palette of earth tones and potato browns under spirals of wood smoke. The Danzig sentences flow like the Vistula, chock-full of the flotsam that Grass loves to describe.

Grass fiercely denies that he writes autobiography. In preparation for *The Tin Drum*, he revisited Danzig briefly and researched the story of its Polish post office besieged by the SS Home Guard. Yet he only recently received a stack of photographs of the city that he shuffles through, making precise identifications. "This is the school in *Cat and Mouse . . .* Here's the cemetery in *The Tin Drum.*"

When a Grass protagonist leaves Danzig, the world starts at once to turn into a nightmare. It is as if a malediction had been pronounced. Homey realism begins to tear apart into fantasy. Characters are likely to change not only their names but their personalities — thinning out, abstracting, becoming jeering ghosts of their former selves.

Grass has succinctly outlined his own journey into that nightmare: "At the age of ten, I was a member of the Hitler Cubs; when I was 14, I was enrolled in the Hitler Youth. At 15, I called myself an Air Force auxiliary. At 17, I was in the armored infantry." Grass left Danzig as a soldier in 1944. He was wounded on April 20, 1945, and the end of the war found him in a hospital bed at Marienbad. He was one of the first

Germans to be marched through Dachau for a whiff of what the infernal was really like. He has not forgotten.

Patriotic Ideology

Call those the live-or-die years. Grass characters are nothing if not survival artists, and Grass survived. He estimates that 80% of the Danzig he knew was bombed out. He had to abandon, naturally, the patriotic ideology he once held as a self-styled "dutiful youth." Like Mahlke, the schoolboy hero of *Cat and Mouse*, he once could identify most German warships by class. Unlike Mahlke, Grass admits: "I myself was thinking right up to the end in 1945 that our war was the right war."

How did a grocer's son from Danzig ever put together the nerve, the innocence, the cold fury, the sheer talent to play tin drummer to the most traumatic decade in modern history? The general pattern was one of slow maturing and lots of retreat time in the desert — the training rules of artists and saints. Grass did not exactly step out of P.W. uniform with calling in hand. He worked as a farm laborer, then in a potash mine — the scene of the climactic *Walpurgisnacht* in *Dog Years*. There followed further preliminary skirmishes among the ruins, more rehearsed handholds on life tentatively resumed.

Grass's sense of direction became firmer when he, like Oskar, apprenticed himself to a tombstone cutter in Düsseldorf — an almost too perfect school for the artist, considering Grass's bent. One imagines him, teeth bared in a macabre grin, ferociously attacking stone angels. In 1949 it all began to come together. Grass was accepted at Düsseldorf's Academy of Art, to study painting and sculpture. He played drums and washboard with the local jazz band ("to fill my stomach"). He began to write poetry ("to ease my soul"). He met Anna in 1952 on a hitchhiking vacation in Switzerland. They were married two years later, after she had moved to Berlin to dance. When, in 1953, he got into the Berlin School of Fine Arts, he also began to write plays.

In 1955, Anna entered a selection of her husband's poetry in a radio contest. He won third prize. More important, he earned a meeting with Group 47, once described by Grass as "the ambulant literary capital of Germany." It was a monumental encounter that must rank in literary legend with the day Hemingway first visited Gertrude Stein for tea.

Group 47, named after the year it was founded, had been established as a forum where young German writers could read works-in-progress and have them appreciated, or criticized. (The reader's chair is known as the electric chair.) "That noisy horde of smart alecks," the last guardian of German *Kultur*, Thomas Mann, called them. But in the cultural power vacuum of postwar Germany, Group 47 had the influence of an intellectual Mafia. Unshaven, in working clothes and a peaked cloth cap, as

veteran Group 47 members now recall him, Grass stood in the doorway
and announced: *"Ich bin* Grass." The tin drummer was on his way.

Condemned to Limbo

To this young man with the absolutely undefeatable lower jaw, what
did it matter that his first published book of verse fell into instant
oblivion? In search of personal isolation and a new environment, Grass
picked up his wife and moved to Paris. There he wrote, living on a
monthly income of 300 marks (about $75) from a German publisher that
he eked out by selling strong-minded but simple drawings. In 1958, Grass
read the first chapter from the electric chair. It is the custom for Group 47
to award an annual prize. Grass won in a landslide, getting more than
75% of the vote. *The Tin Drum* was published the following year, with an
advance sale—then an astounding figure in Germany—of more than
40,000.

Every artist kills the middle class he loves, and Grass can seem
merciless. "The truth is," he writes of Oskar's presumptive father before
killing him off, "he had never been anything but a blue-eyed boy, smelling
of cologne and incapable of understanding." Obedient in war, complacent
in peace, the blue-eyed little nobody is the villain of all Grass's pieces, the
real god that failed. Grass does not spare him.

Yet the members of the middle class remain Grass's wary hope too,
and the object of his unspoken compassion. Seldom good enough, but
never really bad either, they are condemned to the limbo of Dante's
trimmers. Grass shares the pain he gives them because, finally, he knows
he cannot save them or himself. Or can he?

That is why Grass goes apoliticking. "My fame must have some use,"
he says grimly, and plods around Germany, an earnest Apollonian,
devoting himself to what he calls "the boring, laborious task of reasoning."
And of repeating himself. Günter Grass, concerned-citizen-on-the-stump,
bears little resemblance to Grass the nightmare poet of past and present.
He comes on anti-charismatic and plainspoken. Gruffly he explains that
there are only "limited opportunities." Then he pleads for bigger pensions
for war widows, bigger inheritance taxes on estates over $1,000,000, some
sort of reconciliation with East Germany—in short, Social Democrat
Willy Brandt's program.

Grass worries about the moral absolutism of the revolutionary young
who seem willing to destroy society in the hope of curing it. Though much
better motivated, he believes, such apocalyptic thinking could prove as
dangerous as the absolutism of the Nazis. Grass worries about the posters
of Che Guevara and Martin Luther King Jr. that he finds on his son's
bedroom walls. "Public mythology," he grumbles. "Che never wanted to

be a picture that people pray before." (Grass himself is a lapsed Catholic, but he is letting his children be brought up in the church.)

The Establishment, of course, has never been able to abide Grass. The lower middle class has never forgiven his desecration of the Iron Cross. For his antimilitarism, his stand against sweeping Nazism under the rug, his insistence that a consumer society soon consumes far more than goods and services, he was for long a great hero of leftish intellectuals and the radical young. After all, the latter felt about their World War II parents the same way their American counterparts now feel about parental acquiescence to Viet Nam.

Grass, however, has spoken slightingly of the cloistered attitudes of writers in their "heart-warming velvet jackets" who walk their "freedom and independence like lap dogs." Four years ago, he lost the intellectual left for good by writing *The Plebeians Rehearse the Uprising,* a play that implicitly criticized Leftist Cult-Hero Bertolt Brecht for not supporting the 1953 workers' rebellion against the Communist regime in East Germany.

That left youth, the one group that Grass cares most about, the one group for which, essentially, *Local Anaesthetic* was written. Almost as much as the young do, he detests the dentist's pet philosopher Seneca whose stoic acceptance of the status quo, however horrifying, the elder generation in Germany and elsewhere has unwittingly come to adopt: "Let us train our minds to desire what the situation demands."

On Greece and War

Like the young of Germany, Grass deplores materialism and hates the repressive power of the Soviet Union. Like them, he is enraged by U.S. support of a bad government in Greece. Viet Nam, he has said, is a tragedy for postwar Europe because it has turned idealistic youth away from the U.S. — once hopefully looked to as a symbol of freedom and democracy. If anyone can or could speak to the Scherbaums of today, Grass can. But for how long? Morally, Grass is a liberal with a radical conscience. In politics he is a step-by-step progressive and a practicing Social Democrat. However, much as he wants change from deep inner conviction and bitter experience, he is against all apocalyptic self-delusions, supersystems, magic social cures and high-flown notions that human society is swiftly perfectible. In sadness he speaks out against youthful extremists and what he calls the "blind activism of a pseudo-revolutionary movement." In anger he sees Neanderthal reaction setting in by men who speak with grim relish of restoring law and order. Tirelessly, subtly, he preaches the folly of posturing.

Pain eats up energy. Politics does not encourage precise thought. "When you begin to shout and find the smile fixing itself on your mouth," Grass says, "you know you're really in politics." Political campaigns are also distracting—as Norman Mailer, the one major writer in the U.S. whose recent course seems to parallel Grass's, recently found out. There are critics who say that Grass will turn from writing to action for good if Willy Brandt should offer him a big enough job in the new government. Grass denies that. As proof, he holds up not only his work in progress but a completed body of writing, some of it done during his political period in the past five years, that has placed him beyond Mailer and Alexander Solzhenitsyn, at least in creative range and staying power.

It is a measure of Grass's seriousness that he has chosen to make a novel out of a theme as spectacularly unappealing as that of *Local Anaesthetic*. It is a measure of his honesty that he persists in giving the young the one answer they do not want to hear: "There is no answer." It is a measure of his abilities that he succeeds—touchingly, amusingly, agonizingly. Since *Local Anaesthetic* came out in Germany, Grass is often confronted by bitter high school and college students. "You only criticize," they complain, "you only show us how things are. Why don't you show us the way?" "I'm not a prophet," he growls in response, "I'm a writer." In the long run, that will probably have to be enough.

A Snail's Eye View [*From the Diary of a Snail*]

François Bondy*

In 1959 the publication of *The Tin Drum* brought sudden fame to a thirty-two-year-old sculptor and poet from Danzig named Günter Grass. The novel signaled a resurgence of that rich German language whose "death" the critic George Steiner had recently announced. Here was an abundance of reality in precise and picaresque detail; here, too, was an abundance of imagination centered on the mythical figure of a dwarf: a boy who refused to grow and who now sees literally "from below" and with a jaundiced eye the dubious fruits of Germany's awakening and Hitler's victories.

Since that auspicious debut thirteen years ago, Günter Grass has remained in prominent public view not only as a novelist but also as a playwright, essayist, and political polemicist. It was hardly surprising, therefore, that the recent publication of his fifth novel, *Aus dem Tagebuch einer Schnecke* (*From the Diary of a Snail*), should be hailed in Germany as a major literary event.

The hero of this new novel is none other than Günter Grass himself, a writer living in Berlin and conducting at his own expense an electoral campaign for the benefit of the Social Democrats. This, Mr. Grass tells his

*Reprinted from *World*, 24 October 1972, 50–51, by permission of the author.

four children (the oldest being fourteen-year-old twin boys), is what he is up to. He also tells them about Germany's past—about the Nazis, the murder of the Jews, and the war. Along with these elements of reality, the author introduces an imaginary character, the schoolteacher Hermann Ott, nicknamed Zweifel ("doubt"), who had helped the Jews during the Nazi years and had survived the war in the cellar of a bicycle trader. The fate of the Jews in Danzig (interconnected with the story of Zweifel), the progress of the electoral campaign, and the preparation of a lecture for the Dürer anniversary year in Nuremberg are woven together with a fourth theme introduced later: the suicide of a pharmacist during a political meeting and the attempt of the author to fathom the reasons why. This last theme is again entirely non-fictional: The suicide actually did take place as described. Here literal exactitude seems to be the mark of literary truth.

Yet the new book amounts to considerably more than the slightly *romancé* diary of Günter Grass. It is not to be compared, for example, to the recently published diary of Max Frisch (which includes, by the way, a remarkable chapter on "Günter Grass as VIP"). Grass himself does not give us the "inside" view corresponding to the "outside" view provided by his friend Frisch. *From the Diary of a Snail* is unquestionably a work of creative fiction—opinionated, polemical, argumentative—in which the speech patterns of our consumer and protest society are strikingly conveyed. Grass makes frequent use of unfinished sentences, which the reader familiar with current clichés will know how to conclude. Although there is much more of present-day reality here than in any previous work by Grass, the book is far from a mere chronicle, and its "true stories" serve a genuine artistic function of collage. The relationship between storytelling and history in this novel is comparable to the same relationship in the novels of Stendhal and Balzac. Stories and history, *Geschichten und Geschichte*, go together.

What is the meaning of the snail (or slug—the German word *Schnecke* can signify either animal)? Like the "drum" and "dog" in Grass's earlier novels, the snail has at once several literal and analogical meanings. Quite early in the book the narrator tells his children that the snail means progress, but that one has to move just a bit quicker. Later we get a report from an electoral meeting in the imaginary town of Schnecklingen (Snailsburg), where Hermann Ott appears to be a collector and student of snails. But the main function of the snail is philosophical. The snail is opposed to the *Weltgeist* on horseback that appeared one day to Hegel wearing the features of Napoleon. A race is going on between this horse and the snail; it is the snail who wins—at horns' length, I suppose. The slow, earth-bound, "sluggish" advance beats the dialectical "jump."

As he did in *Dog Years* with Martin Heidegger, Grass in this way makes fun of Hegel. But his dislike of Hegel and his concomitant admiration for Hegel's enemy Schopenhauer seem rather odd. Arthur Schopenhauer never stood for progress, even at a snail's pace, and he was certainly not interested in history. It is to Günter Grass's everlasting credit that he attempts in his novels to give a new intense consciousness of history to his German contemporaries, most of whom are quite indifferent to it and who prefer to live in the present or wildly in the future while blotting out the past. Whatever Hegel's *hubris* — as the narrator calls it — he is the one philosopher who gave history its philosophical dignity. To write on history as a thoughtful, committed German democrat and to root at the same time for Schopenhauer somehow seems contradictory — a discrepancy that has not escaped West Germany's foremost Marxist critic, Hans Mayer.

However, the contradiction is perhaps not as blatant as may appear. The lecture in Nuremberg that closes the book is called "About Stasis in the Midst of Progress." Here Grass discourses on the need for progress while at the same time recognizing the limits and ambiguities of all progress — the need for optimism balanced by the sadness that belongs to knowledge. Let us not forget that Grass in this novel tells his children about Auschwitz (indeed, an article of some years ago was called just that: "How to Tell My Children About Auschwitz"), describing for them the mass shootings, the deportations, the gassings. Over the years Grass has conducted research in Danzig, in Israel, and in West Germany to inform himself as fully as possible about the fate of the Jewish neighbors of his childhood. When I told him that I was reading his book, he referred me to a recently published history of the Danzig Jews, advising me to compare it with his own use of this material.

To present such a tale of suffering, humiliation, and destruction is to show an acute awareness that, despite the "economic miracle" and despite the success of decent, militant anti-Nazis like Willy Brandt, things are not all right, even if they seem so today. There is no comfort after such a tragedy. Next to history as a movement, there is always history as a past, to be relived in memory and awareness. A novelist turns backward, even when he is politically committed to progress.

In certain respects this *Diary of a Snail* seems rather remote from current trends in modern fiction, even if the mixing of fiction and nonfiction is familiar. The art of novel writing does not, it seems, follow a straight line. Occasionally "regressions" become necessary. Grass would rather risk losing out on the unity of his work than losing out on the richness of its component strands. Neither does he want to lose his right to introduce reflections and polemics.

How the new novel will stand up in years to come remains a matter of conjecture. Many of the events and persons mentioned are familiar to today's newspaper readers and television watchers in Germany. However, in years hence many allusions may need to be elucidated in footnotes. Even now, readers outside Germany will need them. Grass's previous novels included within their pages all the information necessary to any reader, but this one relies on some outside knowledge. It will be worthwhile to revisit the *Diary of a Snail* in a couple of years to see how the passing of time has affected this strange—and brave—piece of work, whose very core is the contrast between progress and melancholy, between the improvable present and the unredeemable past.

An Epic, Ribald Miscellany
[*The Flounder*]
Morris Dickstein*

A gargantuan fable that spans a period from the Stone Age to the 1970's, *The Flounder* is Günter Grass's first major novel in 15 years and one of the most exuberantly inventive works in recent European fiction. The books that made Mr. Grass's literary reputation—the brilliant, quasi-autobiographical *The Tin Drum*, his novella *Cat and Mouse*, and the mammoth Joycean *Dog Years*—were all first published between 1959 and 1963. By 1965 Mr. Grass had merrily plunged into West German electoral politics as a one-man Chatauqua on behalf of the Social Democrats and his good friend Willy Brandt.

Since then, along with his fellow novelist Heinrich Böll, Mr. Grass has remained an irrepressible gadfly of German society, a liberal democrat opposed to both the doctrinaire left and the anti-terrorist authoritarian backlash. Admirable as this is in a country whose writers and intellectuals have traditionally (and catastrophically) kept away from politics, it proved no benefit to his writing, though he produced a steady stream of poems, plays, essays, speeches and some minor fiction.

With the publication of *The Flounder* all this has instantly changed; even if it were a disaster it could hardly be minor, for everything in it runs to excess. *The Flounder* is one of those monstrous miscellanies like Rabelais's *Gargantua and Pantagruel*, Burton's *Anatomy of Melancholy*, Sterne's *Tristram Shandy*, Melville's *Moby Dick* (a Grass favorite), Flaubert's *Bouvard and Pecuchet*, and (in our century) Joyce's *Ulysses*, that can take on the guise of narrative fictions but whose wilder energies lie elsewhere—as inflatable vessels of bizarre information, vehicles for all kinds of encyclopedic, mythological, and historical lore. (Pynchon's and Barth's long novels are recent American contributions to this genre.)

Frequently these are scabrous and scandalous books, more blatantly obscene than other kinds of fiction—Mr. Grass is no exception here—yet they're also the work of intensely bookish men, anal types, collectors and compilers, shy but lecherous antiquarians. One of the things they collect is

*Reprinted from the *New York Times Book Review*, 12 November 1978, 12 and 66. © 1978 by the New York Times Company. Reprinted by permission of the New York Times Company and the author.

words, language; they have a passion for lists as well as facts, for epic catalogues and literary parodies. Where many novelists use language as a transparent medium for picturing the familiar world, these novels are more directly entranced with language itself and are written in a spectrum of styles as wide-ranging as their subject matter.

Within the framework of a modern fable, Mr. Grass tells and retells an assortment of historical anecdotes, ribald tales, and full-scale novellas — all variations on the battle of the sexes through the ages (but each also keyed to a particular food staple!). The framing story is a free adaptation of the famous Grimm fairy tale "The Fisherman and His Wife," in which a greedy woman forces her husband to keep asking a talking flounder (really an enchanted prince) for more and still more, until she asks for the sky and they wind up in the same miserable pot where they began.

Mr. Grass expands this slanderous parable of nagging womanhood into a raucous treatment of women in history: from primitive matriarchy, in which "mother right" supposedly held sway, to the women's liberation movement, which puts the principle of male dominance on trial. That principle is embodied in the legendary Flounder himself, whom we see on the dust jacket, sketched by Mr. Grass, whispering mischievously in the masculine ear.

Attached to that ear is the nameless narrator of the book, whose present life bears some resemblance to that of Günter Grass. Married to Ilsebill, the nagging wife of the fairy tale, now pregnant and asking for dishwashers and the like, the narrator keeps running off to do things a famous writer must (like visiting Calcutta as a cultural emissary and narrating a TV documentary about his native Danzig, now the Polish city of Gdańsk). In previous incarnations, however, the narrator, always with the advice of the Flounder, has been involved with nine (or eleven) women, all of them cooks, each belonging to a different phase of history or prehistory. With the Flounder's aid the narrator — and society — have managed to overcome matriarchy and put women in their place, in the kitchen, in bed, while men learned to make history by advancing technology and pursuing war and conquest.

Eventually, as the modern world grows more insanely destructive, Flounder becomes disenchanted with the male cause and finally, late in the 20th century, offers his services to some feminists, who instead of using him put him on trial for his past sins. Before a satiric Bertrand Russell-style tribunal, where splintering factions of militant feminists preside, we hear tales from the lives of all those cooks and the men they served (and sometimes dominated). These stories are served up to us with large helpings of popular anthropology and German history, along with staggering quantities of culinary information for each period. Mr. Grass evidently believes that society travels on its stomach; a rough but elaborate historical cookbook could be extracted from his mounds of out-of-the-way data.

Finally, with much ideological phrasemaking, the Flounder is convicted, but a moderate faction prevails and the talking fish is thrown back into the Baltic rather than killed and eaten. Meanwhile the narrator's wife, who had conceived in the opening pages — the book is divided into the nine months of her pregnancy, which parallel the nine cooks of history — at last gives birth: to yet another girl, another omen of female continuity.

This sounds almost as confusing as a summary of Joyce or Rabelais would. It contains as dazzling a variety of dishes as any literary menu since *Gravity's Rainbow*, but is the meal digestible? As in many such unusual concoctions, some of the ingredients come out half-cooked and a few of the courses seem to go on forever, such as the send-up of anthropological lore in the opening chapters and the increasingly tedious gibes at women's lib as the book goes on. But the risks of tedium and excess are built into this kind of encyclopedic satire. "At first I was only going to write about my nine or eleven cooks," says the narrator, "some kind of history of human foodstuffs — from manna grass to millet to the potato. But then the Flounder provided a counterweight. He and his trial." Only gradually, I take it, did the female question impose itself as the framework of the stories, and then without the insistence, the inevitability, of the prewar and Third Reich material so impressive in Mr. Grass's first three novels.

Mr. Grass was born and grew up in the Free City of Danzig, a Baltic seaport 96 percent German, surrounded by Poland, under the doubtful "protection" of the League of Nations. One of the world's most frequently besieged and contested cities (as Mr. Grass loves to emphasize), Danzig in the 1930's was a symbol of Germany's lost territories and a focus of Nazi agitation. By the end of the war it was buried in rubble with all its German population driven out. It is a truism to say that, except for Southerners like Faulkner, who inherited the consequences of the Civil War, American writers have a relatively undeveloped sense of history. But even among Europeans Mr. Grass was unusually well situated to learn how history buffets and battles local dreams and individual lives. A comic epic stuffed with maniacal research and ingenious analogies, *The Flounder* is by far the most audacious product of his historical imagination. Not in its feminist theme however: by temperament Mr. Grass seems attached to his masculine prerogatives though depressed at the havoc they have wrought in the world. But the challenge of feminism does not possess his imagination the way the spectacle of the Nazis once did. The sardonic ferocity of *The Tin Drum* turns more pensive and playful here.

What stands up as vividly authentic in *The Flounder* is its original conception, the use of culinary history and sexual history as a vehicle for history. As in Joyce, Mr. Grass's sweeping panoramas of human life are more effective for being concretely localized. But Mr. Grass is an exile, an orphan. Like the shtetl that haunts the Yiddish writer, German Danzig has come to exist exclusively in his work. "Men survive only in the written word," saith the Flounder. In this novel Mr. Grass undertakes to record and preserve not only the lost world of his childhood, as in *The Tin Drum*, but all of Danzig's history back to the Stone Age.

This is where the nine or eleven cooks prove so ingenious a device, like that other protagonist, the dwarfish Oskar banging his tin drum, who adamantly refuses to grow after his third birthday — and hence develops an unusual perspective on the adult world, which in its own way is more stunted and freakish than he is. Mr. Grass is an earthy writer with a coarse sense of humor, a bubbling sensual gusto, and an infectious appetite for life. Not a conventional realist, he diffracts history through symbols and parables, using distortion and exaggeration to limn essential reality all the more sharply. He revels in the traditional German affinity for the grotesque, but he has eschewed the solemnity of Gothic painters and expressionist playwrights; instead, with a special mixture of comedy and horror — as when Oskar's father died swallowing his Nazi Party pin — he became one of the tutelary spirits of the comic apocalyptic mode of the 1960's.

But where American black humorists sometimes settle for a casual nihilism, a send-up of history as an absurdist joke, Mr. Grass, despite his comic extravagance, remains a serious socialist obsessed with what history means and where it is going. This impels him to his political work, though it damages him as a writer. He has Chile on his mind, Watergate, the Yom Kippur War, the slums of Calcutta, and this can easily dilute his writing into topical discursiveness. Mr. Grass's cooks save him, for they give body to his politics and unite them with his gustatory temperament. Though comic creations, Mr. Grass's cooks, like Oskar, are all unyielding obsessional types, hedonists, ascetics, patriots, all mute but enduring witnesses to the special horrors of their age. Cooking tripe, boiling potatoes, hunting for mushrooms or ladling out soup at every stage of Europe's history, the cooks bring together Grass the novelist and Grass the socialist, for they make it possible for this burly Falstaffian imagination to write "history from below." Under the sign of the animal appetites, which no social coercion has ever managed to stifle, Mr. Grass recovers the point of view of the anonymous masses and rooted impulses usually left out of official history. In other words, he has written a real novel.

Elbe Swans and Other Poets
[*The Meeting at Telgte*]
Stephen Spender*

The date is 1647 — or perhaps Herr Grass would prefer to say 1647 / 1947. The meeting of German poets at Telgte, between Osnabrück and Münster, takes place while the Thirty Years War is drawing to a close, three years before the signing of the Treaty of Westphalia, and during the period of prolonged negotiations. The 200 states and sees which constituted the Germany of that era are devastated. The war which began as the culmination of the Counter-Reformation has fanned out into a multiplicity of wars, not all of them between Catholics and Protestants, some between co-religionists. For many years:

> The military lineup of the contending parties was not determined by religious allegiance: Catholic France, with papal approval, had fought against Spain, the Habsburgs, and Bavaria; the Protestant Saxons sometimes had one and sometimes the other foot in the imperial camp; a few years earlier, the Lutheran Swedes had attacked the Lutheran Danes. In deep secret Bavaria was bargaining for possession of the Palatinate. . . .

Some armies had mutinied, others had changed sides. Luckily for the rest of Europe, England was much taken up with civil war. "The thing that hath been tomorrow is that which shall be yesterday," runs the first sentence of Günter Grass's novel; and this Europe resembled much the world of sides constantly changing sides within a setting of unceasing war which Orwell foresees as the state of the world in 1984. 1647 / 1947 / 1984 then.

In 1947, under the sponsorship of the German writer Hans Werner Richter, a group of German writers held meetings to discuss the state of German literature and the German language after Hitler, in a Germany whose cities were heaps of ruins. Herr Grass invents in *The Meeting at Telgte* a parallel for Richter's meeting — a projection back into the past — which, he certainly manages to persuade us, might well have taken place. A meeting of German poets "to rescue their cruelly maltreated language and to be near the peace negotiations. There they would sit until everything, the distress of the fatherland as well as the splendor and misery of poetry, had been discussed." The writers who met were overwhelmingly of the Protestant persuasion; the members of Hans Werner Richter's group were overwhelmingly pro-Western (there were no writers from the Soviet zone).

The Meeting at Telgte contains none of the ambitious devices of Herr

*Reprinted from the *New York Review of Books*, 11 June 1981, 35–36, by permission of the *New York Review of Books* and the author. © 1981, Nyrev, Inc.

Grass's earlier novels. There is none of the symbolic machinery of tin drum or flounder drawing the strands of the characters and their narrations together. Instead, at the center of the novel there is a featureless, anonymous, timeless "I" — the author as abstract tricentennial witness.

The narration is in appearance a straightforward account of what was discussed, of poems read at meetings. The writers consider form, subject matter, language. The poet August Buchner, professor of poetry at Wittenberg, Prince Hamlet's university, talks about dactyllic measures. Siegmund von Birken reads a chapter from his manuscript of *German Rhetoric and Poetic Art*, in which he draws up directions for the treatment of characters in poetic drama: children should speak childishly, old people wisely, women chastely and gently, heroes bravely and heroically, peasants crudely. This view is repudiated by the realists, one of whom — Christoffel Gelnhausen — remarks that on an occasion when he met the devil at a crossways, this gentleman was most soft-spoken.

Although this book has a very crowded canvas, no detail seems irrelevant. It is a powerful historic construction built round one piece of historic invention, like Schiller's apocryphal confrontation between Queen Elizabeth and Mary Queen of Scots in *Mary Stuart*. Poets are lights signaling to one another across black distances; so the discussions between them which Günter Grass invents are implicit in their consciousness of one another's work. *The Meeting at Telgte* fits comfortably into what is plausible as history.

The dominating character here is undoubtedly Christoffel Gelnhausen, an undisguised portrait of the poet and fiction writer Johann Jakob Christoffel von Grimmelshausen, with a certain degree of self-portraiture by the ebullient Günter Grass himself thrown in. Grimmelshausen was author of the famous picaresque narrative *Simplicissimus*, about the Thirty Years War. An extension to this was the story *Courasche*, "a paper monument to a sturdy and unstable, childless yet inventive, vulnerable and embattled woman, man-mad in skirts, manly in breeches, making the most of her beauty, a woman both pitiable and lovable." The Brechtian Courasche, here called Libuschka, landlady of the Bridge Tavern at Telgte where the poets meet, has a long-standing impassioned relationship with Gelnhausen, compounded in equal proportions of love and hatred.

Gelnhausen is the embodiment of the violence and rhetoric of the soldier-adventurer-troubadour produced by the time; and he rough-hews the circumstances surrounding his fellow poets during the time of their meeting. Drawn together by the magnetism of poetry in times of chaos, in response to the invitation of the most paternally benign of their number, Simon Dach, they have booked rooms at Oesede but, having got there, they find their quarters already commandeered by a contingent of Swedes. Gelnhausen, who arrives with his troop of soldiers of the emperor, evicts a bunch of merchants from the Bridge Tavern and, at first to their shock, installs his colleagues there. In this action, he displays, as always, rhetorical panache:

> When the merchants asked for a written statement justifying their eviction, Gelnhausen drew his sword, called it his goose quill, asked to whom his first missive should be addressed, and added that in the name of the emperor and his adversaries he must urgently—by Mars and his ferocious dogs!—request the departing guests of the Bridge Tavern to observe the strictest silence concerning the reason for their sudden departure.

Gelnhausen also makes a raid with his troops on the local citizens in order to provide the poets—who have been living for days on barley soup—with a banquet of five geese, three suckling pigs, and a fat sheep. The poets consume all this but when they come to hear how it was obtained, they consider the possibility of putting Gelnhausen on trial before an extempore court of honor. Of course this plan evaporates in words. Some poets are conservatives, some moderns, some professors and academics. They belong to various associations which have delightful names: German-minded Association, Order of Elbe Swans, Fruit-Bearing Society, Pegnitz Shepherds, Cucumber Lodge, Upright Society of the Pine Tree. Names more colorful than Beatniks or Hippies.

Above all they are concerned with language, questions of dialect, Low German or High German. They themselves illustrate the fragmentation of language in Germany.

> Though he had been living and teaching mathematics in Danish Zeeland ever since Wallenstein's invasion of Pomerania, Lauremberg expressed himself in his native Rostock brogue, and Rist the Holstein preacher answered him in Low German. After thirty years of residence in London, the diplomat Weckherlin still spoke an unvarnished Swabian. And into the predominantly Silesian conversation, Moscherosch mixed his Alemannic, Harsdörffer his peppery Franconian, Buchner and Gerhardt their Saxon, Greflinger his Lower Bavarian gargle, and Dach a Prussian kneaded and shaped between Memel and Pregel.

The younger poets in their hay loft contrive to bed down with the tavern's maid servants, changing sleeping partners between dreams. And there is always talk of war and its horrors:

> How when Breisach was besieged homeless children were butchered and eaten. How in places where order had been put to flight, the mob set themselves up as masters. How the most flea-bitten yokels swaggered about in city finery. And everyone knew of highwaymen in Franconia, in Brandenburg, behind every bush.

On the outskirts of Telgte, corpses, swollen and putrescent, float down the river Ems, sometimes coupled together in grotesque parody of the love-making of the poets with the maids in the hay loft.

The poems they write portray destruction in language of lamentation: "O, empty dream whereon we mortals build. . . ." "Everything went sour. Horror clouded the mirrors. The meanings of words were reversed. Hope languished beside the silted well. Built on desert sand, no wall stood firm." This is the burden of the poets' songs at Telgte while they go on with their meeting, eating, and love-making. On one level this book is an ironic comment on poets.

Each of the guests comes to Telgte with his life story as part of his luggage. And the narrating "I" is very good at following these up. With the skill of Brueghel or Teniers painting an immense canvas of villagers in their surroundings, each distinct in appearance and involved in his own particular idiosyncrasies, Grass keeps his characters distinct in their behavior, beliefs, and circumstances. Simon Dach, convener of the meeting, a father-figure who regards the poets as his children, is depicted as in a portrait by Hans Memling. The pietistic Paul Gerhardt, who prays for the schism-torn world and for his colleagues, stands slightly apart from the rest. Perhaps the most moving portrait of many is that of Heinrich Schütz, the great composer of mostly religious music (cousin of the poet Heinrich Albert), who comes uninvited to the meeting in order that he may hear poets and read their works, with a view to setting these to music. With his austere listening and judging appearance, he awes the poets, and pains them when he observes that Italians provide much better texts than the clogged German rhetoric: witness Maestro Rinuccini's libretti written for Monteverdi. Schütz seems a portrait by Albrecht Dürer.

The poets are convinced that it is their duty as practitioners of their art to produce a manifesto: an overwhelmingly moving appeal to the great powers, its princes, to make a lasting peace which will not lead to further war. It must begin with a throbbing reminder of the ruinous condition of the nation — "Germany, the most glorious empire in the world, is now bled white, devastated and despoiled." The poets must stand above the disputing parties, claiming that they alone represent the true Germany.

However, as happens with artists when they go into public affairs, they fall back on those very attitudes of partisanship that they deplore in statesmen. When the manifesto prepared by two of them was read out to the assembled poets:

> As was to be expected, Gerhardt took exception to the special mention of the Calvinists. Buchner criticized the over-sharp condemnation of Saxony. Such "scribbling," said Weckherlin, would neither move Maximilian to take a single step against the Spaniards, nor spur the landgravine of Hesse against the Swedes.

In politics, each poet is a representative of the local interests of his region.

At the end, partly as the result of the intervention of Schütz, they produce a high-minded, ineffectual document, based on awareness of their dignity as artists, an appeal "to all parties desirous of peace not to scorn the preoccupations of the poets, who, though powerless, had acquired a claim to eternity." Shakespeare expressed the same despair at the powerlessness of art (in Sonnet 65):

> Since brass, nor stone, nor earth, nor boundless sea,
> But sad mortality o'ersways their power,
> How with this rage shall beauty hold a plea,
> Whose action is no stronger than a flower?

Günter Grass tells home truths about poets in their behavior and their personalities, as applicable to 1947 as to 1647. Perhaps the famous vanity of poets lies in their assumption — and their letting themselves be flattered by the same assumption in others — that they display in daily life the same qualities of discrimination and idealism as are revealed in their poems. But of course there is a disjunction between the poet as man in his life and as man in his poems. The fact is that someone who happens to write poems may have the character he realizes there only when actually writing them — if then. He is indeed only intermittently a poet, much less a perambulating personification of his poetry. At other times he may be an insurance executive or a thug.

There is a wonderful description in Thomas Mann's *Lotte in Weimar* of Goethe waking from a dream of Greece and being for a few moments identical with his poetry — imagination and genius incarnate — before he resumes the garb of the great bureaucrat and dictator of taste at court. In Grass's book too there are glimpses of one or another of the poets alone with his inspiration, the glory and the horror and the boredom. Yet with all the debates about prosody and other matters going on here one feels more informed than enlightened about the nature of poets and poetry. Oh for a touch of Virginia Woolf, I found myself sighing at intervals, wading through so much clanking of tankards and brawling in taverns and taking of maidens in the straw. I am quite glad not to be a poet living in the seventeenth century.

Nevertheless this is a brilliant entertainment and there is much to be grateful for. In the end we are at any rate reminded that despite the bustling rhetoric of poets, "poetry makes nothing happen." Here also is a nobly consoling demonstration that "It survives . . . a way of happening, a mouth," an assertion which Grass's drawing on the jacket, of a hand holding a quill pen and emerging from a mass of rubble that looks like broken thumbs, emphatically demonstrates.

Günter Grass: King of the Toy Merchants [*Headbirths*]

John Irving*

There is still a youthful restlessness to the work of Günter Grass — an impatience, a total absence of complacency, a shock of unexpected energy that must be gratifying to those German writers who, in 1958, awarded Grass the prize of the Group 47 for his first novel, *The Tin Drum*. In the more than 20 years since its publication, *Die Blechtrommel* — as it is called in German — has not been surpassed; it is the greatest novel by a living author. More than 14 books later, Grass himself has not surpassed *The Tin Drum*, but — more importantly — he hasn't limited himself by trying. He has allowed himself the imaginative range of an international wanderer, while at the same time, at 54, he has remained as recognizably German as he was at 31 when he wrote *The Tin Drum*.

One reason Grass remains forever young is that he exercises no discernable restraint on the mischief of his imagination or on the practical, down-to-earth morality of his politics. Grass is a writer whose political activism has included writing almost 100 election speeches for Willy Brandt (in 1969), and whose recent fictional undertakings have included a dense, short but crammed-full historical novel — *The Meeting at Telgte*, set at the end of the Thirty Years' War (1647) — and a huge, discursive novel — *The Flounder* — that begins in the Stone Age and resides in the present at a most contemporary "Women's Tribunal," where a talking fish is on trial for male chauvinism.

Fortunately, for the pleasure of his readers, Grass has not acquired a single gesture of literary detachment or intellectual pompousness. He remains engaged — at once dead-serious and a tireless prankster. He is our literature's most genuine eccentric. Writers as unique as Gabriel García Márquez and as derivative as Jerzy Kosinski are under the shadow of what Grass does better than anyone: Against the authoritative landscape of history, he creates characters so wholly larger than life, yet vivid, that they confront the authority of history with a larger authority — Grass's relentless imagination. He does not distort history; he out-imagines it.

Perhaps, one day, he'll slow down and write an introduction to his work — either to something new (if he feels old enough), or (if he feels patient enough to offer us some hindsight) to something old: perhaps to a new edition of *The Tin Drum*, or to one of the less popular, more difficult works, *Local Anaesthetic*, *From the Diary of a Snail*, even to *Dog Years*. (The last is an expansive odyssey of a novel set in war-time and postwar Germany; it suffered, popularly — and wrongly — by being ill-compared to *The Tin Drum*.) But until such a time, when Grass is willing to check his astonishing forward progress with the necessary calm required of reflec-

*Reprinted from *Saturday Review*, March 1982, 57–60, by permission of the author.

tion, we have no better, *general* introduction to the methods of his genius than *Headbirths*.

Written in late 1979, shortly after Grass returned from China (from a trip with the film director of *The Tin Drum*, Volker Schlöndorff), *Headbirths* is first a political speculation — set just before the 1980 German elections, when Helmut Schmidt of the Social Democrats (Grass's party) defeated the Christian Democrat and Bavarian Prime Minister, Franz Josef Strauss. It is also the creative musings for a film Grass never made (with Schlöndorff) about a fictional German couple who travel to Asia to investigate how that part of the world is living, carrying with them the loaded political and personal problem of world population growth and their own ambivalent feelings about having a child. The premise of this slim, innocent-appearing book is what Grass calls a "speculative reversal." "What if," he writes, "from this day on, the world had to face up to the existence of nine hundred fifty million Germans, whereas the Chinese nation numbered barely eighty million, that is, the present population of the two Germanys." As Grass mischievously asks, "Could the world bear it?"

The title of the book, and the would-be film — *Headbirths* — refers to the god Zeus, "from whose head the goddess Athene was born: a paradox that has impregnated male minds to this day." The subtitle, *The Germans Are Dying Out*, originates from Franz Josef Strauss — a fear-inspiring notion meant to provoke the anxiety, among Germans, that other, less-restrained nations were out-reproducing them and would overtake them. "And since fear in Germany," Grass writes, "has always had a high rate of increment and multiplies more quickly than do the Chinese, it has provided fear-mongering politicians with a program." Thus right-wing election tactics and a trip to China provide Grass with an insight to a moral and political global concern: world population growth, world starvation, and the complicated, personal dignity that is called for in a conscientious, contemporary couple's decision to have or not to have a child. With the accessibility of a diary or a journal — an accessibility rare to the writer's more recent work — Grass constructs a fictional couple and imagines *their* trip to Asia (on the eve of the German elections in which they are seriously, and liberally, involved).

Within this deceptively plain narrative, Grass uncovers insoluble, irreducible complexity; he writes at his baroque best. "A couple straight out of a contemporary picture book," he calls his invented family — he, named Harm; she, Dörte. "They keep a cat and still have no child." They met at a sit-in against the Vietnam War. They're serious; their political consciousness is keen. She belongs to the Free Democrats; he lectures about the Third World at Social Democratic meetings. Regarding China — their Asian adventure — they are schoolteachers traveling for their education; they care about being informed, and about being right. This problem about having a child or not having one—it nags at them, personally and politically:

> The child is always present. Whether they are shopping at Itze-hoe's Holstein Shopping Center or standing on the Elbe dike at Brokdorf, bedded on their double mattress or looking for a new second-hand car: the child always joins in the conversation, makes eyes at baby clothes, wants to crawl on the Elbe beach, longs at ovulation time for the sprinkling that fructifies, and demands auto doors with childproof locks. But they never get beyond the whatif or supposingthat stage, and Harm's mother (as surrogate child) is alternately moved to their apart-ment and shipped to an old-people's home, until some forenoon shock derails their single-tracked dialogue.

Like so many motifs in Grass's work, the couple's dilemma is repeated, is used as a refrain, is compounded—sometimes it is converted into elegy, sometimes it is mocked. That he is writing a book as instruc-tions for a film provides Grass with the opportunity to *visualize* the couple's indecision. He accomplishes this with characteristic irony and compassion:

> This time Dörte's laugh is really a bit too loud. And just as spontaneously, she can take the contrary view. "But I want a child, I want a child! I want to be pregnant, fat, round, cow-eyed. And go moo. Do you hear? Moo! And this time, my dear Harm, father of my planned child, we're not calling it off after two months. So help me. As soon as we're airborne, hear, as soon as we have all this here, that's right, as soon as we have you jugheads over there in your atomic concentration camp below us and behind us, I'm going off the pill!"
>
> The director's instructions are roughly: Both laugh. But because the camera is still on them, they do more than laugh. They grab hold of each other, roughhouse, peel each other's jeans off, "fuck," as Harm says, "screw," as Dörte says, each other on the dike among the cows and sheep, under the open sky. A few guards at the still-future construction site of the Brokdorf nuclear power plant may be watching them, no one else. Then two low-flying pursuit planes. ("Shit on NATO!" Dörte moans.) In the distance, ships on the Elbe at high tide.
>
> A note on one of the slips I took with me to Asia and then home again says, "Shortly before landing in Bombay or Bangkok—breakfast has been cleared away—Dörte takes the pill." Harm, who only seems to be asleep, sees her and accepts it with fatalism.

And, intricately woven through his would-be screenplay, Grass re-veals his actual Asian travels with Schlöndorff. "In every city we stopped in I read simple chapters from *The Flounder*: how Amanda Woyke introduced the potato into Prussia." In every great novelist's mind, everything *is* related to everything else; the history of *food*, Grass notes, "is timely in present-day Asian regions." It takes a cook, which Grass is reputed to be—and a good one—to give food the honorable role of subplot, which a German liver sausage is given here. A "plot-fostering sausage," it is rightly called. Harm and Dörte are stuck with a kilo of it to take with them to Asia, a typically German gift intended for some obscure relative of a friend of a friend, supposed to be living in Java and pining away, of course, for liver sausage from the Fatherland. And so our German tourists, despite their serious-mindedness, carry a sausage with them, a sausage that never finds its customer. In countless, hot hotel rooms, deprived of refrigeration, the sausage sits, grows green and dubious, gets packed up and travels again. Finally, this world-traveling sausage returns to Germany—in somewhat the same state as the accompanying couple, a little the worse for wear, and symbolically undelivered: Dörte and Harm, at the book's end, *still* don't know whether or not to have a child. "Even in China," Grass chastises them, *they* wouldn't know "whether or not to bring a child into the world." It's not an easy question.

As with the characters in his other books, Grass makes fun of Harm and Dörte without ever removing his sympathy from them. As with the masterful handling of the subplot of the liver sausage, he demonstrates—even in this little book—his scrupulousness of detail, which is the truest indication of a writer's conscience. On a "wide sandy beach . . . a stranded turtle becomes a photograph"; in a village of 5,000 inhabitants, 3,000 are children ("worm-ridden, visibly ill, marked by eye diseases. They don't beg, they don't laugh or play; they're just quietly too many").

Of his travels, Grass writes that he "loyally wrote 'writer' on the profession line of my immigration card. A profession with a long tradition, if the word was really in the beginning. A fine, dangerous, presumptuous, dubious profession that invites metaphoric epithets. An East German apparatchik, a Chinese Red Guard, or Goebbels in his day might have said what Franz Josef Strauss, leaving his Latin on the shelf, said a year ago in German. Writers, he said, were 'rats and blowflies.' " Of himself and Schlöndorff, Grass remarks: "What did we drink to? Since our glasses were often refilled, we drank to contradictions, to the repeatedly contested truth, naturally to the health of the people (whoever they may be), and to the white, still-spotless paper that clamors to be spotted with words. And we drank to ourselves, the rats and blowflies."

He calls himself "childlike like most writers." Perhaps this is why the mischief lives in him still. He is serious enough to know what any truly serious person knows: that the confidence for enduring mischief can come from only the greatest seriousness. In *The Flounder* he writes, "Fairy tales only stop for a time, or they start up again after the end. The truth is told, in a different way each time." And at one point in *Headbirths*, he keeps Dörte and Harm "circling over Bombay without permission to land, because I forgot to inject something that's in my notes and should have been considered before the takeoff: the future."

As for the future, Grass is wisely cautious about *ours*. He even speculates that the Germans *may* be dying out. "And is it not possible that

German culture (and with it literature) will come to be prized as an indivisible but manifold unity only after and because the Germans have become extinct?" Although he is *fun* to read, Grass is never so insecure as to be *polite*. In praising the work of Céline, Kurt Vonnegut has written: "He was in the worst possible taste . . . he did not seem to understand that aristocratic restraints and sensibilities, whether inherited or learned, accounted for much of the splendor of literature . . . he discovered a higher and more awful order of literary truth by ignoring the crippled vocabularies of ladies and gentlemen and by using, instead, the more comprehensive language of shrewd and tormented guttersnipes. Every writer is in his debt . . . no honest writer . . . will ever want to be polite again."

Grass also knows how to be harsh. Of his character, Dörte: "Now that she wants a child—'This time my mind is made up!'—she has been tiptoeing on religious pathways. With Balinese women she offers up little flower-patterned bowls of rice in temples under holy trees, in each of which a white, fertility-bestowing woman is said to dwell." On the other hand, she stops sleeping with Harm (" 'I haven't got to that stage yet' "). Of the limitations of the movie art: "The cave breathes what a film cannot communicate: stink." Of Dörte and Harm's whole generation, which is my generation, the student-protest generation: "They have found themselves knee-deep in prosperity-determined consumption and pleasureless sex, but the student protest phase left sufficient imprint to keep the words and concepts of their early years available to them as an alternative, as something they can relapse into wherever they may be sitting or lying." Of us all: "Our complexities and neuroses are mass-produced articles."

He writes (in 1979):

> There's no shortage of great Führer figures; a bigoted preacher in Washington and an ailing philistine in Moscow let others decide what they then proclaim to the world as their decision. Of course we still have (as trademarks of salvation) good old capitalism and good old communism; but thanks to their tried and true enmity, they are becoming more and more alike . . . two evil old men whom we have to love, because the love they offer us refuses to be snubbed.
>
> And so we grope our disconsolate way into the next century. In school essays and first novels, gloom vies with gloom.

But the gloom that Grass perceives is always underlined with wit, and elevated by it:

> My proposal to my Eastern neighbor-dictator would be that the two states should exchange their systems every ten years. Thus, in a spirit of compensatory justice, the Democratic Republic would have an opportunity to relax under capitalism, while the Federal Republic could drain off cholesterol under communism.

Grass asks, "How will Sisyphus react to Orwell's decade?" To Orwell, he writes: "No, dear George, it won't be quite so bad, or it'll be bad in an entirely different way, and in some respects even a little worse." Of Sisyphus he asks: "What is my stone? The toil of piling words on words? The book that follows book that follows book? . . . Or love, with all its epileptic fits?" The writer's stone, he says, is a "good traveling companion."

Headbirths also provides us with some terse, shorthand insights into Grass's earlier work. "It was a mistake to imagine that *Cat and Mouse* would abreact my schoolboy sorrows. I never run out of teachers. I can't let them be: Fräulein Spollenhauer tries to educate Oskar; in *Dog Years*, Brunies suck his cough drops; in *Local Anaesthetic*, Teacher Starusch suffers from headaches; in *The Diary of a Snail*, Hermann Ott remains a teacher even when holed up in a cellar; even the Flounder turns out to be a pedagogue; and now these two teachers from Holstein . . ." his Dörte and Harm, who take up teaching, Grass admits, "with the best intentions." What prevents him from letting his teachers be, he writes, is "that my growing children bring school into the house day after day: the generation-spanning fed-upness , the to-do over grades, the search, straying now to the right and now to the left, for meaning, the fug that stinks up every cheerful breath of air!"

For such a small book, this is such a rich one. And he is not speaking only of Germans when he writes, "In our country everything is geared to growth. We're never satisfied. For us enough is never enough. We always want more. If it's on paper, we convert it into reality. Even in our dreams we're productive. We do everything that's feasible. And to our minds everything thinkable is feasible."

And of that truly German question—its divided East and West parts—he says, "Only literature (with its inner lining: history, myths, guilt, and other residues) arches over the two states that have so sulkily cut themselves off from each other." It is what Grass provides us with every time he writes: "Only literature." His gift for storytelling is so instinctually shrewd, so completely natural. If it's true—as he says—that he never runs out of teachers, he never stops *being* a teacher, either. In *The Flounder*— which is, he writes, "told while pounding acorns, plucking geese, peeling potatoes"—he doesn't resist indulging his irritation with the world of fools on whom fiction is largely wasted. "A good deal has been written about storytelling. People want to hear the truth. But when truth is told, they say, 'Anyway, it's all made up.' Or, with a laugh, 'What that man won't think up next!' "

Scherbaum, the favorite student in *Local Anaesthetic*, tries to reach the conscience of Berliners by setting fire to his beloved dachshund. He observes, with a sad truthfulness, that human beings are more apt to notice the suffering of animals, and be moved, than they are likely to care for the suffering of fellow-humans. It's possible that in the character of Scherbaum Grass was thinking of the radical Rudi Dutschke, whom Grass calls (in *Headbirths*) a "revolutionary out of a German picture book."

(Following an epileptic fit, Dutschke drowned in a bathtub.) "What makes me sad?" Grass asks. "How he was carried away by his wishes. How his ideals escaped him at a gallop. How his visions degenerated into paperbacks." At the time of his death, Dutschke was 39 — my age. "Seldom has a generation exhausted itself so quickly," Grass writes. "Either they crack up or they stop taking risks." How true: We are a generation lacking in staying power.

Headbirths is not the literary jewel that Grass's second novel, *Cat and Mouse*, is. That gem is as fine a short novel as *The Tin Drum* is a triumphant major undertaking. And *Cat and Mouse* remains the best book with which a new reader might introduce himself to Grass, the *novelist*. But in all of Grass's work (and abundant, even, in this fictional, nonfictional, would-be movie of a book) one finds that flowering honesty that V.S. Pritchett calls fundamental to the Russian novelists of the 19th century ("the call to bare the breast and state one's absolute convictions"). Turgenev, Pritchett reminds us, believed that "art must not be burdened with all kinds of aims," that "without art men might not wish to live on earth," and that "art will always live man's real life with him." Grass celebrates this *Russian* conviction with everything he writes.

In 1920, seven years before Grass was born, Joseph Conrad wrote in his introduction to *The Secret Agent* (published 12 years earlier): "I have always had a propensity to justify my action. Not to defend. To justify. Not to insist that I was right but simply to explain that there was no perverse intention, no secret scorn for the natural sensibilities of mankind at the bottom of my impulses."

Like Conrad, Grass freely indulges in such a "propensity to justify" *his* action — *and* his work. It was unnecessary for Conrad to conclude his introduction as he did, claiming that he *never* "intended to commit a gratuitous outrage on the feelings of mankind." Of course he didn't! Gratuitousness is a charge fashionably aimed at good writers by squeamish and second-rate critics.

Writers today need to be thicker-skinned than Conrad, somehow more immune to such moralistic posing in intellectual garb — though we aren't. "We all bear wounds," as Thomas Mann has noted. "Praise is a soothing if not necessarily healing balm for them. Nevertheless," Mann wrote, "if I may judge by my own experience, our receptivity for praise stands in no relationship to our vulnerability to mean disdain and spiteful abuse. No matter how stupid such abuse is, no matter how plainly impelled by private rancors, as an expression of hostility it occupies us far more deeply and lastingly than the opposite. Which is very foolish, since enemies are, of course, the necessary concomitant of any robust life, the very proof of its strength."

Like Mann's, Grass's literary self-confidence is always present. He seems somehow born knowing that *any* violence done in the course of a novel's discovery of the truth is *never* gratuitous. In *The Tin Drum*, when the Nazis force the Jewish toy merchant, Sigismund Markus, to kill himself, little Oskar Matzerath knows he has seen his last tin drum. For poor Herr Markus, for himself—for a Germany forever guilty for its Jews—little Oskar mourns: "There was once a toy merchant, his name was Markus, and he took all the toys in the world away with him out of this world."

For readers who found *The Flounder* and *The Meeting at Telgte* too inaccessible, *Headbirths* will seem warmer, more personable and approachable. For the hard core of Grass's fans—those of us who have tolerated (indeed, loved) each of his excesses—*Headbirths* has the clear voice and familiar consciousness of a letter from an old friend. And to those nonreaders, if there still are any—to those moviegoers who know of him only through Volker Schlöndorff's admirable rendition of *The Tin Drum*—this little book would be a mild, wise, mischievous starting place: a view of Grass, the good artist, taking notes, setting his shop in order.

Some readers find that the diary-form offers access to a fiction writer's mind by exposing components rarely made available in the fiction (more often, concealed). Personally, I'd still recommend that one's initial experience with Grass be *Cat and Mouse*, but *Headbirths* is broadly entertaining enough to satisfy the most strenuous and demanding of Grass's faithful readers, and it is accessible enough to be inviting to the beginner. In whatever category of reader you see yourself, you can't be called well-read today if you haven't read him. Günter Grass is simply the most original and versatile writer alive.

ARTICLES

Günter Grass's Uniqueness
J. P. Stern*

With the deaths of Thomas Mann in 1955 and of Bertolt Brecht and Gottfried Benn in 1956, a major era in the history of German literature comes to an end. These three are not only the greatest writers of their age, they are also its witnesses. Each of them worked in a different genre: Thomas Mann in the convoluted, partly essayistic prose of his novels, Bert Brecht in the drama and narrative poetry of social dialectics, Benn in the lyrical poetry of radical Modernism. Each went through a different political development and reacted differently to the ruling political ideology. Yet the questions they ask have a family likeness; and the answers they offer remind us forcibly that theirs was an age of terror.

Any author whose literary gifts and moral disposition lead him towards this contemporary turmoil and who tries to come to terms with it creatively, with the best that is in him, is bound to have to face very special formal and compositional problems. These problems are likely to be different for a writer like Günter Grass, who faces the same world at one remove, reporting on the way the dead buried their dead. This is our first premise. The other is that, quite irrespective of that era, the German novel at its most characteristic has not been renowned for its contributions to the "Great Tradition" of European realism, which dominated French, English and Russian prose literature throughout the 19th and well into the 20th century. Realism as we know it from Stendhal, Dickens, Tolstoy onwards entered German literature relatively late in the day and has been powerfully challenged by other modes of writing. Thus Thomas Mann's very last work, the unfinished *Confessions of Felix Krull, Confidence Man* of 1954, is a picaresque novel whose main narrative devices are a direct challenge to the verisimilitude of realistic fiction.

Chief among the literary and cultural patterns of Thomas Mann's novels had been the classical German *Bildungsroman*, the novel of initiation and development, in the course of which a young hero is led from adolescent self-absorption and egocentricity on the margins of the

*Reprinted from *London Review of Books*, 5–18 February 1981, 11–14, by permission of *London Review of Books* and the author.

69

social world through a variety of instructive experiences—often a mixture of the erotic and the aesthetic—to a state of adulthood and responsibility at the centre of contemporary society. True, Thomas Mann's use of the *Bildungsroman* and its main theme had never been unambiguous and unproblematic, had always been informed—or undermined—by a spirit of irony; in *Felix Krull* this is radicalised to a point of fantasy and farce.

The pattern from which *Krull* evolves is the picaresque novel which, in German literature, goes back to the 17th century; 1668, to be precise, when Hans Jacob Christoffel von Grimmelshausen published his *Adventures of Simplicius Simplicissimus*, a novel which, in sharp contrast to the contemporary courtly novel, is set among soldiers, actors, servants, beggars, robbers and whores. There are characters exemplifying the Christian virtues, but the notion of moral and spiritual development recedes behind a rich and colourful series of adventures on the pattern of "one damn thing after another." Purposeful teleology gives way to the rule of fortune, spiritual uplift goes hang, cunning for the sake of mere survivals is the order of the day, and when salvation does come, it comes in as untoward and unmotivated a manner as do the temptations of the flesh and of the devil. All this, as we shall see, is grist to Günter Grass's mill. The picaro he will create from some of the elements of the traditional rogue novel is as radical a response to Thomas Mann's genteel Felix Krull as Krull is to Grimmelshausen's Simplicius. Very strong affinities of atmosphere connect the Germany of the Thirty Years War, which Grimmelshausen portrayed, with the Germany of the 1930s and 1940s which is the obsessive concern of Grass's "Danzig Trilogy." These are affinities which are not encompassed by Mann's imagination, or by the imagination of many writers of Mann's generation apart from Brecht.

Günter Grass was born in a suburb of the Free City of Danzig in 1927, then under the protection of the League of Nations, and like Charles Dickens, Jan Neruda, James Joyce, Theodor Fontane and his acknowledged exemplar Alfred Döblin, he places his native city at the centre of his creative imagination. Grass's best work so far is given over, again and again, to its evocation: a very special piety ties him to the streets and places of Danzig, its beaches, its inhabitants and their desperate, murderous national conflicts. For even more than the London, Dublin, Berlin and Prague of the authors I have mentioned, Grass's Danzig is an intensely political city: the place, from the 12th century onwards, where Prussia and Poland, the Knights of the German Order and Polish patriots, Germans and Slavs encountered each other in rivalry. In 1933, Hitler was appointed Chancellor of Germany. At this time, when Danzig was experiencing growing unemployment, a deterioration of its maritime trade and an upsurge of nationalism, the people of the deeply divided city elected a Senate with a National Socialist majority and the local Party Gauleiter as its President.

To paraphrase a sentence of Brecht's Galileo, happy is the country that has no land frontiers. With the conflict of Ulster in the forefront of our minds, we now find it less difficult to imagine the protracted bitterness and violence of the Polish-German relationship that is epitomised in the history of Danzig—the intensity of the passions, the internecine strife of centuries, which come to a head and lead directly to the outbreak of the Second World War in the first days of September 1939, and to the city's death in the last week of that war. The rhythms of the threnody which the narrator-hero of *The Tin Drum* chants for the city illustrate that special *pietas loci* which informs Grass's prose, and give us a first idea of its innovatory energy:

> After that we seldom emerged from our hole. The Russians were said to be in Zigankenberg, Pietzgendorf, and on the outskirts of Schidlitz. There was no doubt that they occupied the heights, for they were firing straight down into the city. Inner City and Outer City, Old City, New City and Old New City, Lower City and Spice City—what had taken seven hundred years to build burned down in three days. Yet this was not the first fire to descend on the city of Danzig. For centuries Pomeranians, Brandenburgers, Teutonic Knights, Poles, Swedes, and a second time Swedes, Frenchmen, Prussians, and Russians, even Saxons, had made history by deciding every few years that the city of Danzig was worth burning. And now it was Russians, Poles, Germans and Englishmen all at once who were burning the city's Gothic bricks for the hundredth time. Hook Street, Long Street, and Broad Street, Big Weaver Street and Little Weaver Street were in flames; Tobias Street, Hound Street, Old City Ditch, Outer City Ditch, the ramparts and Long Bridge, all were in flames. Built of wood, Crane Gate made a particularly fine blaze. In Breechesmaker Street, the fire had itself measured for several pairs of extra-loud breeches. The Church of Saint Mary was burning inside and outside, festive light effects would be seen through its ogival windows. What bells had not been evacuated from St. Catherine, St. John, St. Brigit, Saints Barbara, Elizabeth, Peter and Paul, from Trinity to Corpus Christi, melted in their belfries and dripped away without pomp or ceremony. In the Big Mill red wheat was milled. Butcher Street smelled of burnt Sunday roast. The Municipal Theatre was giving a premier, a one-act play entitled "The Firebug's Dream." The city fathers decided to raise the firemen's wages retroactively after the fire. Holy Ghost Street was burning in the name of the Holy Ghost. Joyously, the Franciscan Monastery blazed in the name of St. Francis, who had loved fire and sung hymns to it. Our Lady Street burned for Father and Son at once. Needless to say the Lumber Market, Coal Market and Haymarket burned to the ground. In Baker Street the ovens burned, and the bread and rolls with them. In Milk Pitcher Street the milk boiled over. Only the West Prussian Fire Insurance Building, for purely symbolic reasons, refused to burn down.

The fate of the city and its surrounding countryside becomes for a boy born of a German father and a Cashubian (Slav) mother, a part of his intimate personal history. As a member of the German lower middle class that was particularly receptive to the new racist and nationalist ideas, at the age of ten he entered the "Jungvolk," from which he was promoted to the Hitler Jugend, joining a tank regiment as a gunner when he was barely 17. When, at the end of the war, on being wounded, he was taken prisoner-of-war by the Americans, he still felt, as he says, "that our war was all right." Then came the shock of a guided tour through the concentration camp at Dachau and the gradual realisation "of what unbelievable crimes had been done in the name of my . . . generation and . . . what guilt, knowingly and unknowingly, our people had brought upon themselves."

Here, then, are the elements present in this exacting setting: lower-middle-class life with its hybrid linguistic milieu and its charged atmosphere of rival nationalisms, with a small Jewish minority the butt of both sides, and a strong and highly ritualised religious tradition — in Grass's case, Roman Catholic; the smells and shapes of a small grocery store; the Party — its ideological slogans, colourful ritual and sordid practice; school life, swimming in the Baltic Sea; the war in its last, hopeless stages; and the true face of the regime disclosed at last. On his release from the American POW camp, aged 19, Grass does not go back to school but finds himself a job as apprentice miner in a potassium mine near Hildesheim, listening during the breaks for salami sandwiches to the last echoes of the political quarrels that had begun long ago, in the Weimar Republic, and in which embittered Communists and disillusioned and resentful National Socialists together ganged up on "the dry-as-dust" SPD who "taught me how to live without an ideology." Grass's activism and his allegiance to the SPD date from those early post-war days before the German economic miracle, and this allegiance was later strengthened by his friendship with Willy Brandt. When, in December 1970, Brandt as German Chancellor went to kneel before the monument to the victims of the Polish resistance in Warsaw (a gesture that appalled the troglodytes on the far Right), Grass was among those who accompanied him. Yet he acknowledges, in his major works, the need to separate his fiction, not from politics, but from political advocacy. A strong political concern goes through his novels, a deep, mature and tolerant understanding for the predicament of the little man at the mercy of huge political forces. But his understanding goes further, beyond this sort of tolerance, to major satirical sorties against the trimmers and fellow-travellers and profiteers, culminating in that very special grotesque presentation of the horrors of war, and of totalitarian regimes, which yields the most remarkable passages of his prose so far and is his outstanding contribution to post-war German literature. The tolerance that informs his portraits of the lower middle classes must not obscure the fact that he is not content, as many of his contemporaries are, to present the predicament of the individual man as though it were caused by a stroke of fate: it is part of his purpose to show the political sources and consequences of that predicament.

After two years of mining, Grass became an apprentice in a monumental mason's workshop in Düsseldorf, and then, after a brief period in a jazz band, he won a scholarship to study drawing and sculpture at the academies of Düsseldorf and Berlin. He is a gifted draughtsman, and has produced some fine illustrations and the stunning designs for the dust-jackets of his books. After his time at the Academy he went, penniless, on a series of extensive hitch-hikes through Italy and France. It was in the course of these journeys that he seems to have moved, quite imperceptibly, from drawing and sculpture to writing, and from huge and impracticable epic effusions to prose-poems, and hence to a highly rhythmic and rich, metaphor-studded prose. To this day, the early plans of his novels tend at first to be set out either like blueprints in multicoloured graphs or in the form of brief, usually unrhymed poems.

Both the interest in the visual arts and the unfussy, easy way in which he moves from genre to genre — creating pictorial patterns and shapes in his literary fictions and complex literary allusions in his drawings — all this ease of transition between different kinds of creativeness is reflected in his prose. Not only that. These transitions have their parallel in the movement of his novels from the present to the past and back again, from the historical to the political, from the concrete to the abstract; and in the disconcerting and apparently arbitrary way in which he is apt to slip from the first- to the third-person narrative, from the point of view of one character to that of another, as though all men, even in their solitude, even in their moments of murderous enmity, were yet unable to deny the fact that they are made of one flesh, consubstantial, and as though the world of things, too, were solid yet not inanimate, an extension of the living substantiality of men. And all this, which I present here as though it were an abstruse, excogitated aesthetic doctrine, is of course nothing of the sort: it is, for him, a literary practice, extensively reflected on, which enables him to match and make his vision of the world. He was 17^1/$_2$ when the war ended in May 1945. The compulsion exerted on him comes, not from the events of the past, but from a recollection of those events. In Grass's early novels it is converted into a prose which turns out to be the only major source of liberation from an unmanageable literary past that post-war German literature has known.

The past as time and life irretrievably lost, and the past in the light of the present; the *grand guignol* of history and the actuality of its politics; the complex relationship of eros and food, and the special place of the disgusting and the sentimental in the recesses, the oubliettes, of consciousness; the religious and the blasphemous, the pious and the obscene; things, animals and men, concrete objects and conceptual abstractions — all these parts of an acute sense of life are set out in Grass's prose, not, however, in some ghastly Hegelian dialectic of antitheses and radical contradictions, but in continuities and prismatic rainbow patterns.

More than one critic has called Grass a humanist. I am not sure the word has much meaning left. He *is* one in the sense that there is no human experience too odd, too alien, to be made a part of one of his prismatic patterns. But he seems, as the author of certain substantial fictions, too diverse, too uncompromisingly interested in the fate of these fictions and in the process that gives rise to them — in short, too free — to be classifiable under any -ism or ideology. Literature is made of many different brews and dispositions, in freedom and in bondage, by the most doctrinaire no less successfully than by the least attached. But in his time and place — our assessment has the wisdom of hindsight — in that moment of defeat and dishonour, of shame and the posturing that tried to hide the shame, in that moment when the past could be neither forgotten (though it was denied) nor allowed to paralyse the present, a man without ideology was what was wanted, and Grass was and has remained that man. I mean here not Grass the political man and responsible Bürger of what has become one of Europe's exemplary democracies, but Grass the author of the most passionately contended books in post-war German literature, books which were attacked, not just on moral grounds (like *Ulysses* or *Lady Chatter-ley's Lover*), but also on political and patriotic grounds (like the works of Sinyavsky and Daniel): I mean the author of "The Danzig Trilogy."

The three works — *The Tin Drum* (1959), the novella *Cat and Mouse* (1961) and *The Dog Years* (1963) — were not planned as a single whole: the collective title comes, as far as I know, not from Grass himself, but from a perceptive critic, John Reddick, who used it as the title of a study (1975). What the three works have in common is, above all, the locale and the historico-political theme of Danzig at war (a theme which, oddly enough, is not central to Reddick's book). It is as if "the Hellish Breughel," his attention caught by the intricate pattern of one of his own landscapes with figures, had decided to devote two further panels to the subject: one small, exploring a single detail, the other on a larger and less intimate scale than the original picture.

In the first work, *The Tin Drum*, Oskar Matzerath — inmate of a mental hospital, which he describes, rather more euphemistically, as *"eine Heil- und Pflegeanstalt,"* a sanatorium and nursing home — Matzerath is writing his memoirs. The time covered takes us from the bizarre scene when his mother was conceived under her Cashubian mother's fourfold skirts in a potato field at harvest time in 1899, through Oskar's own birth in 1924, through his arrest and hospitalisation 28 years later, in 1952, when (with the help of Bruno, his warden) he begins writing his memoirs, to his 30th birthday and the conclusion of his manuscript in 1954.

Narrative coherence, in *The Tin Drum*, is achieved by a complex but relatively unified point of view, the "I-he" narration of Oskar Matzerath. In the novella *Cat and Mouse* (1961) — an adventure story of wartime adolescence, an offshoot of one of the episodes of the first novel — the point of view remains that of a single narrator, Pilenz, but because it is a confessional tale, involving a sequence of schoolboy jealousies and betrayal, the reliability of Pilenz as first-person narrator is constantly undercut. The truth of his narration remains as uncertain as does the character of the problematic hero and object of Pilenz's betrayal, "the great Mahlke" himself. German *Novellen* are built around a single momentous event. Here the event is Mahlke's theft of one of Germany's highest military decorations, the Knight's Cross of the Iron Cross. Every German schoolboy's dream, a coveted toy loaded with immense mystical, patriotic and sexual connotations, that Knight's Cross serves, in an almost physical sense, as the means of Mahlke's desperate self-defence and arrogant self-assertion (as the tin drum does for Oskar Matzerath); its ambivalent function — it commemorates the Knights of the Teutonic Order, yet it is a creation of Hitler's — corresponds to the narrator's unreliability and unstable point of view.

Finally, and again emerging from the episodic material of *The Tin Drum*, the mammoth undertaking of *The Dog Years* (1963). This is the story (among a great many other things) of the friendship between Walter Matern, the son of a German miller from the Danzig hinterland, and the half-Jewish Eddi Amsel, alias Haseloff, alias Brauxell (in several different spellings). The account of three decades — from 1925 to the mid-Fifties — is presented by various authors, including a whole post-war collective of them in the pay of the now baptised Amsel-Brauchsel, the artist-entrepreneur-manufacturer of Art-Déco scarecrows, who (like most other characters in the novel) is in pursuit of a past he hopes he will never catch up with.

The coherence of *The Dog Years* is provided neither by the action nor by its characters: the discontinuous narrative, especially in the last section of the book, is a part of its programme — one might almost say of its ideology. The action is frozen into metaphors and images, which provide such unity as the book possesses. To say this, though, is liable to lead to a misunderstanding. Critics who point to the importance of images in novels often argue as though the patterns these images form were patterns in the book and nowhere else. This is called "non-referential" — I think nonsensically. The genealogy of black dogs from which the book takes its title and which is reiterated throughout —

> Pawel . . . had brought Perkun with him from Lithuania and on request exhibited a kind of pedigree, which made it clear to whom it may concern that Perkun's grandmother on her father's side had been a Lithuanian, Russian or Polish she-wolf. And Perkun begat Senta; and Senta whelped Harras; and Harras [covered Thekla von Schüddelkau] and begat Prinz; and Prinz made history [because Prinz was given to the beloved Führer and Chancellor of Greater Germany for his birthday and, being the Führer's favourite dog, was shown in the newsreels . . .]

— this genealogical list, for all its symbolical overtones, is made up of the sequence of generations of actual SS black dogs and is the emblem of a historical experience. Similarly, the ontological blatherer with totalitarian collywobbles and attacks of authenticitis of the cervical membrane called Martin Heidegger is an identifiable caricature of the philosopher of that name; and the mountain made of human bones which lies between the outskirts of the city and the lunatic asylum at Stutthof, which everybody sees and nobody has seen, which everybody smells and nobody knows anything about—that mountain, expressed in Heideggerian gobbledygook, is "being that has come into unconcealment" and "the ontological disposition toward the annihilating nothingness of German history."

There is no end to the strings of bizarre images which create the unity of the book. They all raise the same question: why is there no continuous action? Why the bizarrerie? For an answer to this central question of Grass's early work, we had better return to his first and most accessible novel, *The Tin Drum*.

Here, certainly, there is something like a central character, depicted with a modicum of psychological coherence—a coherence which is undercut, but not fatally, by that opening confessional statement made in the haven of a lunatic asylum. Oskar Matzerath is presented—and presents himself—in a series of unstable and unnervingly ambiguous relationships with the people and events around him, mainly victim but occasionally victimiser of a bizarre world, a "world upside down." Even as an embryo, he anticipates that his entry into the world is bound to be disastrous—not because it is *his* entry, but because it is the world. (The heroes of the classical *Bildungsroman* similarly hesitate whether to enter the social world or to remain safely hidden in the caul of their solipsistic imagination, but similarly, too, we read in one of Grass's favourite novels: "My Tristram's misfortunes began nine months before ever he came into the world.") And when Oskar's wish to return into limbo is not fulfilled (the midwife—I mean Oskar's midwife, but it could be Tristram's—having done the irreversible and cut the umbilical cord), Oskar does the next best thing: he throws himself through the trapdoor into the cellar at the age of three, and there and then wills himself to stop growing. End of *Entwicklung* with a vengeance.

What this fairy-tale of outrageous absurdity suggests is that there is no other way of coping with, and making sense of, the hideous events and encounters of the adult world, and also that this is really no way either, because, by becoming a freak with every *appearance* of a gravely retarded development, Oskar is liable to fall a victim of the state-controlled euthanasia action which the National Socialist regime practised in order to implement its racial policy: it is only the collapse of the postal service at the end of the war (when even the Prussian bureaucracy ceased to function) that prevents Father Matzerath's letter, in which he consents to the eugenic killing of Oskar, from reaching what is so quaintly called the Reichs Ministry of Health. And this world, in which Oskar wills himself to stop growing, still pays lip-service to the Classical Weimar values of spiritual growth and development that had been central to the ideology of the *Bildungs-* or *Entwicklungsroman.*

These outrageous assaults on the reader's sensibility dominate every part of the novel. Oskar has a mother who dies, hideously, of a surfeit of fried lampreys and eels, some of which, we are told, may be the descendants of those Baltic eels that may have eaten her Polish grandfather, assuming, which is never entirely certain, that he was drowned and didn't disappear in the United States. Her death, like so many deaths in the novel, is the sign of a botched life. And Oskar has two fathers: an elegant Polish one, who is his mother's lover, and a German one, the hefty grocer Matzerath, with whom he will eventually share a mistress. Jan Bronski, the Pole, is involved in "the famous battle for the Polish post-office" at the outbreak of the War, which he spends playing a difficult game of three-handed skat—difficult because one of the players, the janitor Kobyella, is wounded and dies in the course of it, and has to be propped up against baskets full of blood-stained letters to prevent him showing his hand. At the end of the battle, Bronski is executed with 30 other Poles, "in the courtyard of the post-office, with arms upraised and hands folded behind their necks . . . they were thirsty and having their pictures taken for the newsreels . . . In Jan Bronski's upraised hand he held a few skat cards and with one hand holding the queen of hearts, I think, he waved to Oskar, his departing son." At the graveside of Matzerath, his other father, in 1945, Oskar wills himself to grow again, ready to assume the responsibilities of an adult, but after another three years, in the course of which he has merely succeeded in growing a hump, he decides (shades of Uncle Toby) that the sickbed in the asylum is the only safe haven and worthwhile goal, after all.

A child with an adult mind, a freak that combines the insights, feelings and sexuality of an adult with the guile and the scotfree licence of a child, Oskar has only two means of making an impact on the adult world: one is his drum, or rather series of drums, made of tin, the sides painted with red and white triangles, the colours of the Polish Army. (The present writer recollects a string of grey stallions of the Polish cavalry, a couple of tall red-and-white drums slung from each, parading on a brilliant Sunday morning in August 1939 along the cobbled street of a little town in Polish Silesia, less than thirty miles away from the German frontier, less than three weeks away from their doom.) The tin drum is the instrument of Oskar's art and self-expression, his defence—with it, he can disrupt political meetings *and* entertain Wehrmacht audiences—and the means of his brief flights of freedom: all-powerful and compelling at one moment, useless in competing even with the noise of carpet-beating the next, an instrument of pure, disinterested *l'art-pour-l'art* at one point, a source of cheap and meretricious entertainment at another.

In the course of defending his drum from seizure by his exasperated family, Oskar discovers a second defence: his capacity to aim his voice at any glass area that is visible to him and to sing it to bits. And this talent, too, is used ambivalently, now as the desperate protest of a child that is being unspeakably maltreated by other children, now as a manifestation of aesthetic decadence and manneristic art: during his stay in German-occupied Paris, Oskar devises an art-historical scheme following which he systematically destroys the contents of an exhibition covering the history of glass from Louis XIV to Art Nouveau. The identifications of author with hero are as grotesque — and as outrageously explicit — as all the other ploys.

There are a good many story-lines one might follow through the novel, but a better way of conveying its extraordinary achievement, *and* the formal difficulties that lie in the way of that achievement, is to concentrate on a single episode. Before doing that, though, the most obvious objection to the novel (and indeed to *The Dog Years* too) must be faced.

The reader may have gained the impression that here is a fictional monster — or a monster fiction — of six or seven hundred pages where anything goes — heedless fantasy let loose on unresistant material, with no discernible unifying meaning or coherence of any kind. Or else he may suspect that, German fictions being notorious for their highflown meta-physical messages, the critic will now pull the rabbit out of the hat and demonstrate the transcendental meaning of it all.

There is (as far as I can see) no such transcendental meaning or message, and yet the novel is much more than a series of self-indulgent or author-indulgent images and random episodes. Its meaning is to be wrested from its compositional difficulties, and they in turn may best be approached from the perspective of another great favourite of Grass's, Melville's *Moby Dick*. In the very deeps of that other monster creation you may stumble across a rumination in which the narrator anticipates the charge of self-indulgence and of excessive preoccupation with the customs and the bits and pieces of the whaling craft: "So ignorant are most landsmen of some of the plainest and most palpable wonders of the world, that without some hints [!] touching the plain facts, historical or other-wise, of the fishery, they might scout at Moby Dick as a monstrous fable, or still worse and more detestable, a hideous and intolerable allegory." Grass is in a similar predicament. The story he is writing is deeply, irreversibly steeped in the history of its time — or rather, not in that history, but in the crude and gory facts of the past from which such a history will have to be fashioned. These facts are notorious for offering the utmost resistance to interpretation of whatever kind. This is both the experience of readers of a different generation or culture *and* the understanding which Grass himself has of his national past and which he shares with his own generation of readers. Yet his impulse to write a historical fiction is clearly every bit as strong as the impulse to understand and come honourably to terms with that impossible past: in the creative act the two are to be united.

The work, therefore, is threatened by two difficulties. On the one hand, there is the danger of creating a sequence in which one "monstrous fable" follows another and the whole ends up as little more than a series of metaphors gone wild. The other, "still worse and more detestable," is that the impossible past gets swallowed up by "a hideous and intolerable allegory."

Again and again, we are likely to return to the question: can the unspeakable obscenity that called itself the Third Reich be fictionalised at all? Clearly, such an undertaking will require a certain imaginative freedom from the past — a freedom which was not available to Thomas Mann and his contemporaries, and which many critics may not be willing to grant. Yet "unspeakable" is itself a descriptive adjective and a legitimate part of the critic's vocabulary; and it is one thing to say (as some critics have said) that the novel cannot be interpreted, that it is incapable of yielding a meaning, and another to say that its meaning is hedged in with meaninglessness, with the grave difficulty of making sense of apparently senseless horror. True, we cannot interpret the story that is told in its fantastic episodes in simple, unambiguous terms, but this isn't due to some degeneracy of its author's sensibilities (as was predictably claimed by its indignant right-wing critics), but, on the contrary, to the immense difficulty he is bound to face when devising the underlying strategy of his novel. For what it aims to convey is the paradox that the daily practice and horrors of the Third Reich went on side by side with the daily practice and horrors of the ordinary world; that these things were and are and always have been a part of the human situation; and that this knowledge — I mean that monstrosities are human and that humankind is monstrous — must be grasped to the full, undiminished by the lethargy that comes from repetition and familiarity, yet without allowing it to destroy both the feeling of outrage and the capacity for interpretation, the capacity for giving a fictional account of it all. What Grass's novel in its own blasphemous way aims to convey is the paradox (whose supreme illustration is the death of Christ) that everything is ordinary and everything is special.

The two dangers that beset the work may now be restated: it is threatened either by a trivialisation of its material or by a demonisation of it. On the one hand, there is the risk that the metaphors, set out to convey the terrible, "unspeakable" evil, will turn out to be of an intolerable obscurity, incomprehensibly transcending all mundane experience — which is what, in *The Dog Years*, Grass satirises in the oracular utterances of Martin Heidegger. And there is the opposite risk — of the story slopping over into a mood of ghastly tolerance, a mood in which we are asked to accept every infamy as part of the human condition, for no better reason than that (as the great Hegel observed in one of his less great moments) in the night all cows are black, boys will be boys, men will be men and that's how it's always been. These are the two dangers attending Grass's prose when things go wrong. They are reflected in his readers' reactions — a sudden switching over from blank incomprehension to bored *déjà vu*.

But of course, at its best — as in "Faith, Hope and Love," the last chapter of the first book of *The Tin Drum* — the narrative emerges from those twin dangers with supreme success. The heading from the First Epistle to the Corinthians provides the chapter with its leitmotif. It begins in fairytale fashion, with a phrase that will be repeated throughout the chapter: "There was once a musician: his name was Meyn and he played the trumpet too beautifully for words." Meyn has been a friend of Oskar's, and of Oskar's friend Herbert, at whose funeral he blows the trumpet, as always when he is drunk, too beautifully for words. But Meyn is also a Storm Trooper, a member of the SA, a psychotic who, when sober and deeply disturbed, tries to kill his four cats and bury them in his garbage can, but "because the cats weren't all-the-way dead, they gave him away." And so the man Meyn was expelled from the party "for inhuman cruelty to animals" and "conduct unbecoming to a Storm Trooper," even though "on the night of November 8th [1938], which later became known as Crystal Night, he helped set fire to the Langfuhr Synagogue in Michaelisweg. Even his meritorious activity the following morning, when a number of stores, carefully designated in advance, were closed down for the good of the nation," could not halt his expulsion from the Mounted SA. Later, Meyn joins the SS.

This 8th of November is also the day when Oskar goes to visit his friend and chief supplier of red-and-white tin drums, the toyshop owner Sigismund Markus. He finds the shop full of SA men, in uniforms like Meyn's, but "Meyn was not there; just as the ones who were there were not somewhere else" (this is the phraseology of post-war alibis). The shop is full of excrements (this connects with a lengthy disquisition on the colour of brown, which is also the colour of the party) and:

> The toy merchant sat behind his desk. As usual he had on sleeve protectors over his dark-grey everyday jacket. Dandruff on his shoulders showed that his scalp was in bad shape. One of the SA men with puppets on his fingers poked him with Kasperl's wooden grandmother, but Markus was beyond being spoken to, beyond being hurt or humiliated. Before him on the desk stood an empty water glass; the sound of his crashing shopwindow had made him thirsty no doubt.

The detail of the dandruff is no more grotesque than the spectacle of the men letting down their trousers or the picture of the dead man.

Oskar leaves the shop, and, outside, "some pious ladies and strikingly ugly girls" were handing out religious tracts under a banner with an inscription from the 13th Chapter of the First Epistle to the Corinthians:

"Faith, hope, love," Oskar read and played with the three words as a juggler plays with bottles:

> Leichtgläubig, Hoffmannstropfen, Liebesperlen, Gutehoffnungshütte, Liebfrauenmilch, Gläubigerversammlung, Glaubst du, dass es morgen regnen wird? Ein ganzes leichtgläubiges Volk glaùbte an den Weihnachtsmann. Aber der Weihnachtsmann war in Wirklichkeit der Gasmann. Ich glaube, dass es nach Nüssen riecht und nach Mandeln
> . . .

The sequence is by definition untranslatable, but this is how the punning on the three saintly virtues ends:

> "Faith . . . hope . . . love," Oskar read: faith healer, Old Faithful, faithless hope, hope chest, Cape of Good Hope, hopeless love, Love's Labour's Lost, six love. An entire credulous nation believed; there's faith for you, in Santa Claus. But Sant Claus was really the gasman. I believe — such is my faith — that it smells of walnuts and almonds. But it smelled of gas. Soon, so they said, 'twill be the first Sunday of Advent. And the first, second, third, and fourth Sundays of Advent were turned on like gas cocks, to produce a credible smell of walnuts and almonds, so that all those who liked to crack nuts could take comfort and believe:
>
> He's coming, he's coming. Who is coming? The Christ child, the Saviour? Or is it the heavenly gasman with the gas meter under his arm, that always goes ticktock? And he said: I am the Saviour of this world, without me you can't cook. And he was not too demanding, he offered special rates, turned on the freshly polished gas cocks, and let the Holy Ghost pour forth, so the dove, or squab, might be cooked. And handed out walnuts and almonds which were promptly cracked, and they too poured forth spirit and gas.

This is the horrendous side by side with, but undiminished by, the practices of the ordinary world.

"Ask my pen," says Tristram Shandy, when questioned about the design of his strange book: "Ask my pen; it governs me; I govern not it." What is being undertaken in Grass's equally strange book is something very new but also, going back to Laurence Sterne, very old. However different the mood of the two novels, they both disdain narrative order and live by extravagant metaphor.

We are accustomed to think of word games, situational games, and the detailed working out of bizarre images, as the conceits of humorous novels. But they are not necessarily and exclusively so. *Tristram Shandy* is certainly a humorous novel, but so, in parts, is *The Tin Drum*; where the humour of the one shades off into sentimentality, the other veers into tragi-comedy; and where *Tristram Shandy* is concerned to guy and illustrate causal propositions and absurd inferences from Locke's philosophy, *The Tin Drum* guys causality and replaces it by verbal association. Its humour and its seriousness are not polarised in some inhuman Hegelian dialectic: they are made continuous with each other, as the everyday and the monstrous are continuous in our experience.

Our conventional terminology, which moves within the squirrel cage of symbols and allegories, won't quite do. Oskar isn't the symbol of anything, just as Uncle Toby or Corporal Trim aren't the symbols of anything. Oskar is what he is, a freak, because freaks alone (according to the logic the author compels us to accept) can be brought into some sort of meaningful relationship with this world—and that relationship is one of metaphors, puns, and of the logic that is built from metaphors and puns. The word-game on faith-hope-love, on the Spirit (pneuma) and gas, Santa Claus and the holy gasman, may suggest elements of satire (German love of Christmas, the Church's comforting concern for the spirit of everyone except those who were gassed, Hitler's role as self-appointed Saviour, etc), but the satirical element is subsidiary to the main undertaking of the novel, which is to match an almost unbelievable, inexplicable past with almost unbelievable and inexplicable metaphors, and thus to make it believable and explain it without reducing its tragic pathos and without explaining it away. And it is an added grace that all this is done without succumbing to that ghastly tendency (so characteristic of post-Nietzschean Germany) to justify and vindicate everything by adverting to a "tragic view of life."

There are traces and analogies of a Christian concern in the novel. At their most obvious, these traces are to be seen in the negative religiousness of blasphemy, such as the exegesis of "Faith, Hope and Love," or the repeated scenes of Oskar Matzerath's imitation of the Christ Child. It is as if blasphemy were the only form of social religiousness available to blasphemous times. But there are also analogies pointing to a religious meaning. The precarious stylistic balance I mentioned, between the obscurity of demonisation and the triviality of "all's grist to the human mill," involving a full acknowledgement of the horrors of the past which the creative conscience prevents from turning either into complacent tolerance or annihilating despair—this balance is surely seen at its clearest within such a framework as is provided by St. Augustine's exhortation, often quoted "with particular relish and sadness," as Christopher Ricks observes in his introduction to *Tristram Shandy*, by Samuel Beckett: "Do not despair, one of the thieves was saved; do not presume, one of the thieves was damned." If, in post-war literature, other literary ways were devised of coming to terms with the past, without presumption and without despair, I have failed to notice them. So far, Grass's achievement is unique.

Aspects of the Absurd in Günter Grass

W. G. Cunliffe*

In his *Deutsche Literatur der Gegenwart*, Walter Jens[1] claims that postwar literature in Germany should be dated from 1952. He even assigns an exact time and place to the new start — a meeting of the Gruppe 47 held in the Spring of 1952 at which Paul Celan, "in a singing voice, very remote from the world," Ingeborg Bachmann and Ilse Aichinger read extracts from their works to the assembled company, routing and putting to shame the "verists," the competent but uninspired story-tellers who had preceded them. In his mythopoeic fashion, Jens is stating his conviction that serious postwar literature requires detachment from the overwhelming events of the recent past. Until that detachment was achieved, there could be only factual reporting (possibly with a little subjective coloring), no true artistic mastery of the material.

Günter Grass, whose first novel *Die Blechtrommel (The Tin Drum)* appeared in 1959, is of the generation of writers who employ the indirect approach as the only one adequate to the modern scene for the novelist's purpose. Thus in *Die Blechtrommel*, he is apparently concerned with the inconsequential adventures of a mad dwarf, born in Grass' native Danzig, but now confined in a West German mental hospital. *Katz und Maus (Cat and Mouse*, 1961) is, at first sight, a preposterous story about a Danzig schoolboy who wears objects (screwdrivers, medals, etc.) around his neck to conceal a large Adam's-apple. The fall of the Third Reich in *Hundejahre (Dog Years*, 1963) is reflected in the adventures of a runaway dog. In the same way, Wolfdietrich Schnurre, in his novel *Das Los unserer Stadt* (1959), does not describe the rain of bombs on Berlin and its subsequent occupation by conquering armies, but composes a surrealist vision of a town taken over by natural forces. Uwe Johnson's first novel *Mutmassungen über Jakob (Speculations about Jacob*, 1959) does not give a straightforward account of life in Eastern Germany, but is concerned with a highly conjectural story about a railway worker. Johnson's second novel *Das dritte Buch über Achim* (1961), brings out into the open the difference between a factual report and a novel. The narrator of Johnson's novel is a West German journalist who wishes to write a report on an East German racing cyclist, but his task turns out to be impossible. What can be told straightforwardly is not the novelist's concern, rather it is his business to find an equivalent (Jens uses T. S. Eliot's term "objective correlative") for his subject-matter. Grass finds this equivalent in the grotesque (a possible literary development foreseen by Friedrich Schlegel in 1799) and, frequently, in the obscene. Now, as George Orwell remarks: "Obscenity is a

*Reprinted from *Wisconsin Studies in Contemporary Literature* 7 (1966):311–27, by permission of *Wisconsin Studies in Contemporary Literature* and the author.

very difficult question to discuss honestly. People are too frightened either of seeming to be shocked or of seeming not to be shocked."[2] The critic of the *Kölnische Rundschau* would seem to be typical of the latter category: "After reading *Die Blechtrommel*, one is overcome by a longing for a lot of hot water and for some good soap." Even Günter Blöcker in the *Frankfurter Allgemeine Zeitung* and Marcel Reich-Ranicki in *Die Zeit*, unmoved by the enthusiasm of other critics, condemned *Die Blechtrommel* on its first appearance for its pointless obscenity, although the *Zeit* critic conceded Grass "considerable gifts of style."[3] This question of obscenity may serve as an introduction to Grass' methods.

A chapter of the second book of *Die Blechtrommel*, which Blöcker singled out for contempt, bears the title "Brausepulver" (Lemonade Powder). Grass sets out, in accordance with his practice, from the object itself, the cheap lemonade powder, dwelling on its characteristics with a wealth of verbs that recalls Rabelais or Fischart and displaying, incidentally, an exact knowledge of his humble subject:

> Lemonade powder. Does that mean anything to you? Once it could be obtained at all times of the year in little flat bags. In our shop my mother sold little bags of woodruff-flavored powder of a sickly shade of green. One sort that had borrowed its color from oranges that were not quite ripe was called: Powder (Orange Flavor). Then there was powder with raspberry flavor and powder which, when plain water was poured on to it hissed, bubbled, became excited, which, when you drank it, before it calmed down, remotely, very faintly tasted of lemons, and had the same color in the glass, only somewhat more eager: an artificial yellow that gave itself the air of being poison.[4]

This effervescent, artificial powder plays an important part in the erotic passages between the hero, Oskar, and Maria, the young shop assistant. They experiment and find that, poured into the palm of Maria's hand and brought to effervescence, it causes delicious sensations. The seething powder is an objective correlative, and equivalent of adolescent love — the phrase "that had borrowed its color from oranges that were *not quite ripe*" is not a mere random detail. More than this, it also presents an equivalent of the spirit of the 'thirties (the setting in which the incident takes place) and the period's heady, dangerous enthusiasms — "an artificial yellow that gave itself the air of being poison." The historical connotations clearly emerge when, in Western Germany after the War, Oskar attempts to buy lemonade powder in the vain hope of recalling youthful ecstasies. An elderly stall-owner informs him:

> It's a long time since there was any of that about. Under Kaiser Wilhelm, and right at the beginning, under Adolf — then it was still sold. Those were the days! But if you'd like a Coca-Cola?[5]

It requires no great critical astuteness to appreciate what Grass has done here. Starting from the lemonade powder as a presiding genius, he has passed on to a human relationship and then to a nation-wide movement. It is as if the whole world were controlled by the powder, just as, in another episode, the crowd on the Danziger Maiwiese dances to the beat of Oskar's tin drum. Cheap lemonade powder, adolescent love and the Nazi movement are closely linked in a pattern of associations. Without any liberal-minded argument or display of enlightened anti-Fascist sentiments, the Nazi movement is placed firmly in an unmistakably petit-bourgeois context of cheap, fizzy chemical pop. Wagenbach, in his brief portrait of Grass, notes the dominant part played by objects in Grass' fiction, and characterizes this stylistic feature as "Objektzwang" (compulsion through objects). He also observes that the method involves a neutral, amoral attitude on the part of the narrator to what he observes:

> The objects are . . . so to speak, ruled by an object. In this way no judgment is passed on an object by a subject; things keep themselves to themselves. It is hardly possibly to consider such a text under the categories of disgust or delight, of the ugly or the beautiful.[6]

For all its grotesqueness, Grass' neutral approach to human activities eliminates certain distortions. While attacking the Nazi movement, for example, Rolf Hochhuth in *Der Stellvertreter* (*The Deputy*), presents it in a light of demonic grandeur. Such spurious glory is eliminated from Grass' object-dominated world. Thus the arrival of the Russians in Danzig in *Die Blechtrommel* is presented in a scene preposterously dominated by the party badge of Alfred Matzerath, Oskar's father. As in a music-hall sketch, Matzerath tries to hide the incriminating object. But the badge controls events and resists (with Oskar's help) all attempts to hide it. In desperation, Matzerath tries to swallow it and chokes to death as Russian soldiers enter the cellar where he is sheltering with his family. This is Grass' version of the end of the Third Reich.

Grass places his reliance on objects because, as he makes plain, moral and logical categories have little relation to the actions of individuals or to the monstrous events of history. To take a simple example — Hitler was fond of dogs (Hitler does not actually appear in *Hundejahre*, but his dog substitutes for him at the last minute). Meyn, of *Die Blechtrommel*, a member of the Danzig SA mob that smashes and plunders Jewish-owned shops and houses during the so-called Kristallnacht of November 9, 1938, is a fine trumpet-player. In a kind of remorse, he kills his four pet cats with a fire-iron, and is expelled from the Party for cruelty to animals. The vicious Nazi girl, Tulla, who plays an important part in *Hundejahre*, and also appears in the other novels, is permanently surrounded by a concentration camp aura of bone glue from the carpenter's yard where her father works. Yet she emerges as a figure of beguiling impulsiveness, while her victim, the gipsy-girl Jenny, is kindly, shy and unenterprising. Only together could they make a complete woman: they stay apart, one to vanish and the other to wither away. The main theme, to which Tulla and

Jenny are a kind of counterpoint, is the relationship between Walter Matern and his half-Jewish blood-brother Eddi Amsel. Matern, together with eight other members of the SA, beat up Amsel and leave him to die in the snow. Yet this relationship is not simply that of the persecuted and persecutor, but something far more ambiguous. Amsel has the firmer character; Matern is, by descent, the moody Slav, the waverer—now Communist, now Nazi, now Catholic, now violently against all those persuasions. Closing his eyes to his own guilt, he travels about postwar Germany seeking revenge on former Nazis. His revenge takes the form of disseminating gonorrhea, and Matern ends, pathetically, as an exhausted victim in a cause not his own. Amsel, with his mocking talents, is resurrected, first as Haseloff, creator of a scarecrow ballet, and later as Brauxel, whose underground scarecrow factories tunnel under affluent Western Germany. To some extent, then, Amsel, the survivor, creator, organizer and endurer is the Spirit, while Matern is also, certainly, the Flesh. But these categories, too, do not really fit—Matern has a metaphysical bent, while Amsel is not averse to social and sensual pleasures.

The objects that preside over the action of *Hundejahre* are the scarecrows that recur as a leitmotif. Eddi Amsel, the victim of persecution, is, ironically enough, the master scarecrow builder. As a child he constructs scarecrows whose presence is anathema to birds and, later, to other creatures and to people. During the War he creates mechanical scarecrows that enact the folly of Nazism. Finally, he turns worldwide supplier of scarecrows that re-enact and travesty human history, politics, social customs, normal and abnormal psychology—in fact, every human emotion and attitude. There is a mock theological controversy: the scarecrow is made in the image of man, and man in that of God—is not then the scarecrow the image and likeness of God? The scarecrow is, in fact, an equivalent of man's inventive and creative activities that may also destroy him, for the artist is a blackbird (Amsel), whom his artefacts may expel.

The dogs, too, which provide the title, exert a strange control over the situation. "Der Hund steht zentral"—"the dog stands in the center"—is the running refrain. Harras and Prinz, sire and whelp, are descended from a Slav she-wolf. Harras is a good, lower-middle-class watch-dog, a typical German, dependable if somewhat rough in his ways. He sires Prinz, who becomes Hitler's pet, whereupon Harras becomes celebrated and a bit of a Nazi. But Prinz, when he senses the downfall of the Third Reich, deserts to the Allies and ends up as Matern's companion on his mission of revenge, under the name of Pluto. This harmless Walt Disney reminiscence shows another facet when a strange reincarnation of this dog becomes Pluto's hell-hound, Cerberus, in Brauxel's scarecrow mine. The dog, then, is the equivalent of Man's animality, a force neither good nor evil (to use unacceptable categories) which can, above all, be exalted or made a scapegoat of. Thus, when Prinz is escaping, Hitler mobilizes his hardpressed forces to recapture the emblematically German "Führerhund," but on another occasion Matern, consumed by self-disgust and his own dalliance with the Catholic faith, shouts at Harras: "You black Catholic swine! . . . Dominican! Christian dog!"[7]

In the same way, much of the action in *Die Blechtrommel* is governed by Oskar's drum, an equivalent, independent of good and evil, of the infantile dynamic force that resides in Oskar and his era. Oskar first offers the services of his drum to the Nazis, where it plainly belongs, on the advice of the Goebbels-like clown, Bebra. But Löbsack, leader of the Danzig party, fails to see beyond the three-year-old boy whom Oskar deceptively resembles, and pats him absent-mindedly on the head. In revenge (and Oskar's revenge is as little justified as Matern's), Oskar employs his powers to break up a Nazi meeting by hiding under the speaker's tribune and beating his drum. Instead of listening to inflammatory speeches, the audience responds to the rival magic and waltzes; later, the trumpeters of the Hitler Youth are hopelessly confused by unaccustomed jazz rhythms. The Church, too, has its share in these sources of power. This is proved on a later occasion, towards the end of the War, when, with the Nazis visibly weakening, Oskar hangs his drum around a statue of the infant Jesus, who proceeds to beat it with his chubby fists. Even on an earlier occasion, when Jesus fails to beat the drum, Oskar's piercing voice that can shatter windows — a prelude to the coming destruction of Danzig — fails to harm the windows of the Catholic Church. In the white-enamelled hospital ward of Western Germany, Oskar still obeys the dictates of his drum. When he has completed a bizarre account of the death of Herbert Truczynski in the embrace of a wooden figurehead, another masterful object that embodies all the disasters of Danzig history, Bruno advises Oskar not to play so loudly in future, for he is disturbing the other patients. Oskar promises that the next chapter of his chronicle will be more restrained. But the matter is out of his control. The next chapter "Faith, Hope and Charity" deals with the events of Kristallnacht and is the wildest of all, so that the coming War is ushered in at the end of the First Book with the effect of a roll of drums — a series of sentences beginning with the fairy-tale "Once upon a time."

This domination on the part of objects recalls the methods of the theater of the absurd — I quote Peter Löffler's *Theater — Wahrheit und Wirklichkeit:* "In contrast to this depreciation of the human being, the objects acquire an added value. Modern drama tends to endow the objects with at least a potential power, which at times can become a magic power."[8] One thinks, for example, of Eugène Ionesco's plays, of the furniture that takes control in *Le nouveau Locataire,* or the chairs in *Les Chaises.* Indeed, before *Die Blechtrommel* was published, Grass wrote a number of absurd plays (not very successful). In *Onkel, Onkel* [*Mister, Mister*] the murderer is frustrated by his own revolver, which prevents him from committing a murder and finally shoots him. In Grass' one-act *Noch zehn Minuten bis Buffalo* (*Ten Minutes to Buffalo*), the lives of the two

dilettante railwaymen, Krudewil and Pempelfort, are entirely subordi-
nated to the abandoned locomotive they serve in the absurd hope of
reaching Buffalo. The effect is summed up by Wolfgang Hildesheimer in
his Erlanger Address on the absurd theater; here he mentions this play and
describes it as "a small diabolical disturbance, an announcement, so to
speak, of the instability of the world."[9] It is this uncertainty and radical
doubt characteristic of the absurd theater that is basic to Grass' work.

Indeed, Grass' statement of literary principle in the essay "Inhalt als
Widerstand"[10] ("Content as Resistance") insists on constant doubt and
revision. The first section of the essay, "a distrustful dialogue" between
Pempelfort and Krudewil, now more congenially employed as poets,
concludes with Krudewil rejecting his companion's ecstasies over flowers
and sitting down to knit a new, sober Muse: "Our new Muse is a skilled
housewife. A faulty upper part would annoy her. She would dismiss us
without mercy, have herself unwound and re-knitted on a machine." In the
final section, Grass uses an illustration from one of his favorite fields —
cooking and eating — to demonstrate the need for constant vigilance:
"Where eggs are served as softboiled, it is best to convince oneself with the
spoon." The vigilance has the purpose of ensuring that the poet remains
close to the object and that he does not depart from it to make large
statements about life. Grass assumes that a poet chooses as his subject a
close-mesh wire fence. A bad poet will rave enthusiastically: "the cosmos
must be included, the motor elements of the meshed wire should swell to a
supertemporal, supersensual staccato, completely dissolved and fused into
a new system of values." He would be better advised, says Grass, to stay
with the original wire fence, as supplied by Lerm and Ludewig, Berlin.
The essay ends with the poet tapping distrustfully at his egg.

The constant vigilance against statements that fail to ring true is
sustained in Grass' novels by his manipulation of time. The events of the
past are constantly checked and impressions revised against events, in
the narrator's present the comparison of "then" with "now." The opening
chapters of *Die Blechtrommel* serve as an example of this technique. The
novel opens, strikingly: "Admittedly, I am the inmate of a nursing
home. . . ." The narrator, Oskar, describes the hygienic hospital ward
with its white bed. Piously declaring his intention of beginning his tale in
the traditional manner with his grandparents, Oskar shifts the scene to a
late October in 1899, when his grandmother was sitting at the edge of a
potato-field in the region of the lower Vistula. The landscape is conjured
up in a masterly fashion. The grandmother's location is precisely determined by means of a wealth of long-vanished local place-names. There
follows the story of the grandmother's meeting with her husband-to-be,
one Joseph Koljaiczek, who, fleeing from the police, takes refuge under
her wide skirts. After a hasty marriage, Koljaiczek provides himself with
false papers and finds work as a log rafter. His subsequent adventures take
him far afield, through Germany (as it then was), Poland and Russia,

along the Vistula and Bug to Kiev. He is finally recognized by his Prussian foreman and presumably drowned fleeing from the police during the launching of a liner in Danzig. This far-ranging narrative is interrupted and concluded by brief returns to Oskar's hospital ward. The ward is in Western Germany — it is, in a sense, Western Germany — and present and past confront each other. The confrontation is of a nature to make the reader revise his perspective. The old world is earthy, yet full of drama and history, while Oskar's present is confined, clean and occupied with neurotic trivialities. In the narrator's present time lingers, while Oskar ponders over the purchase of 500 sheets of paper; in the past the narrative moves swiftly through time and space.

The vanished world that came to an end in 1914 is well known to have been, as Stefan Zweig expresses it, "the Golden Age of Security." Grass brings this cliché to life by objectifying it in the wide skirts of Oskar's grandmother; she possesses five of them, of which she wears four, one over the other. Every week, in accordance with a comforting, regular routine, the dirtiest of the current four is changed for a clean one. It is here that Joseph Koljaiczek and, later, Oskar, seek refuge from a cold world.

At times, Grass extends his range of vision far back into German and European history. This occasions further doubt and unease, for everywhere, in the manner of Thomas Mann's Serenus Zeitblom, he sees disturbing associations between the past and the Nazi era. This is especially true of *Hundejahre*, which acquires its shape from the historical theme; the central story emerges from and ends in a welter of history. The novel opens on the banks of the Vistula, outside Danzig. Two boys are playing on the dikes, Eddi Amsel, partly Jewish, and his protector and potential murderer Walter Matern. The river bears past the rubble of a long history in which they will both be caught up. The panorama extends to the gods of the Prussian Slavs, the Teutonic Knights, Frederick the Great and the Princes of Pomerania. Myths and legends are included — one about twelve headless nuns and twelve headless knights recurs through the novel to communicate horror and violence from the past into the present (horror and violence that are embedded in a chivalrous and sacred past). The river dikes, however, are not dependable; mice are in them and there is danger of flooding.

The main plot is the flood that follows. It covers roughly the period of the Third Reich, which lasted about the lifetime of a dog. At the end of the novel we are brought back to the starting-point. For the second time Matern throws Amsel's pocket-knife into the river (this time not the Vistula but the Landwehrkanal in Berlin) and insults him. The story comes to rest in a mine near Hanover where Amsel, resurrected as Brauxel, manufactures scarecrows that enact a pageant of German history.

The circular structure is not peculiar to *Hundejahre*. All three novels set out from the narrator's present in Western Germany, explore the history of the last forty years, with digressions into the remoter past, and, gradually narrowing the gap between the narrator's present and narrative present, return to the jumping-off point. But the journey has been made in vain: the traveller has really wandered round in a complete circle. The postwar Düsseldorf where Oskar settles bears a strong resemblance to the Danzig he has fled from—there is even a similar eccentric character haunting the cemetery. The thirty-year-old Oskar at the end of *Die Blechtrommel* remains as childish as ever, and, in the concluding nursery rhyme of the Black Cook, with its refrain "Ist die schwarze Köchin da—ja, ja, ja" terror continues to dominate. As Enzensberger expresses it: "Oskar takes leave of his readers, cites the shadow that has always been there and which will not leave him and us."[11] The hero Mahlke in *Katz und Maus* disappears from Danzig, unappreciated and unrecognized; the narrator searches in vain for him in postwar Western Germany. At the end of *Hundejahre*, Krupp, Flick, Hoesch and the other captains in industry are back in business. Yet commentators on Grass' work, such as George Steiner, who see in Grass a liberal-minded satirist, rubbing German noses into their nasty past and exhorting them to change their ways, have, I believe, missed the point, misled perhaps by clumsy, repetitive attacks on, for example, *Der Spiegel* magazine or the "Wirtschaftswunder" at the end of *Hundejahre*. Grass is no satirist; he has none of the satirist's absurd hope that the world can be improved. Rather, he is doubting whether progress is possible at all in human affairs, whether there are any goals to aim at. This, again, is the view of life expressed in the absurd theater; the disturbing possibility broached in Beckett's *Waiting for Godot* that the tramps will go on waiting (for what?) for the rest of eternity.

Grass is not a satirist, but he is a most accomplished parodist. *Die Blechtrommel* is a parody of the Entwicklungsroman, the novel, of the type of Goethe's *Wilhelm Meister*, which gives an account of the education of a young man to maturity. At an early stage, Oskar takes a look at the world and decides to cease development at the age of three; his education, however, includes even the theatrical training that was an essential part of Wilhelm Meister's preparation for maturity—in Oskar's case with a group of midgets entertaining troops in France. On his return to Danzig he claims, not very convincingly, to be the father of a son born to Maria Matzerath. His development reaches its peak in his grotesque pose as Jesus. A gang of young hooligans, "die Stäuber" [The Dusters], appoint him as their leader and steal church furnishings during the last phase of the War. But it all comes to nothing. The gang is caught red-handed, while Oskar takes advantage of his outward form, that of a three-year-old boy, to escape scot-free, abandoning his companions to their fate. The optimistic principles of the Entwicklungsroman clash with and are defeated by the principles of the absurd theater that reflects the inconclusiveness of life itself. The only development that Oskar attains is a growth of some ten centimeters on the refugee train that takes him from Danzig to the West.

Even this modest result is achieved at the expense of his energy; he is a hunchback, no longer able to shatter glass with his voice and incapable of the erotic adventures of his vigorous three-year-old youth—a mocking parallel to the development of the Bundesrepublik after the defeat of 1945.

The middle section of *Hundejahre* parodies the epistolary novel. It is in the form of love-letters written by Harry Liebenau to his cousin Tulla, an unchaste Lotte, who is willing to grant her favors to everyone except Harry. The epistolary convention is treated with increasing perfunctoriness, until finally it is abandoned and the letters are simply headed "Once upon a time. . . ." The kinship between Nazism and other currents of thought is expressed by parody, especially Heidegger parodies, of which there are many in *Hundejahre*. Thus the messages sent to and from Hitler's Berlin bunker during the last days of the War in Europe are progressively distorted until they become a strange mixture of military and philosophic jargon (Hitler is, at this stage of the Götterdämmerung, represented as tracing his runaway dog with the aid of Fü-Hu-Su-Trupps). An "exlocution" issued by the Führer's supreme headquarters, dated April 26 could be rendered:

> Dread impedes apprehension of Nothing. With effect from now Dread will be surmounted by speeches or song. Negation of Nothing attuned to distantiality continues prohibited. Never must the Reich capital in its locus-wholeness be infirmed by dread.[12]

In fact, Grass in *Hundejahre* shows himself as accomplished a parodist as Joyce. There is, for example, a striking dramatic monologue in which a genteel, worldly anti-Semite delivers himself of every highflown cliché about the Jews.

The pointlessness of the revenge which Matern seeks in that section of *Hundejahre* entitled "Materniaden" is underlined in various parodies. On one occasion Matern pays a visit to his former Commanding Officer. The latter is amused, and takes the wind out of Matern's sails by pointing out the resemblance he (Matern) bears to Beckmann in Wolfgang Borchert's *Draussen vor der Tür*. The search for revenge culminates in the parody of a radio interview (which is, in addition, a parody of *Faust*) in which Matern is exposed as the persecutor of Amsel.

Die Blechtrommel includes a parody of the Schelmenroman, the picaresque novel. The hero, in the manner of Grimmelshausen's Simplicissimus, ends his wandering life in a hermitage, or, at least, in the seclusion of a sanatorium. The device of placing the narrator in seclusion is frequent in modern novels—Max Frisch's Stiller speaks from a prison cell and the narrator of *Das Los unserer Stadt* writes his chronicle in a monastery. Such seclusion is a convincing method of enabling the narrator to employ a variety of perspectives, from that of participant to that of impartial judge, and, in his remote reflectiveness, to fuse realism with fantasy. Oskar takes full advantage of these various possibilities. He frequently changes from first into the third person, sometimes within a single sentence: "May I remind you of the Great and the Small Tattoo, and, further, indicate Oskar's previous attempts."[13]

The wide range of Oskar's point of view is indicated at the very beginning of *Die Blechtrommel*. Oskar's simple-minded attendant, Bruno, regards his charge anxiously through the peep-hole in the door, while the latter conjures up childhood memories on his drum. From the stories that Oskar tells him, Bruno creates fantastic shapes out of string and plaster, which may or may not have some artistic merit. The author is both Bruno peering inwards and creating what may be works of art and Oskar, looking outward at the surrounding world. The reader is allowed no certainty as to which point of view is prevailing at a given moment. Yet Oskar insists that what follows his introduction is to be a straightforward, old-fashioned novel, and he says of Bruno and himself: "We are both heroes, quite distinct heroes, he behind the peep-hole and I in front of the peep-hole, and when he opens the door, both of us are still, in spite of our friendship and loneliness, no nameless and heroless mass."[14] Oskar's claim to be "in front of" the peep-hole, while his attendant is "behind" it, only adds to the uncertainty.

The same range and uncertainty of point of view marks the opening of *Hundejahre:*

> You tell the story. No, you tell it. Or you could tell it. But, then, should the actor begin? . . . Should the scarecrows all at once? . . . Someone must begin. You or he or the other or I.[15]

Oskar regards pre-war Danzig society subjectively and objectively from both sides of the peep-hole and from all angles. He climbs to the top of the Stockturm to survey the doomed city, and he crawls under the table while the family is playing Skat and from there obtains a scurrilous, worm's-eye view of human affairs. On the surface, *Die Blechtrommel* has much in common with Grass' next, short novel *Katz und Maus*, and this fact has caused some commentators to dismiss the latter work as a mere supplement to the longer novel. Both works, for example, contain a variety of grotesque episodes involving a main character distinguished by a deformity and eccentric habits — in *Die Blechtrommel* the dwarf with his tin drum, in *Katz und Maus* the schoolboy Mahlke with his oversize Adam's-apple which he tries to hide by wearing objects on a string around his neck (with the Knight's Cross as the culminating object). There is an important difference, however, in the point of view from which events are observed. In *Die Blechtrommel* the central character observes a broad field of activity. In the novella the eccentric central character is the focus of attention. He is observed from the point of view of a narrator, a schoolfriend named Pilenz who, himself, in his lack of comprehension of the hero, is a representative of the society they both move in. In one case we look at society from the point of view of an individual, with consequent dispersal of attention; in the other society looks at an individ-

ual, giving the author better opportunity to impose form and pattern on
his material.

Through the ingenious device of employing a narrator who is only
dimly aware of the hero's virtues, but constantly aware of the ridiculous
figure he cuts in the eyes of the world, Grass succeeds in revealing Mahlke
convincingly as a true hero, with the hero's traditional attributes of
bravery, modesty, honesty and chastity, without abandoning the inconse-
quence and absurdity which are essential to Grass' approach to human
affairs. The reader is never allowed to forget Mahlke's Adam's-apple, the
"mouse" of the title, a reminder that Mahlke is different from his fellows
and a victim and martyr to the cat of society. In the very first scene
Mahlke is shown in the posture of a martyr: he is one of a group of boys
lying at the edge of a playing-field, when some unknown hand, possibly
that of the narrator, sets a cat on to Mahlke's mouse. Events reach their
carefully prepared climax in the exact mid-point of the novella in Chapter
VII, when Mahlke attends a lecture delivered by a submarine commander.
The sight of the commander's medal inspires Mahlke to heroism that wins
him the same decoration to adorn his neck, but he ends, as he began, a
mouse to the world's cat. Just before the fall of Danzig, he deserts and
disappears mysteriously in the manner of the legendary hero.

The essence of Mahlke's heroism is its unpretentiousness. He expresses
this quality in a manner absurd in its concreteness, by eating repulsive
foods. In summer, Mahlke and his companions swim nearly every day to a
wrecked Polish minesweeper lying in Danzig bay. With a screwdriver hung
around his neck, Mahlke performs feats of salvaging that arouse astonish-
ment and admiration. Where the other children are content to eat
seagulls' droppings scraped from the rusty deck, Mahlke, on one occasion,
dives deep and salvages a can of frogs' legs which he consumes, to the
horror and admiration of them all. Such scenes involving the consumption
of repulsive foods recur throughout Grass' works, and Wagenbach[16] sees in
them a suggestion of atonement, whereby the absurd domination of the
object is maintained. The motif is interpreted in a poem included in the
collection *Gleisdreieck* entitled "Askese" ("Asceticism"). The speaker is a
cat, who recommends a sober, matter-of-fact manner of life in these
terms:

> Du sollst, so spricht die Katze weiter,
> nur noch von Nieren, Milz und Leber,
> von atemloser saurer Lunge,
> vom Seich der Nieren, ungewässert,
> von alter Milz und zäher Leber,
> aus grauem Topf: so sollst du leben.[17]

(Thou shalt, the cat went on to say, live only on kidneys, spleen and
liver, on breathless, sour lung, on the urine from the kidneys, undiluted,
on old spleen and tough liver from a gray pot: so shalt thou live).

In *Hundejahre*, Tulla's mourning for her younger brother takes the form of sharing with the dog similarly repulsive offal from his bowl. She refuses to move from the dog's kennel until her period of mourning is completed — the dog allows no one to approach her. The most memorable of the scenes involving repulsive foods occurs in *Die Blechtrommel*, in the chapter "Good-Friday Diet." Oskar's parents, accompanied by his mother's lover, Jan Bronski, encounter during a Good-Friday walk along the seafront an elderly longshoreman, who, while they are watching him, pulls up from the sea a horse's head on the end of a long rope. He is fishing for eels, and this is the bait. Eels, some of them covered with particles from the horse's brain, emerge from all orifices, the big ones last of all and with some difficulty. Oskar's mother is sick, a fact which the ever-present seagulls take full advantage of. To show his courage, Matzerath feels compelled to buy some eels and take them home to cook for supper. Oskar's mother is horrified at the idea, and begs him to do nothing of the sort. Yet, from that day on she eats fish of all kinds in huge quantities:

> She began with sardines for breakfast, and two hours later, if there were no customers in the shop just then, she attacked the plywood case with the Bohnsack sprats, demanded for lunch fried flounders or pomuchel in mustard sauce and in the afternoon there she was again with the can-opener in her hand: jellied eels, rollmops, fried herrings, and if Matzerath refused to fry or boil fish again for supper, then she didn't waste any words, she didn't grumble, she got up quietly from the table and came back from the shop with a piece of smoked eel. . . .[18]

The result is that she dies soon afterwards from fish-poisoning. It is as if she were atoning in this way for her lack of moderation, her excessive love for Jan Bronski, a love which itself is expressed in terms of food: "My mother and Jan Bronski didn't leave a single crumb. They ate everything up themselves. They have the appetite that never ceases."[19]

Repulsive food has a religious significance in the play *Die bösen Köche* (*The Wicked Cooks*). There are two rival factions of cooks, and they are after the secret of a mysterious gray soup consisting of cabbage soup with some kind of ashes added. The holder of this secret is a certain Count alias Herbert Schymanski. The cooks allow him to marry the nurse Martha in return for his secret, but he fails to keep his part of the bargain and commits suicide, excusing himself by claiming that the secret is not communicable, but a matter of living knowledge.

The same comment could be made about much of Grass' highly personal, grotesque imagery. The scarecrows, the tin drum, the nuns and cooks are suggestive without being essential, defining, discrete and definitive. Grass is presenting his own sense of being, his individual intuition of the human situation. The grotesqueness of this vision contrasts with the minutely observed petit-bourgeois background, depicted to the last potato-dumpling. In spite of his bizarre visions, Grass has all the virtues of an old-fashioned novelist. He knows and can describe with meticulous accuracy the smell and appearance of a pre-war elementary school, the life of a log rafter at the turn of the century, what it is like to serve as a waiter in a dock-side tavern, or how a small grocer's shop was run during the War. The variety of tones and dialects is equally impressive; the speech of Skat players, of gypsies, of minor Party officials, of the patriotic Oberstudienrat exhorting his charges to be clean and hard—all are captured. Grass' fiction can be classified with that of a large group of modern authors whose works are bound up with a certain locality: Joyce, Faulkner, Pavese.

In Grass' poetry, where the grotesque images appear without the exactly observed environment, these images often seem mere surrealist trifling—thus "Musik im Freien" (Music in the Open Air") from the first volume of poems:

> Als der gelbe Hund über die Wiese lief
> verendete das Konzert.
> Später fand man den Knochen nicht mehr.
> Der Kapellmeister nahm sein Luftgewehr
> und erschoss alle Amseln.[20]

(When the yellow dog ran across the meadow, the concert came to an end. Later the bone was no longer to be found. The conductor took his air-gun and shot all blackbirds.)

Readers of *Hundejahre* will recognize the attempt to find an equivalent for terror in images that are both familiar and bizarre. On the other hand, where Grass abandons absurdity, as he does in his latest play *Die Plebejer proben den Aufstand* (*The Plebeians Rehearse the Rising*), on the theme of the Berlin rising of June 17, 1953, he does not appear to be very successful. Critics were unanimous in finding the play weak as theater, nor was the audience enthusiastic at the Berlin premier in January, 1966. It is in his novels, where Grass places his grotesque imagery and other absurd effects in context that his absurd vision of the world is most effective. The accuracy of the background springs from the fact that the exile remembers his lost home with barely-suppressed nostalgia for its speech, customs and place-names. Yet the same accuracy forces the narrator to include, for example, the concentration camp of Stutthof, near Danzig, which duly appears in Grass' picture of the region. Reality precludes the attitude of nostalgia at the same time as politics and history justify, or at least make inevitable the loss of the homeland. The situation is one of confusion and pervasive doubt that finds its adequate expression in the various absurd features noted here—the subjective imagery, obscenity, the domination of the neutral object, the circular structure, the atmosphere of parody and the indefinite perspective. The only conclusion that Grass allows himself (or his reader) to draw is the recommendation of unpretentiousness and modesty embodied in the grotesque food imagery. In concrete political terms, this modesty of attitude would seem, from Grass' political addresses, to include the renunciation of all ideas of regaining German territory lost in Eastern Europe—a striking example of the principle of the absurd serving the cause of unpalatable reality.

Notes

1. (Munich, 1961), p. 150.

2. George Orwell, *Collected Essays* (London, 1961), p. 214.

3. H. L. Arnold, "Grass-Kritiker," *Text und Kritik*, I (1966), 32.

4. Günter Grass, *Die Blechtrommel* (Neuwied and Berlin, 1959), p. 330. Translations included in this paper are my own.

5. *Die Blechtrommel*, p. 345.

6. Klaus Wagenbach, "Günter Grass," in *Schriftsteller der Gegenwart*, ed. Klaus Nonnemann (Olten and Freiburg, 1963), p. 124.

7. Günter Grass, *Hundejahre* (Neuwied and Berlin, 1963), p. 293.

8. (Zürich, 1962), p. 95.

9. Wolfgang Hildesheimer, "Erlanger Rede," *Akzente*, 7 (1960), 543.

10. Pub. in *Akzente*, 4 (1957), 229.

11. H. M. Enzensberger, "Wilhelm Meister auf Blech getrommelt," *Frankfurter Hefte*, 11 (1959), 833.

12. *Hundejahre*, p. 419.

13. *Die Blechtrommel*, p. 50.

14. Ibid., p. 12.

15. *Hundejahre*, p. 7

16. Wagenbach, p. 126.

17. Günter Grass, *Gleisdreieck* (Neuwied and Berlin, 1960), p. 57.

18. *Die Blechtrommel*, p. 190.

19. Ibid., p. 118.

20. Günter Grass, *Die Vorzüge der Windhühner* (Neuwied and Berlin, 1956), p. 17.

The End of Innocence: Günter Grass's *The Tin Drum*

Robert Maurer[*]

In one's end is one's beginning. The Candide who cultivates his garden in the last paragraph of Voltaire's comic masterpiece is prefigured on the first page, in the circumstances of Candide's birth and in the peculiar quality of his personality. Candide finally reaches the point where he no longer listens with goggle-eyed wonder to Dr. Pangloss's monotonous revelations about this best of possible worlds, but until the last Candide's "givens" demand his patient tolerance of philosophical nonsense and his everlasting loyalty to an unworthy Cunégonde. He must perforce maintain

*Reprinted from *Bucknell Review* 16, no. 2 (1968): 45–65, by permission of *Bucknell Review*.

the foundations of his basic self. While the predominant line of his development is from innocence to awareness, his awareness, unlike Voltaire's, can never be more than partial, his initiation never more than incomplete.

In *The Tin Drum*, as in so much contemporary fiction, Voltaire's kind of developmental, chronological history is turned topsy-turvy. Oskar Matzerath is discovered in the first paragraph to be at his wit's end — in an insane asylum, thirty years old, at home in neither the realm of the sacred nor the realm of the profane, in an utter muddle about his future after his impending release. His end is his beginning in another sense. For Voltaire, Candide's end must be consistent not only with starting assumptions made about the hero but also with the logical, necessary line of his development through a series of clearly delineated circumstances; whereas for Günter Grass, Oskar's end initiates an investigation, one blurred by such mysteries as that surrounding his birth (for who is Oskar's real father?) and by the labyrinthine, often conflicting, always interpretable maze of events lived through. Where with Voltaire a reader is drawn forward by the question of how Candide will end, with Grass he is absorbed by what made Oskar end as he did. To locate a metaphor in mathematics: if Voltaire's task was to work through a problem, somewhat syllogistically, from its assumptions to inevitable conclusions, Grass's is to begin with conclusions and to determine thereafter the very nature of the problem.

More is involved in this contrast than differences between old and new manners of treating fictional chronology and causation. Such differences have been often noted, and between authors less separated in time. Grass calls attention to them himself, when, always acutely aware of exactly what he is doing, he sardonically catalogues some questionable modern storytelling methods that deliberately create temporal confusions or pretend to have "solved the space-time problem" (p. 17).[1] By implication Grass intends to abjure such methods; however far his basic structure is from Voltaire's, he ridicules mere pretentious technical virtuosity. The contrast leads to a more fundamental issue: what is the possibility in our day of an author's treating the theme of a hero's progress from innocence to awareness?

The term "initiation" has been used to describe Candide's adventures; quite clearly it fits that hero's gradually growing knowledge of the world's ways. It involves a rite of passage from actual or figurative childishness to membership, however reluctantly sworn to, in the club of adulthood. Oskar, on the other hand, is born knowing. As he drums out the story of his birth, having just recorded its otherwise normal obstetrical details, Oskar stops to note its unusual side: "I may as well come right out with it," says he; "I was one of those clair-audient infants whose mental development is completed at birth and after that merely needs a certain amount of filling in" (p. 47). From that point Oskar's dilemma is caused by a superfluity of natal wisdom. Candide's sort of initiation is for Oskar not merely unnecessary but impossible. An initiate knows too little; Oskar knows too much. As child and child-man, connections—association not so much discovered as simply recognized—pose the problem. For what do they mean? How validly may they be interpreted? What do they say about what one should do? Is there a garden like Candide's that the mature Oskar can cultivate besides the figurative one of his hospital bed, around which he wishes that the bars were built higher to prevent anyone's coming close to him?

Such questions occur to the Oskar newly popped from his mother's womb. The moth that flies around the two sixty-watt light bulbs in the room where he is born "chattered away as if in haste to unburden itself of its knowledge" (p. 47). Still only minutes old, his umbilical cord uncut, Oskar can already identify himself with this insect, associating it with his own enormous need to rid himself of his troublesome load of wisdom. The huge book that Oskar drums out—and that we read—is therefore a purgation, a testimony to that need. It is one with many other modern fictional catharses, with "confessions" of protagonists as far separated as Céline's Ferdinand Bardamu, Salinger's Holden Caulfield, or Nabokov's Charles Kinbote, all glutted with their end-point knowledge, all from their beginnings enlightened beyond the possibility of initiation. It may be true, as Norman Podhoretz has claimed, that fiction is now severely limited because it has no novel news for its jaded readers; it may be equally true that our fictional heroes are so stuffed with news that discovery and resultant change in them are ruled out. The novel of initiation may be more than necessarily naive if The Tin Drum is a representative example. It may be passé.

The above-mentioned moth passage deserves quoting at length, to indicate both the density of associations Oskar recognizes and the problems raised for an infant who, if he does not exactly enter the world trailing clouds of glory, is father to the man in more ways than Wordsworth ever imagined:

> I observed and listened to a moth that had flown into the room. Medium-sized and hairy, it darted between the two sixty-watt bulbs, casting shadows out of all proportion to its wing spread, which filled the room and everything in it with quivering motion. What impressed me most, however, was not the play of light and shade but the sound produced by the dialogue between moth and bulb: the moth chattered away as if in haste to unburden itself of its knowledge, as though it had no time for future colloquies with sources of light, as though this dialogue were its last confession; and as though, after the kind of absolution that light bulbs confer, there would be no further occasion for sin or folly. (p. 47)

"Today," says the thirty-year-old Oskar directly after this paragraph, "Oskar says simply: The moth drummed . . . that moth was Oskar's master." Throughout his own drumming, but particularly during his later life, Oskar is unsure of his associations, as he is here. In order to offset his tendency to locate questionable complications of all sorts, he at times simplifies, forcing himself to stick close to verifiable statements: the moth drummed; he was my first teacher. Or, looking back on one of his synthesizing simplifications, he sometimes admits its inadequacy; as when, having narrowly centered his reading on two authors, Goethe and Rasputin, and having composed from them a "conflicting harmony" (p. 90), a Manichean worldview polarized between good and evil, his "filling in" leads him to question his former assertions: "I began to read avidly, no longer satisfied, now that I had grown, with an oversimplified world evenly divided between Goethe and Rasputin" (p. 436). To the end of his story, however, he never stops making analogies, is always associating with his own experience parallels of history, commonplace symbols, literary allusions, myths. The comic villain, Oskar's friend Vittlar, giving evidence during Oskar's trial for the murder of Sister Dorothea, may attempt to check the fulsomeness of such parallels: "To this day," Vittlar writes. "I cannot understand why, just because I was lying in a tree, he [Oskar] should have taken me for a symbolic snake and even suspected my mother's cooking apples of being the Paradise variety" (p. 565). Inevitably the associations do seem suspiciously symbolic, and Oskar persists. For after such knowledge as he is born with, neither forgiveness nor innocence is possible.

At birth Oskar is already creating a bewildering set of connections, some with parts of his future life, some with thematic motifs established elsewhere during his drumming, some available from the common stock of everyday metaphor that, owing to the texture of the novel, each reader is also encouraged to draw on, both for meaning and for the sheer pleasurable kick that comes, as it does with books like *Finnegans Wake*, from extending possible interpretations. In the moth passage are connections between the moth's drumming with "such disciplined passion" and his; between both their existences in light and dark; between its innate knowledge and his; between its need for religious rituals, confession and absolution, and his own; between its attraction to light — and all light's commonplace associations with truth, vision, divinity, innocence, and beatific salvation — and his own; between the moth's instinctive immersion in the destructive element of light and his own constantly expressed desire for self-extinction; between his and its sense of mutability, of the niggardly distribution of time to men and beasts; between its miniscule size and his; between the dark shadows it casts, so disproportionate to its seeming capabilities, and his own.

The moth with appear repeatedly elsewhere during Oskar's later adventures, in which memories accumulate in geometrical progression, and in which for him no past association ever seems to fade or to lose significance. His knowledge dates even from the time before birth, when Oskar was still a foetus, and back beyond that.

Once well on with his story, lying in the hospital bed, Oskar uses his drum to recall the scars on the back of his friend Herbert Truczinski, that half-comic, half-tragic, much knifed tavern bouncer who finally, fatally, meets his conqueror straight on, as he tries to rape a wooden statue of Niobe. As inspiration for this recollection, Oskar sets before him, as he drums, the pickled ring finger of Sister Dorothea, and with the aid of this prop the associations tumble out headlong:

> Whenever I wanted to recall Herbert Truczinski's back, I would sit drumming with that preserved finger in front of me, helping my memory with my drum. Whenever I wished—which was not very often—to reconstitute a woman's body, Oskar, not sufficiently convinced by a woman's scarlike parts, would invent Herbert Truczinski's scars. But I might just as well put it the other way around and say that my first contact with those welts on my friend's broad back gave promise even then of acquaintance with, and temporary possession of, those short-lived indurations characteristic of women ready for love. Similarly the symbols on Herbert's back gave early promise of the ring finger, and before Herbert's scars made promises, it was my drumsticks, from my third birthday on, which promised scars, reproductive organs, and finally the ring finger. But I must go back still farther: when I was still an embryo, before Oskar was even called Oskar, my umbilical cord, as I sat playing with it, promised me successively drumsticks, Herbert's scars, the occasionally erupting craters of young and not so young women, and finally the ring finger, and at the same time in a parallel development beginning with the boy Jesus' watering can, it promised me my own sex which I always and invariably carry about with me— capricious monument to my own inadequacy and limited possibilities. (pp. 178–179)

Scars, ring finger, secret parts of women, umbilical cord, drumsticks, Jesus' penis and his own—all these "symbols" are somehow linked in Oskar's mind, scanning the past to make it understandable, shedding prophetic light forward that will focus on future symbols. For the symbols are not complete with this passage; later other oddments will be added: the eels caught by the fisherman during the stroll Oskar takes with his family (p. 494); Sister Dorothea's black belt, which he finds in her cupboard (p. 494); and the cartridge case, handed to him by Leo Schugger in the Saspe Cemetery, from the bullet that killed his perhaps father, Jan Bronski (p. 568). Each of these Oskar forthrightly relates (in the pages referred to) to an already formidable stack of elongated objects that could, if they only would, reveal to him some awesome meaning, some solution to the mystery of what he is.

Back beyond the womb lie other vast expanses of interpretable wisdom—of fact and fancy, the incontrovertible and the magical. These too the clair-audient Oskar knows, who shares his creator's encyclopedic knowledge of everything ranging from the bright history of sailing ships to the dimly lighted rituals of the Roman Catholic faith; who is continuously ready to see beyond the purely verifiable into mystery, and, at the same time, to question the revelatory miracle. Astrology, thus, that sibling of voodoo and parent of an exact science, tells him much about the mysterious determination of one's being—his mother's, his own, his son Kurt's. "Neptune," he says of the starry influences on his own personality, "moved into the tenth house, the house of middle life, establishing me in an attitude between faith in miracles and disillusionment" (p. 48). Astrology, itself based on faith in the mysterious concatenation of heavenly bodies and human beings, annoyingly prestructures in Oskar the skepticism that causes him to distrust miracles.

Like astrology but different from it in its mundane verifiability, history provides another means for Oskar to explore the nature of his end. History, familial and national, though it may veer at times into the legendary and apocryphal (as it does in the variant fables of Oskar's grandfather, Joseph Koljaiczek, and his wondrous escape from under a logger's raft) is another determining force. The history of Polish nationalism has deep roots in Oskar's self. The devilish incendiary blood that flowed through Koljaiczek's veins also flows through Oskar's, but it is at least partly fired by blessed causes. The emblematic red and white on Oskar's drum are more than coincidentally historical colors: with it he once summons up a ghostly cavalry squadron of Polish Uhlans, flying red and white pennants, to rescue a patriot from Nazi assassins (p. 574). Familial traits are inherited: Koljaiczek's propensity for hiding is shared by Oskar's mother, and in turn finds expression in his own desire for higher bed bars. And there is always the historical vision of his grandmother's four skirts, pointing out to him the dark, warm, moist nature of his blood source, beckoning him to a possible destiny: "to take refuge beneath her skirts and, if possible, never again draw a breath outside of their sheltering stillness" (p. 215).

Astrology and history, two far-separated sources of self-discovery for Oskar, two more sixty-watt filaments of light, can serve as well to illuminate the fundamental division in *The Tin Drum* between the material in it that is purely fantastic and that rooted in a recognizable reality. Oskar's willed act to stop growing at three, the weird effects of his drumming, his eerie ability to smash glass with his voice—these clearly lie in the province of magic and fairy tale. The fall of Danzig's Polish post office under the Nazi sledgehammer in August, 1939, greengrocer Greff's service as an air warden during the war, or even the autobiographical correspondences between Oskar's career and Günter Grass's—these just as clearly exist in a world we might read about in the daily papers and *Current Biography*. The relation between these two seemingly separated modes of vision needs to be established in any interpretation of the novel, any revelation about Oskar's end-beginning.

Oskar's assertion that his character is astrologically determined, located midway between faith in miracles and doubt, accounts for much of the wavering back and forth from fantasy to fact. So too does Grass's own compulsion to use any degree of expressionistic distortion to force coherent meaning from the jumble of moths and scars. For above all, what Grass seeks is some key, some unifying, organizing viewpoint that will open the way to clarifying insight about Oskar's end. "Obviously," said one reviewer of *The Tin Drum* upon its first appearance in English, "there is a vast parable in these 600 pages of grotesquery, but I, for one, would not like the job of supplying a point-for-point interpretation of Grass's symbols."[2] No one would, not even, one suspects, Grass himself; for "a vast parable," with all its implications of singular story line and universal applications, belies the structure of the novel and Oskar's very nature. Grass, it must be assumed, would move at his work from another direction.

II

As Oskar tries at the end of the novel to decide on his future, all sorts of opportunities are open to him. He can settle down and marry; he can inspire artists, along with Muse Ulla, with his modeling; he can go to America to find his grandfather; or, accepting the role of Christ that he assumed at the time of his arrest, he can found a sect. The dilemma of choice should say something about Oskar's, or even Grass's final inability to disentangle 600 pages of associations. In fact, to follow the last choice requires of Oskar an impossible point-for-point interpretation of his career, the crazy medley of events and objects in it. "Just because I happen to be thirty," he speculates, "I go out and play the Messiah. . . ; against my better judgment I make my drum stand for more than it can, I make a symbol out of it" (p. 585).

Oskar's reluctance to turn his personal attributes and possessions into public, universal symbols should also be our own. It should prevent us from equating Oskar totally with either a resurrected Christ or a contemporary Germany; with either the Artist as a Young Dwarf or modern man pursued by Satanic forces and guilt. Such interpretations are all partially valid, but none of them is sufficient, and there are others that demand inclusion with equal persistence. Confusion and complexity, not singular clarity of interpretation, are the price that Oskar pays for his innate wisdom; questions and contradictions are more attuned to Oskar's drumming, and to Oskar's end, which, though it is surrounded by such broad figures of parable as The Black Witch and the Satanic Vittlar, is also infused with an individuality that is Oskar's alone.

So much of the novel is determined by that individuality. In the same early passage in which Oskar pokes fun at modern fictional techniques, he also criticizes those authors who say that "a novel can't have a hero any more because there are no more individualists," because "man—each man and all men together—is alone in his loneliness and no one is entitled to individual loneliness, and all men lumped together make up a 'lonely mass' without names and without heroes" (p. 17). Oskar rejects such namelessness for both himself and his keeper, Bruno. They do have names, he declares; and, as if to begin his long tale by asserting his personal distinctness, he launches a history of one set of grandparents, whom no one else can possibly have in common. Besides, he insists, he and Bruno *are* heroes.

In Bruno's case Oskar protests too much. The very degree, the excess of his protestation sets the tone of critical tomfoolery in the passage. To view Bruno as "hero," however much his grotesque plaster-covered knot sculptures may represent primitive creative urges, is to test too severely the limits of the term, in regard to both the minor role that Bruno plays in Oskar's saga and the traditional measuring of a hero's ability to act above and beyond the potentialities of the average man. Even Oskar is not entirely adequate cast as hero; his size upstages him; his end is awry, as is his tone. "Nowadays," says Oskar elsewhere, "every young man who forges a little check, joins the Foreign Legion, and spins a few yarns when he gets home a few years later, tends to be regarded as a modern Ulysses" (p. 346). Yet despite disclaimers, despite Oskar's insistence that his disruptive drumming beneath Nazi rally platforms does not metamorphose him into an intrepid resistance fighter, Oskar's position and his magical powers of drum and voice are somehow cut from the same material as Ulysses' ability to subdue Cyclops and the Sirens. Too, Christ is revealed to him when the infant Jesus comes to life in Mary's arms. As Homeric adventurer or Christian mystic Oskar may not fit the hero's role without qualification, but there is a firm basis beyond irony and tomfoolery for his identification of himself as such. He is and he is not. To locate his position between ridiculous clown and Ulysses, or at either extreme, is one of his hospital bed problems.

The same kind of ambiguous basis exists for his insistence upon his individuality, the peculiar non-mass identification of himself. His Kashubian ancestry is particular and substantial, not conceptual and universal. So are all of the many other circumstances that Oskar shares with Günter Grass. Like Grass, Oskar is a native of Danzig, the son of a grocer, a reluctant Roman Catholic, a one-time jazz drummer and gravestone carver, and a participant in a series of events stretching between two postwar periods. It would be folly, a butting of one's head against a wall of particularity, to try to locate in each of these autobiographical details — and there are many others — definitive archetypal or symbolic referents. Like all well-created, distinctive literary characters, Alfred Matzerath, Oskar's nominal father, inevitably becomes enlarged to typify all sorts of things — the abstract "Father," or the willingly led Nazi horde, or the flatulent bourgeoisie that Oskar refuses to join. Oskar's mother Agnes, killing herself with overeating, trying futilely to stuff "an abyss of emptiness," may be viewed as a mindless victim of a crass social milieu, or as one link in a long chain of nun-nurse figures that Oskar seeks for sanctification and contradictory spoilation. None of these generalized interpretations is abstruse; none makes the character, in Oskar's words, "stand for more than it can"; none leads a reader any great distance from a specific reality—from, in Matzerath's case, a rather stupid grocer who likes to cook; or, in Agnes's case, from a woman who bounces indiscriminately from adulterous bed to confessional box, finally to become unbearably conscious of her inner sordidness by a disgusting display of black, slippery eels emerging from a horse's head hauled out of the sea by a fisherman.

If Oskar at thirty refuses the role of a Christ ready for public life because his individuality will not support such a self-interpretation, it will not do to attempt locating Mary and Joseph in Agnes and Alfred Matzerath (or Jan Bronski, who by all analogical processes should represent the impregnating Holy Spirit). Their huge distance from such sacred stances simply emphasizes the bitter irony of Oskar's whole attempt to reconcile those circumstances that are his alone—that define his unique personality, and that because of their sheer petty literalness refuse to be forced into sublime symbolic interpretations—with others that seem to call for more meaning than logic will allow, for example Christ's miraculous drumming or Vittlar's Satanic first appearance.

The need for a vast point-for-point reading of *The Tin Drum* is obviated by recognition of these splits between individuality and universality, between mundane literalness and burgeoning archetypal significance. However, such recognition does not at all discount the relevance of Oskar's end, and it explains a great deal about Grass's two big novels, *The Tin Drum* and *Dog Years*, both of which are too long, too exhaustively all-inclusive, largely because of Grass's compulsion to fictionalize all the details of his own particular experience, as if fearful of missing the very sort of pregnant associations that Oskar so often tries to make. When interest flags for a reader (as it does through the last third of *The Tin Drum* and through large portions of *Dog Years*) it is often because the material simply will not offer up such coherent connections. Grass's wry, tongue-in-cheek attitude is as often as not a conscious, humorous protection against his own (and Oskar's) failure to find serious significance, meaning that matters, in this perverse mixture of personal documentation and symbolic suggestions. His frequent shifts of technique from diary to history to dramatic dialogue to court testimony; his tendency, increased in *Dog Years*, to allow characters to assume multiple forms and names; his expressionistic distortions of identifiable reality, like the view of post-war Germanic revelry in the Onion Cellar episode; even his inability to locate a firm point of view—all these are explained by Grass's efforts and final failure to come to terms with his own creations.

Reading Grass, one frequently experiences an inability to identify, to bridge the vast gulf separating his hero's particular circumstances and one's own. If despite this, episodes such as the orgy of artificially induced weeping in Schmuh's Onion Cellar café are effective, they are so in the same way as Feiffer cartoons, as trenchant commentaries on social history; or if the tale of Herbert Truczinski's love affair with Niobe sustains interest, it does so largely because of Grass's enormous power to spin any bizarre yarn with compelling Rabelaisian gusto, and not so much because we may link Niobe with all the other fatal Eves in the novel and in the world in which we exist. Yet there is a huge dimension of overlapping between Oskar's end and any modern reader's, for in important ways Oskar's basic problems are also ours.

All of us have our peculiar individuality, which we, like Oskar, persist in maintaining — the specialness of ourselves that distinguishes us from "all men lumped together," from our societies, and from our fathers. At times for most of us — almost always for Oskar — it seems that this specialness alone, when insisted upon, can open doors to miracles of accomplishment and to the clearest vision. Regardless of the negative aspects of this position, the loneliness and sense of limitation and guilt that may come with separation, the compensating rewards are worth the effort required in adopting a role, even if it be of mindless midget, or, along with Hamlet, of fool. Too, proceeding in a direction opposed to that of unique individuality in a mass age, the Oskars of our time — our sensitive artistic and literary minds, each beating his separate drum — possess an overwhelming drive to find in their particularized experience the basis for an hieratic authority, in the degree to which they live out patterns of collective myth, or find in the specific action the archetypal analogy.

Grass understands all this, as well as the morass of pomposity, error, vapidity that can engulf a work when a writer flees from fact into purely maneuvered symbol, or when critics locate in each action some immaculately conceived myth. "Delightful as it may be," Oskar once says, "to see the world and its relationships unfolding inside my own grandmother, to be profound in a limited area. . ." (p. 350); but his thought trails off; he turns deliberately from such delight to deal with a more mundane event, his son Kurt's third birthday. To be profound in a limited area — here is the territory to be thought about with caution, to be tempered with comic irony, if only to indicate the need to treat one's own limited stamping ground with something less than an ear-shattering cry of Eureka!

In many ways, therefore, *The Tin Drum* is both a defense of and a warning against the creed of transcendent individuality. It is also a piece of demonstrative literary criticism. In a period of symbol creation and symbol hunting, Grass has written a work that is tentative, exploring possibilities of interpretation but always aware, elusive, ironic, undercutting assertions with caveats and doubt, simply because neither Oskar nor Grass can accept his own singular or collective relevance without question.

Little wonder, then, that Grass has professed surprise upon finding the novel received, particularly by American critics, with interpretive cleverness and profundity that surpassed his own.

Without denying the fundamental urge of a writer to turn the uniquely personal into universal, widely recognized terms, Grass provides an antidote for over-intense, abstruse symbolizing in fiction. Just as the extent of modern man's natal wisdom has perhaps ruled out the possibility of the novel of initiation, so, he seems to be saying, it is no longer possible to view with sublime seriousness modern substantial man in traditional terms of archetype. Cases for these impossibilities are not made on the basis of a single novel, of course; yet as early as *Moby Dick* Melville found it wise to temper his epical overtones with ironic humor, and in as recent a model as Herman Hesse's *Steppenwolf* we hear that hero's mentor, Mozart, advising: "Learn what is to be taken seriously and laugh at the rest." The problem is to locate the boundaries between the circumstantial and the meaningful, the laughable and the sublime. Failure to solve that problem leaves only one remaining tone, irony, and one mood, the interrogative. This all becomes clearer when one studies some of the principal areas in which Oskar's experiences work outward towards larger ramifications.

III

It may seem odd to question the seriousness of Günter Grass's symbolic strategy in view of Oskar's self-identification with, among others, Adam, Little Claus, Jonah, Tiny Tim, Jack the Giant Killer, David, Odysseus, Goethe, Rasputin, Jesus, Faust, Abel, the Prodigal Son, St. Peter, Hamlet, Quasimodo, St. Thomas, Yorick, and Satan; or in view of his spontaneous outbursts of word play as he explores such vast symbolic extensions of meaning as exist in drums, crosses, colors, or "Faith, Hope, and Love" in Saint Paul's First Corinthian Epistle. Yet the sheer intensity of Oskar's ingenious inventiveness makes him something of a brilliant ham, and there is certainly more humor than substance in his grotesque accumulations. His comparisons and verbal performances are intended as serious modes of self-exploration, but always ringed round with conscious double-takes. So are the three central images with which Oskar is associated—his size, his drum, and his glass shattering.

The ostensible reason for Oskar's decision to stop growing at three is Matzerath's vow that his son will inherit the grocery store. Already lonely and misinterpreted at birth, Oskar realizes "that Mama and this Mr. Matzerath were not equipped to understand or respect my decisions whether positive or negative" (p. 49). Thus begins Oskar's separation from even the most intimate social unit, the family. His size, used to maintain his alienation, is soon fortified by the crude musical instrument chosen for him by his mother; with it he extends his isolation, exercising his "ability to drum the necessary distance between grownups and myself" (p. 64). By the time he joins the juvenile gang called the Dusters, he is waging a fight "against our parents and all other grownups, regardless of what they may be for or against" (p. 374). His continual repudiation of all accepted values, certainly of all the goals that Germany is to goosestep toward in the thirty-year scope of the novel, makes this a typical low-down view of contemporary institutions and of a nation.

Oskar, in brief, may be viewed as the youngest of the world's angry young men. Or, what may be much the same thing, he may be grouped with our modern outsiders, with all those whose perspectives from underground, or on the road, or invisibility, or death-row cells, have revealed how much they are cut off from shared communication, how little they can trust once-cherished beliefs. The alienation maintained by stature and drum may even be extended to a view of Oskar as an existential absurd man, unable to locate rationality in the universe, anxiously conscious of his incertitude and impending death, viewing himself as object possessing no ascertainable essence, often nauseously ill, at once rebellious and impotent. And when we hear Signora Roswitha advising Oskar, "Forgive your fathers. . ." (p. 173), or when Bebra listens to Oskar's confessions as a sort of surrogate father, we seem to be traveling over territory made familiar to us by critical studies about Billy Budd and Stephen Dedalus, two other child-men seeking fathers. Based on the two grotesqueries of diminutive size and expressive drum, Oskar's tale seems firmly set in a modern groove.

All these seemings possess their degree of rightness. Grass is frequently grappling with the commonest, most fashionable themes of our time. The extent of Oskar's wisdom should make this expected, and fashionable issues need not be considered any less significant simply because they are fashionable. If this essay moves toward qualification of these possibilities, it is partly because they so obviously can be explored with profit, partly because what may be easily missed is Grass's comic view of these themes which is perpetually undercutting them.

Consider, for example, the iconoclastic twist that Grass gives to the theme of the father search. When Oskar is trying to figure out his son Kurt's attitude towards *his* father, Oskar confesses that he killed Matzerath "for no other reason than because he was sick of fathers." Perhaps, Oskar muses, Kurt too "could express only by homicide the childlike affection that would seem to be desirable between fathers and sons" (p. 404). Here and elsewhere Oskar wants to have done with the whole overworked issue of father-son traumas, and well he might, considering the half-baked fathers out of which he would have to compose his comparisons with Oedipus's Laius. Oskar is of course also worried that he will be murdered by Kurt for as slight a reason as his own for murdering Matzerath and Bronski; but it is entirely typical of him at such a dangerous moment of realization to speak of patricide in terms of desirable "childlike affection."

For if fathers can't live up to their mythical roles, neither can children, Oskar included. Oskar's undercutting comic irony questions the whole assumption of basically affectionate innocents in search of understanding parents. A firm believer in the doctrine of original sin, Oskar sees the basic ingredient of the child as his devilishness.

The adults in Oskar's world are simply unconscious. Spurred on by Oskar's drum or by the onions in Schmuh's Onion Cellar café, adults may reach a limited point of awareness and become recognizably human; only then, Oskar discouragingly notes, may they speak the essential, recover memories of their atrocities, cry like the guilty they are. Such lapses are momentary and incongruous, supporting Oskar's need for separation from them. When his teacher, Miss Spollenhauer, spontaneously claps her hand to his drumbeat during his first and only day in the classroom, "she became a not unpleasant old maid, who had forgotten her prescribed occupational caricature and become human, that is, childlike, curious, complex, and immoral" (p. 80). But it is that last word, dropped with the timing of a clown's pratfall, that makes Oskar's alienation an ambiguous mixture of virtues that separate him from the machinelike mass and satanic evils that unite him with it.

Caricature is the proper word for Miss Spollenhauer. Again and again one is struck by the Dickensian flatness of the characters peopling Oskar's tale, the Dickensian mechanization of their repetitious gestures. Oskar's three parents, for example, play combined skat and hanky-panky as if they were key-wound toys set in motion by their limited adultness. Even so favored a character as Herbert Truczinski, who at least applies an admirable frenzied zeal to his love affair with a mythical figurehead, is made comical, if not utterly pitiful, by his inability to exercise his will; and such a detestable character as Corporal Lankes copulates with nun and muse with as much sensitivity for their feelings as a robot. Like Dickens' characters, these are possessed by hypertrophied obsessions, which provoke our laughter and determine our negative evaluations.

What we seek in Oskar's size and drum, then, is some relief from such mechanical action, and in his alienation some means of locating standards by which we may affirm. Yet all of these actions—so many of which deal with varieties of love—are not too different, in effect at least, from Oskar's own, from his own complex immorality. It is appropriate, after Oskar's decision to grow in Part III, that when he and Bebra shape plans for capitalizing on Germany's post-war prosperity, they do so in an utterly mechanized office. But long before Part III and Oskar's reluctant surrender to his adult responsibilities to Maria and his son, he has confessed his own inability to view love as more than a tangle of two copulating bodies (p. 279); and his constant exercising of his "watering can," sometimes with the help of commercial fizz powder, and his compulsive drive to kill those closest to him, are testimony to his own mechanical heartlessness, causes of his own guilt.

Oskar's size, then, is the means by which he asserts a most ambiguous separation from the adult world, and by which he tries, not wholly successfully, to maintain that separation. Oskar's drum, besides being a symbol for the imaginative impulse through which he expresses himself, is as well his means of influencing the actions of those from whom he is alienated. However, with all the powers inherent in size and drum, Oskar is neither saint nor savior, teacher nor reformer. Since his imprisonment at the end is self-willed, a favor to Vittlar (and one of the very few favors he does for anyone), he cannot even assume satisfactorily the role of sacrificial scapegoat. Unlike the heroes with a thousand faces who traditionally returned after their arduous journeys to deliver their people and bring society back to a point of stasis, Oskar, with his childlike immorality, is predominantly a destructive force. His glass shattering, first used as a means of self-protection, is twisted into an instrument for tempting stupid people into stealing; his size protects him from possible assailants, but it makes victims of Jan Bronski, Alfred Matzerath, and Roswitha; his drum is a means of protest, but it does no more than transform the rhythms of Nazi rallies into ridiculous waltz times.

Wherever one turns in *The Tin Drum* one is faced by Grass's refusal to align Oskar's adventures with any stock literary-critical response. From the time of Dostoevski, our modern underground outsiders have been strange combinations of righteous indignation against mass hypocrisy and traditional beliefs, plus contradictory self-condemnation, guilt, impotence, and pride. Seen from one slant of the head, Oskar is no exception. Seen from another, Oskar's case is special and peculiar, in a way that keeps throwing a critic slightly off balance. If Oskar seems possessed by Poe's imp of the perverse, which drives him to do the very thing he knows he should not, so Grass, conscious always of what fashion expects, deals with issues from some opposing, startling textural or thematic angle.

Thus Oskar's destructive Satanism is inextricably mixed with his inability to adjust himself to the demands of the sacred realm, to a Roman Catholicism that is as historical and as circumstantial as his Kashubian ancestry or his Polish nationalism. Grass may extend his themes to such universalized ones as the pristine, pre-Christian struggle between the forces of good and evil, but he is not generally using religious myth according to the modern temper, for secular purposes. Grass's religion is not secular but sectarian. His Roman Catholicism *is*; it exists, as palpable and as potent in its particularity as in François Mauriac or Graham Greene. Neither Thérèse Desqueyroux nor Commissioner Scobie can locate a priest adequate to bear their confessions; neither can Oskar, who both ridicules his mother for her ephemeral repentances during her confessions and envies the peace of mind they bring her. The point may seem at first inconsequential, but to the degree that it expresses Oskar's seeking solace from the time of the moth through rituals of a specific church, it again stresses the force of individuality in Oskar's tale. Oskar's confessions to Bebra will not suffice, not simply because in them Oskar distorts his sins, even professing guilt for crimes he did not commit, but also because they are secular.

"I must admit," Oskar says, "that the floors of Catholic churches, the smell of a Catholic church, in fact everything about Catholicism still fascinates me. . . . You will admit that I have maintained a certain Catholic tone" (pp. 137–138). Indeed he has, even in the Black Mass he celebrates with the Dusters just before their arrest, or in his persistent imitation of Christ. "I am Jesus," he replies in three languages to the international agents about to arrest him at the top of the Orly airport escalator (p. 587); and long before that, during his many encounters with the statue of the infant Jesus in the Church of the Sacred Heart, he tries to invert a central mystery of Catholicism, the Incarnation, in which God became man in Jesus and dwelt among men. Where the Incarnation made a man of God, the Word become flesh, Oskar tries to make a man into God, the flesh the Word.

The preponderant force of Oskar's Satanism derives from his futile drive to subvert his basic Roman Catholicism. During his baptism he insists that the reigning deity of the ceremony is Satan. Thirty years later, in his prison bed, he is still blaspheming, declaring that "with a snap of my fingers I can equal if not surpass God the Father, the only begotten Son, and most important of all, the Holy Ghost" (p. 349). But the attempt is futile; during his greatest moments of devilish triumph, his powers leave him. Having once proved the superiority of his self-conceived Christ before the statue of the infant Jesus, he is later withered by a miracle. About to seduce Sister Dorothea on the fiber rug in the name of Satan, he cannot get his fleshly watering can to function. His glass shattering is effective in every place but churches. For fundamentally Oskar is a captive believer, fleeing from the Christ and Church that he pursues. However much, like Lankes, he may seek out repetitive figures of nuns and nurses in order to bring them low, to locate the corrupt body beneath the uniform symbolic of healing and sanctity, unlike Lankes he never can be so unwise as to ignore faith in the miraculous motherhood of Mary or the very miracle of faith. "But, as they say," Oskar realizes, "he who doubts, believes, and it is the unbeliever who believes longest. . . . I was unable to stifle [Christ's] miracle under my doubts" (p. 360).

Oskar's last effort to bring coherence into his experiences is still another attempt to move beyond the symbolism provided by his Catholicism. The Black Witch has haunted him since the time he first heard her name in the children's street song. Now, in the last pages of the novel, as he confesses that he is at last "running out of words," she looms up all around him, in front, in back, present in all the events he has recounted, made manifest in the diabolical Lucy Rennwand, redolent in the name of blessed Goethe, existing even behind the altars in Roman Catholic confessionals. Though he wishes he could have a vision of his grandmother

Anna Koljaiczek, "the exact opposite of the Black Witch" (p. 586), his all-consuming horror is of an omnipresent spirit of darkness:

> Where's the Witch, black as pitch?
> Here's the black, wicked Witch.
> Ha! ha! ha!

Thus *The Tin Drum* ends. Here is black humor indeed, which would perhaps bring some peace if only Oskar were convinced that blasphemous evil was really behind it all. "Forgive your fathers, accustom yourself to your own existence that your heart may find peace and Satan be discomfited," was Roswitha's whole advice. But in the last paragraph Oskar does not even know who the Witch is: "Don't ask Oskar who she is! Words fail me" (p. 589). With all his innate wisdom, his last effort for peaceful resolution is tainted by an admission made much earlier, "For my part, I don't know" (p. 204). Despite his huge knowledge, ignorance is the sixty-watt bulb that turns his last black vision into a comic grey. It is hard even to know, with those ending ha-ha's, who is having the last laugh.

IV

In *The Tin Drum* (1959), Günter Grass began his career in fiction with a rollicking, playful study of an alienated self. It is, in this writer's estimation, the best of his three novels, perhaps because like so many first novels, it may have been fed by the intensity of Grass's indirect exploration of his own life, his own problems. Autobiographical correspondences always provide a soggy, dangerous terrain for critics, and yet it is hard to keep from asking whether or not Oskar's end-point uncertainty about his future was also Grass's own. Having, like Oskar, explored the nature of his individual end, Grass may well have asked, What next?

Cat and Mouse (1961), his second novel, appears now as a brief stopping-off point before the massive forward rush of his last, *Dog Years* (1963), almost a chapter that could be tucked into either of his two big books without unduly upsetting either their texture or structure. For it begins to be clear that Grass is mining more and more extensively the setting and timing of his first novel, creating a sort of Yaknapatawpha County out of the Danzig area and the characters who spread out from there to the parts of Germany Grass knows. The material is even beginning to overlap: Oskar appears fleetingly in *Dog Years;* Tulla Pokriefke, briefly introduced in *Cat and Mouse*, has a major part in *Dog Years;* the Gnasher, Walter Matern, who is merely mentioned in *The Tin Drum*, is a major protagonist in *Dog Years*. Richly peopled, Grass's novels up to this time seem capable of supplying an inexhaustible font of material for an inexhaustible storyteller like Grass.

More important, however, is that Grass has increasingly turned more of his emphasis towards the public issues of Germany, which now occupy so many of his country's writers. As has been mentioned, such things as Oskar's guilt are not at all isolated from national states of mind, and none of the heroes that follow Oskar in Grass's books are unconcerned with their singular, special problems. Yet by the time of *Dog Years*, such issues as the rise of the Nazi state, anti-Semitism and concentration camps, the effects of post-war prosperity, and the condition of much delayed guilt become central. They also become more limiting, strangely enough, and more difficult to handle with Grass's penchant for expansive, torturous imaginative expression. As has been said, identification with the hero of *The Tin Drum* is often extremely difficult; it becomes even harder in the later books, particularly when, as in *Dog Years*, one of its chief protagonists has to an astonishing degree the characteristics of Adolf Hitler. Too, as Grass becomes increasingly absorbed in his country's fate, it becomes harder for him to adjust his sweeping, universal symbolism to his "limited area."

But these are subjects for another essay, one that would try to relate more succinctly the respective dilemmas of self and society. Who knows, the dilemma might turn out to be not so utterly different, for even Oskar says of the many what has been said in this article of the one: "in our country the end is always the beginning" (p. 204).

Notes

1. Parenthetical page references are to the Pantheon Books edition of *The Tin Drum* (New York, 1962).

2. Fred Grunfeld, "*The Tin Drum*," *The Reporter*, 28 (14 Mar 1963), 54.

Günter Grass's *Katz und Maus*   Helen Croft*

The idiosyncratic and complex nature of Günter Grass's *Katz und Maus* [*Cat and Mouse*] leaves any attempt at overall critical explication embarrassingly inadequate. When confronted with this situation some critics have opted for setting up a "myth" framework which, in a rather humourless and disjointed manner, purports to deal with various archetypal situations in the work, but which in no way incorporates the important narrative issue into their criticism.[1] Conversely others build an equally "serious" interpretative system on the function of the narrator while successfully circumventing the problems posed by the abundance of mythic outcroppings;[2] and yet others confine themselves to statements about the work's ambiguity.[3] It would seem therefore that at best it is

*Reprinted from *Seminar* 9 (1973): 253–64, by permission of *Seminar*.

possible to emphasize certain important structural features of the work; at worst to make truistic statements about the novel's apparently "appalling vision."[4] With such qualifications granted, this discussion of *Katz und Maus* will utilize a set of terms provided by Jungian criticism, in an attempt to demonstrate the unity of Grass's distinctly ironic-archetypal patterning, including the narrator's integral position in this ironic structure. This is not offered as any all-encompassing revelation, but merely as a means of emphasizing certain major overall structures and their implications in the novel.

The major informing principle of *Katz und Maus* might be seen then to derive from Joachim Mahlke's operating as a libido-hero figure and "fulfilling" the basic myth cycle required of such a figure. This is not, of course, to deny that into this structure has been incorporated a range of ironies which are continually to qualify the possibility of fertile behaviour crucial for the libido-hero myth. Indeed, at one stage in the novel, even myth structure in general is openly mocked: this occurs during the description of the U-boat commander's speech to the school: ["In conclusion he rose to mythical heights: the homecoming after a successful mission, Ulysses, and at long last: 'The first seagulls tell us that the port is near' " (59 / 63).][5] Nevertheless, the myth-structure, ironised or not, is functional in the work.

The most immediately obvious indication that Mahlke is to work as a libido-hero figure is found in his association with Christ and Christian symbolism:[6]

> [He represented the face as a triangle with one corner at the chin. The mouth was puckered and peevish. No trace of any visible incisors that might have been mistaken for tusks. The eyes, piercing points under sorrowfully uplifted eyebrows. The neck sinuous, half in profile, with a monstrous Adam's apple. And behind the head and sorrowful features a halo: a perfect likeness of Mahlke the Redeemer. The effect was immediate (32–33 / 35).]

Such passages clearly reveal Mahlke's connection with a Christlike sphere of activity. This concept of Mahlke as "redeemer" is a constant one throughout the work: and as if to show that this concept is not based merely on externals, the reader is later told, ["the Redeemer's hairdo was gone. . . . But the countenance was still that of a redeemer. . ." (99–100 / 105)]. The Catholic liturgy is also used to set up important Christ-Mahlke parallels: the "Stabat Mater dolorosa . . ." sequence, for example, is shown to be uniquely and irrevocably associated with Mahlke; ["the Great Mahlke had . . . literally left his name behind him: in the latrine . . . the beginning of his favorite sequence: *Stabat Mater dolorosa. . .*" (93 / 98–99)]. Here, via Mahlke's individual use of the sequence, his relationship to the Holy Mother tends to overshadow and replace that with Christ, thereby pointing to the exchangeable and so parallel natures of Christ and

Mahlke.[7] A further example of such liturgical connection is found during the description of Mahlke's last attendance at Mass: ["Gusewski elevated the host . . . and it rose and rose until at length it fell and passed away, close to the second pew facing the altar of Our Lady: 'Ecce Agnus Dei'. . . . Mahlke was the first to kneel" (108 / 113)]. The sharp juxtaposition of the liturgical sequence "Ecce Agnus Dei" with "Mahlke was the first to kneel . . ." again identifies the Christ-Mahlke relationship.

This common ground shared by Mahlke and the Christ figure, however, emerges time and again on a quite unobtrusive level. The reader is, for example, confronted with this description of Mahlke: ["No hat, but round, black ear muffs, such as those worn by garbage men and the drivers of brewery trucks, covered his otherwise protruding ears, joined by a strip of metal crossing at right angles the part in his hair" (36 / 39)]. While the detail which surrounds this description of course qualifies it, the impression of Mahlke marked with the sign of the cross still remains.

Among these less overt references is the association between Mahlke and the east. A certain amount of emphasis is laid upon Mahlke living in the Osterzeile. After already stating that Mahlke lives in the Osterzeile— ["He and his English screwdriver didn't have far to go—out of Osterzeile. . ." (13 / 15)]—the narrator then continues later to make almost an issue out of this information: ["Your house was on Westerzeile. . . . No, your house was on Osterzeile. . . . He lived on Osterzeile and not on Westerzeile" (17 / 19–20)]. When such description is considered in the light of the overt "Christ" references the connection between the Osterzeile and an "Easter" area becomes more significant. Again in the description of Mahlke's room this "east" pattern emerges: ["From his window Mahlke could see the dial of the east face of the tower" (18 / 20)].[8] (And when it is also remembered that Mahlke acts out his most significant "redeemer" activities by right of his skill in the water even the "Ost" quality of the familiar "Ostee," in which he swims (6/7), assumes greater significance.)

Another "Christ-like" attribute given to Mahlke is the description of him in terms of a fish. The fish was, of course, an important early Christian symbol; and, in general, the fish is "a symbol of renewal and rebirth."[9] When Mahlke first swims with the group, for example, the reader is told that Mahlke's Adam's apple transforms him into some kind of fish, ["the horrid piece of cartilage . . . cut through the water like a dorsal fin, leaving a wake behind it" (8 / 10)]. Also in his prayers to the Virgin Mary he takes on certain "fishlike" characteristics: ["Fishes tossed up on the beach gasp for air with the same regularity" (41 / 43–44)].

Yet while these associations are important as indicators of Mahlke's operating as a libido-hero figure, they are also essentially ironic, for Mahlke does not move in a Christian or a specifically Catholic area, nor does he act as any ultimately productive force. The "east" pattern, for example, can be seen as immediately qualified. Early in the work, when the vital cat-mouse incident is related, the scene is set with ["The wind was from the east, and the crematorium between the United Cemeteries and the Engineering School was operating" (5 / 7)]. Here the "east" motif normally associated with the area of rebirth is shown as operating rather futilely in an area where deadness is all-pervasive. Indeed the life-bringing "wind from the east" is shown to work in conjunction with a corpse-processing unit conveniently situated between the two corpse-producing institutions of the society.

Overall the manner in which Mahlke is given Christlike attributes tends to be as ironic and qualified as it is status-giving. The previously quoted section which assigns to Mahlke the sign of the cross (36 / 39), also reveals him to be, with his dustman ear muffs, his giant safety pin, and protruding ears, a rather pathetic libido-hero specimen. And the general impression made by Mahlke is not that of the transcendent Christlike hero: for while Mahlke is directly set up as a Christ figure through such imagery as that centred on "fish," the description almost always dwells upon the most grotesque and un-Christlike aspects of the image. When, for example, it is stated [that "fishes tossed up on the beach gasp for air with the same regularity" (41 / 43–44)], the Mahlke-fish connection is certainly made, but in the image of the stranded fish's ineffectual gasping it is Mahlke's essential impotence that is really stressed. Again in his extreme and highly idiosyncratic nature he constantly cuts a ridiculous figure. The reader is confronted with him riding a bicycle—["Even before he learned to ride a bicycle—a ludicrous figure with his deep-red, protuberant ears and his knees thrust sideways as he pedaled—" (7 / 9–10)], or with his fastidiousness about his fingernails, or his plastering his hair down with sugar water. Each occasion develops this qualification of the "hero" archetype, so that it becomes difficult ultimately to view Mahlke as anything but a basically impotent figure, a ["pathetic sort of ghost, capable at most of scaring children and grandmothers" (46 / 49)].

It is clear then, that Mahlke is to operate on his own eccentric level as a fertility hero: this is more fully revealed by his basic conformation to the libido-hero cycle. (Again, as in the more general "hero" features discussed above, Mahlke will be seen to fulfill essential "hero" requirements, but to do so in a manner which is ironically qualified.) Mahlke, as hero, conforms to the "dual mother" aspect of the cycle. "The dual-mother motif suggests the idea of a dual birth. One of the mothers is the real human mother, the other is the symbolical mother; in other words, she is distinguished as being divine, supernatural, or in some other way extraordinary . . . He who stems from two mothers is the hero: the first birth makes him a mortal man, the second an immortal half-god."[10] Mahlke certainly does have a mortal mother (see 82–83 / 86); but his divine mother, the Virgin Mary, is more dominant in the work and makes him invulnerable, a super-human being: ["And yet you had both Crosses and some other thing, but no wound insignia: the Virgin had made you invulnerable" (99 / 105)].

A further aspect of this cycle is found in the hero being the ideal masculine type. The application of this to Mahlke's situation can be found in his general vitality[11] as opposed to the group's lethargy, and in his "hero" activities. From the very first day he swims with the group he gains admiration from them for his swimming and diving exploits: ["From the very first day he was tops" (8 / 11)]. His later gaining of the Ritterkreuz is also part of this libido-hero pattern. The masculine emphasis is also brought out by the various references to Mahlke's phallus, that ["looked much more grownup, dangerous and worthy to be worshipped" (29 / 32)].

Nevertheless it is at this point that the irony begins to come through strongly, for the basic ironic double-take at work here is that Mahlke's development into a libido-hero figure, albeit a grotesque one, derives from his desire to be like the others of the group — ["But after we had swum away from him several afternoons in a row and come back telling fantastic stories about the sunken mine sweeper, he was mightily inspired and in less than two weeks he was swimming" (7 /10)]. And while his extraordinary exploits single him out on the one hand as the ideal masculine type, Mahlke's frailty is pointed out to modify again the pattern. The Adam's apple which is referred to in the book as Mahlke's strength, ["Mahlke's motor" (70 / 75)], and which has strong phallic overtones[12] appropriate to a libido-hero, must also in some way be an ironic comment on Mahlke's strength, since a prominent Adam's apple can equally well be characteristic of a thin underdeveloped physique. It is in fact a strain on Mahlke to become a hero figure; and this is brought out and emphasized in the references to Mahlke's shivering. The reader is confronted, for example, with Mahlke immediately after he has proven his heroic status to the group: ["Mahlke shivered. . . . His back, white in spots, burned lobster-red from the shoulders down, forever peeling with fresh sunburn on both sides of his prominent spinal column, was also covered with gooseflesh and shaken with fitful shudders. His yellowish lips, blue at the edges, bared his chattering teeth" (9 / 11)].

At one stage in the cycle the hero "must leave the mother, the source of life, behind him."[13] This finds expression in the Mahlke situations by his breaking away from the protection provided by the certificates to the school informing them of Mahlke's sickliness and inability to participate in gymnastics and swimming: ["He had been excused from gymnastics and swimming, because he had presented certificates showing him to be sickly" (7 / 9)].

However perhaps the most important movement of the cycle derives from the hero's attempts to return to the womb, to experience rebirth, thereby bringing the hope of rejuvenation to the particular situation in which he is operating. In the first half of the novel Mahlke follows this pattern by diving into the submerged hulk of the wreck, which operates on at least one level as a womb symbol. Just by the very act of entering into the submerged body of the wreck and resurfacing, Mahlke establishes himself in the libido-hero pattern. But the situation in which he moves tends again to qualify any optimism inherent in the archetype. For while the boys on the old wreck appear to be merely pre-fertile, as brought out by the constant descriptions of their sitting in a "foetal" position — ["we huddled lean and long-armed between our upthrust knees on the remains of the bridge" (6 / 8)] — the stressed "castration" description of the wreck's empty gunmounts might be seen as a grotesque reference to the fact that the situation in which they are involved is irretrievably impotent and regressive. (If there is a larger society capable of mature and productive responses, Mahlke does not penetrate it.)

Mahlke's attempts to act as a revitalizing agent may also be seen in his removing from the wreck various items, such as the virgin medallion and the gramophone, renovating them, and then returning them to the wreck. He does of course introduce his own belongings into the wreck, along with those he has salvaged and renovated: and the implications involved in this action are quite significant. On one level this tends to emphasize the idiosyncratic nature of Mahlke as libido-hero; and yet it also points to the need for the individual to bring his own unique interpretation to the archetypal situation. However it becomes apparent that the positive claims made by the action are again being treated in an ironic manner. This emerges when the reader comes to consider some of the items, for example, the "snowy owl" with which Mahlke works. It might at first seem appropriate that Mahlke, as fertility-hero, introduces an owl (the symbolic bird of wisdom), which was inherited from his father, into the maternal womb of the wreck. But, of course, the owl is "stuffed" (18 / 21); it is dead and, when it is later described as "decaying" (72 / 80), the entire libido-hero activity is placed in a ridiculous, if pathetic, light.

Mahlke's later attempts to function as a fertility hero can be seen in his wartime activities:

[O thou, most pure. Mother inviolate. Through whose intercession partake. Most amiable. Full of Grace. It's the honest truth. My first battle north of Kursk proved it. And in the tangle outside Orel when they counterattacked. And in August by the Vorskla the way the mother of God. They all laughed and put the division chaplain on my tail. Sure, but then we stabilized the front. Unfortunately, I was transferred to Center Sector, or they wouldn't have been through so quick at Kharkov. She appeared to me again near Korosten when the 59th Corps. She never had the child, it was always the picture she was holding. Yes, Dr. Klohse, it's hanging in our hall beside the brush bag. And she didn't hold it over her breast, no, lower down. I had the locomotive in my sights, plain as day. Just had to hold steady between my father and Labuda. Four hundred. Direct hit. (115 / 121)]

Here the libido hero's function of fructifying the "great mother" figure is revealed in his shooting at the Virgin's abdomen overlapping the womb symbol of the tank.

Mahlke, however, fails in the social extension and application of this pattern, as is revealed by his unsuccessful attempt to communicate his message to his schoolmates and the adult world. Appropriately he returns to the wreck, regresses to a more basic, less specific situation. However, he fails to resurface, fails to confirm the rebirth pattern for Pilenz. Mahlke's rebirth, if it ever happened, was not communicated to this narrator or this society. As Pilenz notes in the final words of the book, ["You didn't surface" (121 / 127).] Mahlke's failure is the ultimate conclusion to Grass's ironic qualification of the libido-hero archetype.

Another technique which the author employs also to qualify the informing archetype is that of the narration of Pilenz. There is an essential unreality connected with the narration of the novel.[14] This is immediately forced on the reader by the initial narrative address: [". . . And now it is up to me, who called your mouse to the attention of this cat and all cats, to write. Even if we were both invented, I should have to write. Over and over again the fellow who invented us because it's his business to invent people obliges me to take your Adam's apple in my hand and carry it to the spot that saw it win or lose" (5–6 / 8)]. This unreal quality of the narration is constantly brought to the surface throughout the work and is again evident in remarks made by Pilenz, such as ["When I had the second sandbank behind me, she was gone, thorn and dimple had passed the vanishing point, I was no longer swimming away from Tulla, but swimming toward Mahlke, and it is toward you that I write . . ." (68 / 72)].

The unreality present in the narration is also revealed by the fact that Pilenz proves to be a doubtful reporter of detail. There is the confusion surrounding the cat and mouse issue and the issue of Westerzeile or Osterzeile (17 / 19). The reader also learns, for example, first that Mahlke has light blue eyes (11 / 14), then later that they are light grey (15 / 17), and finally that "anyway . . . they were not brown" (31 / 34). While this in some way is connected with the projection of Mahlke as a hero, it also functions to lend an unreal and uncertain texture to the situation.

Another aspect of this narrational technique is that it develops an ironic parallel between the failed libido-hero and his "failed" biographer, Pilenz. For the novel even refuses that comfort be drawn from the hope that, through art, it is possible to reach some kind of productive area. For example:

[Of course it is pleasant to pirouette on white paper — but what help are white clouds, soft breezes, speedboats coming in on schedule, and a flock of gulls doing the work of a Greek chorus; what good can any magical effects of syntax do me; even if I drop capitals and punctuation,

I shall still have to say that Mahlke did not stow his bauble in the former shack of the former Polish mine sweeper *Rybitwa*. . . . (71–72 / 76]

and:

[Who will supply me with a good ending? For what began with cat and mouse torments me today in the form of crested terns on ponds bordered with rushes . . . (120 / 126)]

The narrator is completely unable to come into correct relation with Mahlke by incorporating him into any satisfactory literary structure.

Indeed Pilenz as narrator proves to be as significant in the novel as its hero Joachim Mahlke. For just as Mahlke presents the libido-hero aspect of humanity, Pilenz appears to assume the persona aspects of the group: that is, he tends to represent the social, conscious attitude.[15] And as the figure of Mahlke embodies the failure of society to produce an adequate libido-hero, positively to project and channel its creative energies, so Pilenz helps present that inadequate society.

There are, perhaps, some common points of contact between Pilenz and Mahlke which serve to underline their representation of the same issue. They are, for example, the only Catholics in their immediate group. (This fact, however, while drawing attention to a common area shared by Mahlke and Pilenz, also helps illustrate an essential difference between them. Pilenz's involvement with Catholicism is associated at one stage with homosexuality (77 / 82) and, therefore, with a sterility and deadness appropriate to the society which is depicted in the work. Mahlke's involvement in Catholicism is ultimately revealed, by his disavowal of God and Christ, to be an ironic and grotesque reference to the fact that he is a fertility hero.) Further similarities can be found in the fact that they both lack effective father figures; and at one stage even Pilenz tends to confuse Mahlke and himself: ["Mahlke laughingly mentioned his old nonsense about his neck, as he put it, and even went so far — his mother and aunt joined in the laughter — as to tell the story about the cat: this time it was Jürgen Kupka who put the cat on his throat; if only I knew who made up the story, he or I, or who is writing this in the first place!" (84 / 89)].

Yet it is Pilenz's continual association with the group which provides the strongest hint that he operates as a persona figure. Pilenz, especially in the initial stages of the work, refers to "us" as opposed to the individual Mahlke: ["We needed a good three quarters of an hour to get back. No matter how exhausted he was, he was always standing on the breakwater a good minute ahead of us" (9 / 11)]. And again: ["we took to the water and swam out to our barge; from the beach, in the lifeguard's binoculars, for instance, we were six diminishing heads in motion; one head in advance of the rest and first to reach the goal" (15/17–18)]. There are also indications to be found in Pilenz's involvement in social organizing. He organizes a trip out to the wreck for his cousins (36 / 38); he wants to organize an occasion for Mahlke to deliver his speech (102–3 / 108); and he later admits to being an organizing official in his parish church (69 / 73).

It is Pilenz who tries to reason with Mahlke; and it is Pilenz who offers an apology to Dr Klohse: ["I tried to give Klohse something resembling an apology, for Mahlke — and for myself" (105 / 111)]. All these descriptions point to Pilenz's acting on one level as a persona figure to Mahlke's libido-hero. That he is a failure in this persona — i.e. social, conscious — function is brought out in his inability to account for Mahlke by any genuinely conscious insights: ["And as for his soul, it was never introduced to me. I never heard what he thought" (27 / 29)].

Indeed Pilenz tends to allow Mahlke to produce various shadow features[16] in his (Pilenz's) character: the failure to come to terms with Mahlke consciously is conterminous with Pilenz's entanglement with the dark and neurotic aspects of his universe. This can be seen in the antagonism towards Mahlke revealed in Pilenz by the cat-mouse issue, and by the more obvious attempts by Pilenz to eliminate Mahlke. Among the earliest episodes which reveal the dangerous attitude of Pilenz and his world to Mahlke is the one in which Pilenz and his friend describe Mahlke to his cousins — ["Schilling seized on the opportunity and described Mahlke's Adam's apple, giving it all the qualities of a goitre" (39 / 41)]. Here the "disease" attribute assigned to the phallic Adam's apple might be seen as again pointing to this society's inability to conceive of a productive potential in anything but sterile terms. It is also Pilenz who sponges the redeemer image off the blackboard (33 / 35); and significantly, when the group believes Mahlke to be drowned, it is Pilenz who is to tell the mother the news (49 / 52). Pilenz, later in the novel, tries to eliminate Mahlke from his area, by cutting Mahlke's name and the crucifixion hymn out of the beam: ["I took the ax and hacked Mahlke's favorite sequence out of the board and eradicated your name" (94 / 99)]; and this pattern reaches its climax when Pilenz, through various lies and the deliberate withholding of the phallic can-opener, "disposes" of Mahlke to his (Pilenz's) own satisfaction into the body of the submerged wreck.

Another indication of this shadow aspect of Pilenz's function is revealed by Pilenz's continually assigning a left, i.e. sinister, position to Mahlke and his world. Mahlke's house is situated on the left side of the street (17 / 20); and in church Mahlke sits in the left pew. This information is given with Pilenz's point of view stressed: ["Seen from the altar, he knelt in the second pew of the left-hand row" (14 / 17)]. The wreck into which Mahlke dives is situated on the left side of the harbour channel (90 / 96). And when Pilenz visits the Mahlkes it is noted [that a plum tree, "leafless and with whitewashed trunk, could be seen in the left-hand pane of the veranda" (82 / 87)]. Here the plum tree, normally representing the natural and the fertile, is placed in a left or negative area from Pilenz's viewpoint. The negative aspect of the situation is enhanced by the tree being "leafless." All such indications appear to point to a society unable to project the libido-hero area of itself adequately, a society unable to channel its creative impulses positively.

The informing patterns of *Katz und Maus*, built around the libido-hero myth cycle, and the manner in which the persona figure relates to the libido-hero, appear then to offer the reader little occasion for optimism. Nevertheless Grass has provided some balance and relief in the ironic pessimism of the work. Mahlke disappears on a Friday (119 / 125), and since in Christian terms this is the period of blackest despair — a period analogous to the situation depicted in the novel — perhaps there is some hope of a rejuvenation to come. Pilenz himself seems unsure as to whether Mahlke is a failure, and talks of an area ["that saw" Mahlke's Adam's apple "win or lose" (6 / 8)]. He also meticulously avoids stating that Mahlke is dead. Even with regard to the social character of Pilenz and the less specific members of the group, a certain alleviation of the situation's grimness can be found. In spite of the deadness and the "smell of corpses" (82 / 87) permeating their world, life is shown, by the post-war meetings of Pilenz and other members of the schoolboy group, to have at least survived.

This discussion of *Katz und Maus* has attempted to move beyond the type of critical framework which describes the novel in terms, be they Gnostic or whatever, which have already been robbed of their specific structural capacity by Grass's constant ironising. The more general set of terms provided by Jungian criticism perhaps allows this grotesque corruption of human patternings to be more readily perceived. And, moreover, the Jungian framework also manages to accord the narrator's function its integral position within the ironised myth framework. The overall texture of *Katz und Maus* then remains pessimistically ironic. Possible positive aspects, while lending a balance and relief to the work, are definitely underplayed: the ultimate vision is that of a humanity unable to cope, and without any real hope of rejuvenation:

> [During one such intermission, I had the lieutenant in charge of the order squad page you from the music platform: "Sergeant Mahlke is wanted at the entrance." But you didn't show up. You didn't surface. (121 / 127)]

Notes

1. See, e.g., E.M. Friedrichsmeyer, "Aspects of Myth, Parody and Obscenity in Grass' *Die Blechtrommel* and *Katz und Maus*," [*Germanic Review*], 40 (1965), 240–50; Karl H. Ruhleder, "A Pattern of Messianic Thought in Günter Grass' *Cat and Mouse*," [*German Quarterly*], 39 (1966), 599–612.

2. See, e.g., James C. Bruce, "The Equivocating Narrator in Günter Grass' *Katz und Maus*," [*Monatshefte für deutschen Unterricht*], 58 (1966), 139–49; also Johanna E. Behrendt, "Auf der Suche nach dem Adamsapfel," [*Germanisch-romanische Monatsschrift*], 19 (1969), 313–26; Robert H. Spaethling, "Günter Grass: *Katz und Maus*," [*Monatshefte für*

deutschen Unterricht], 62 (1970), 141–53. Spaethling does in fact state that Grass uses "symbolic forms and archetypal patterns" (p. 141), but this statement is as far as he really goes in attempting to incorporate such material into his framework. Instead he prefers to set up the old dichotomy of "timeless patterns of human behaviour" versus "a realistic tale of a contemporary situation" (p. 149), placing Grass firmly on the side of the latter.

3. See, e.g., Kurt J. Fickert, "The Use of Ambiguity in *Cat and Mouse*," [*German Quarterly*], 44 (1971), 372–8.

4. Friedrichsmeyer, p. 249.

5. Günter Grass, *Katz und Maus* (Rowohlt Taschenbuch: Reibek bei Hamburg, 1963). [Ed. note: Page references are given parenthetically and in double form: numbers before the slash refer to the German edition; numbers after the slash refer to *Cat and Mouse*, trans. Ralph Manheim (New York: Signet Books, 1964).]

6. See C.G. Jung, *Symbols of Transformation* (London, 1956), esp. pp. 367–8 and 391–2, for a description of Christ as libido-hero. Karl H. Ruhleder's article also provides interesting information on the following "Christian" associations. However he restricts this information to conform to his "Joachite prophecy" structure without ever adequately building into his discussion the fact that the constant ironising essentially destroys the specificity, and indeed usefulness, of such structures.

7. Admittedly the ironic association of Christ and the Virgin Mary with latrines and graffiti emphasizes the fertility-hero aspect of Christ rather than his transcendence.

8. E.L. Marson has drawn my attention to further evidence for this point. From the narrator's comments about the general layout of the district, both the "front" (northern) *and* eastern sides of the tower ought to have been visible from Mahlke's room. However, since it is the eastern aspect which is stressed, there is some narrational suppression working here to emphasize the Mahlke-east association.

9. Jung, p. 198.

10. Ibid., p. 322.

11. See J. Reddick, "Action and Impotence: Günter Grass' *Örtlich Betäubt*," [*Modern Language Review*], (1972), 563–78. Reddick has also noted this vitality of Mahlke's activities (see p. 563), which enhances the essential libido-hero features of this character. However, his discussion fails to observe that Mahlke actually cuts a ridiculous figure as "the most outstanding athlete of his class," which shows Mahlke's function in an ironic light, at least for this particular society.

12. Ruhleder, p. 604.

13. Jung, pp. 389–90.

14. See Spaethling and Fickert.

15. J. Jacobi, *The Psychology of Jung* (London, 1951), pp. 33ff.

16. Jacobi, p. 130.

Günter Grass' *Hundejahre:* A Realistic Novel about Myth

Scott H. Abbott*

Günter Grass' novel *Hundejahre* [*Dog Years*] begins with the phrases ["You tell. No, you. Or you"].[1] This exchange would remind a Freemason of the passage in Freemasonic ritual — ". . . you begin. No, begin you. You begin."[2] The novel ends with the pointedly Freemasonic initiation of Walter Matern into the mysteries of Brauxel's underground factory.[3] And between the Freemasonic beginning and ending, very near the mathematical center of the novel, we are told that *Studienrat* Oswald Brunies, the teacher of the novel's three narrators, was a Freemason (337 / 287). Roughly parallel to this Freemasonic structure is a numerological structure: the novel begins with thirty-two "Frühschichten" ["Morning Shifts"], ends with a visit to the thirty-two rooms of Brauxel's mine, and has its high point when Amsel's thirty-two teeth are knocked out as he is brutally transformed in the snow scene. And between these Masonic and numerological beginnings and endings, surrounding their centers, are innumerable references to astrology, myth, superstition, magical transformation, divination of the future, and other supernatural activities of the most varied sort.

Given this profusion of related motifs in *Hundejahre*, the modes of interpretation most often resorted to are naturally theological, mythical, numerological, or masonic.[4] Readers conditioned by novels such as Thomas Mann's *Der Zauberberg* [*The Magic Mountain*] (which likewise makes extensive use of symbolic numbers, contains lengthy descriptions of Freemasonic ritual, and features a mythical revelation in the snow), are especially apt to rummage through *Hundejahre* with delight. But these striking similarities, far from inviting similar interpretations, should warn the reader (unless one is dealing with an obviously epigonal work), that the novels should be read differently.

In a speech given in West Berlin at the opening of the exhibition ["People in Auschwitz,"] a speech he called ["The difficulties of a Father in Explaining Auschwitz to his Children"], Grass commented on the history intervening between Mann's work and his own: ["Adorno's comment that one cannot write poems any more after Auschwitz has provided so many misunderstandings that it must be supplemented, at least tentatively, by the interpretation that poems which have been written since Auschwitz will have to be prepared to accept the yardstick of Auschwitz"].[5] The strikingly similar themes and motifs used in Mann's *Zauberberg* and Grass' *Hundejahre* — the Freemasonry, the numerology, the supernatural phenomena, the mythology, and the magical transformations in the snow — must, according to Grass, be measured against different criteria. But just

*Reprinted from *German Quarterly* 55 (1982): 212–20, by permission of *German Quarterly* and the author.

what is the new perspective from which we must view this postwar parody of *Der Zauberberg?*

To answer this question I would like first to examine several of Grass' nonliterary statements on the general subject of myths, ideologies, and symbols, and their relationship to history. Then I shall discuss the narrators of the novel, showing that the similarities between *Hundejahre* and *Der Zauberberg* are due to the propensity of *Hundejahre's* narrators to interpret events in their lives magically, mystically, and mythologically. The point I want to make is that when we fail to recognize the narrators as the producers of the novel, when we think in the same categories through which they view the world, if we interpret the novel mythically or numerologically, if we view it the same way we do *Der Zauberberg*, forgetting Auschwitz, we are abetting the very tendency Günter Grass would subvert.

First, then, Grass' statements about myth and history. When asked about his flounder as a personification of Hegel's *Weltgeist*, Grass answered: "Yes, I was considering a satire on the German preoccupation with assigning hidden meanings to history. History to me is chaos, plain and simple."[6] In a letter published in *Der Spiegel* Grass addresses another facet of the same problem. After referring to Idealism as Germany's basic problem, whether used to support rightist or leftist absolute claims, he writes: [". . . it is always idealistic difficulties that make it impossible for the apostles of salvation to put up with the contradictions of reality and remain face to face with their own impotence"].[7] In other words, Grass is concerned with the fact that men, faced by the contradictions of reality and conditioned by Idealism, turn all too quickly to an ideology, to a mythic history promising a millenium, or to a heroic leader. Grass is not alone in seeing in myth an attempt to reconcile historical contradictions. Indeed, two of the twentieth-century's leading theoreticians of myth— Claude Lévi-Strauss and Ernst Cassirer—touch on this very point.

In his *Structural Anthropology*, after pointing out that "myths are still widely interpreted in conflicting ways: as collective dreams, as the outcome of a kind of aesthetic play, or as the basis of ritual," Lévi-Strauss offers the following as a definition of myth: "the purpose of myth is to provide a logical model capable of overcoming a contradiction (an impossible achievement if, as it happens, the contradiction is real)."[8] Although the attempt to overcome a contradiction with such a logical model is, on Lévi-Strauss' view, a much more positive activity than on Grass' view, the basic concept is the same; and indeed, the parenthetical comment on a "real" contradiction seems very close to Grass' own position. In addition, Lévi-Strauss makes a comparison between "myth and what appears to have largely replaced it in modern societies, namely, politics."[9] Here he contrasts the historian's view of the French Revolution ("a sequence of past happenings, a non-reversible series of events the remote consequences of which may still be felt at present") with that of a politician, who sees in the same events a pattern from which he can infer future developments. This is the very patterning which Grass fears.[10]

A second view of myth comes from Ernst Cassirer, who, in Volume II of *The Philosophy of Symbolic Forms*, defines myth positively as "a unitary energy of the human spirit: as a self-contained form of interpretation which asserts itself amid all the diversity of the objective material it presents."[11] But after having witnessed the political manipulation of myths also described in *Hundejahre*, Cassirer writes of another aspect of myth in *The Myth of the State*:

> In the times of inflation and unemployment Germany's whole social and economic system was threatened with a complete collapse. The normal resources seemed to have been exhausted. This was the natural soil upon which the political myths could grow up and in which they found ample nourishment. . . . Myth reaches its full force when man has to face an unusual and dangerous situation.[12]

Both Lévi-Strauss and Cassirer, then, see in myth an attempt to overcome a contradiction or dangerous situation, often political, and Cassirer specifically refers to the political myths of Nazi Germany as natural attempts to establish order in a chaotic environment.[13] And this is the tendency of which Grass would make us aware. Before turning to *Hundejahre* let me quote Grass once again, speaking about the problem from yet another perspective:

> Only ideologists need symbols to manifest themselves. Nazis with their swastikas, Communists with their hammers and sickles, the Roman Catholics with their arsenals full of images, the capitalists with their trademarks. I am even afraid of turning anti-ideology into an ideology. I just know what I want and don't want — the danger is when these things become a system.[14]

We see here a position diametrically opposed to that of Thomas Mann, whose work is, among other things, a magnificent system of symbols and myths. In the subchapter ["Snow"], for example, confronting the contradictions between Naphta's radical irrationalism and Settembrini's enlightened rationalism, Hans Castorp achieves a synthesis through the mediation of myth. Of course the undercutting irony of *Der Zauberberg* must be taken into account; but the opposition between Mann and Grass set forth here, despite simplification, is nonetheless productive. But the question remains: if Grass, as we have just seen, distrusts ideologies, symbols, and mythical histories, how is one to interpret *Hundejahre*, an extraordinarily complex novel bristling with astrology, numerology, symbols, myths, and ideologies?

Hundejahre is named after a family of German shepherds. They are all black, and fatefully attach themselves to whoever espouses the kind of mystical, mythical, barbaric thought which allowed the Nazis to come to power and which, according to Grass, still flourishes in the postwar world.

Further, the novel is a collection of three accounts of life in a small suburb of Danzig. Eddi Amsel (also known as Brauxel) describes pre-war Danzig in his ["Morning Shifts"], Harry Liebenau tells of the war years in his ["Love Letters"], and Walter Matern reports on postwar Germany in his ["Materniads"]. Amsel, a half-Jew, is an artist whose medium is scarecrows, creations which most often depict mythological figures. Matern is Amsel's friend and protector who turns against him in the Nazi years and knocks out his teeth in a bloody attack in the snow (a parody of Mann's ["Snow"] scene). And Harry Liebenau, a younger acquaintance of the other two narrators, in a bizarre public discussion, brings Matern to trial for his misdeeds as a Nazi. From the very beginning Grass focuses on these three narrators as narrators.

Even the opening sentences of the novel [("You tell. No, you! Or you.")] leave no question as to the primacy of the problem of narration. In the first paragraphs the narrator repeatedly emphasizes the fact that he is the narrator: ["The present writer bears the name of Brauxel at the moment. . . . The present writer usually writes Brauksel in the form of Castrop-Rauxel. . . . The present writer . . ."] — all on the first page! Grass wants to make sure that we are aware that we are dealing with a narrated text. Such an emphasis should lead us to examine the narrators a little more closely. Who are these three men through whose eyes we are viewing a crucial era in Germany's history? How were they educated? And what was the result of that education?

Eddi Amsel, Harry Liebenau, and Walter Matern — the three members of the *Autorenkollektiv* ["authorial collective"] who write the novel — grow up in Danzig in an atmosphere saturated with myth. In their accounts they refer specifically to three men who exert powerful pedagogical influences on them. Herr Olschewski, a ["young teacher with ideas about the school system"] teaches *Heimatkunde* [local history]; but when Eddi asks him about the origin of the name Pluto he lectures for weeks on mythology — Germanic, Greek, and especially Polish myths — about ["all the gods there used to be, who still exist and who existed once upon a time. . . . Ever since"], Brauxel reports, ["Amsel has devoted himself to mythology" (68 / 64)]. A second teacher, Oswald Brunies, is, on the one hand, a grand old humanist who refuses to have anything to do with the Nazis. But on the other hand, he is an absurd rooster, scratching in the schoolyard for rare pebbles. ["With him nothing happened naturally, everywhere he sniffed out hidden forces. . . . Carrying on like an old Celtic druid, a Prussian oak-tree god, or Zoroaster — he was generally thought to be a Freemason" (144 / 129).][15] This *Studienrat*, who is supposed to teach history and German, is addicted to sweets and Romanticism. His students do not learn how to spell, nor do they learn history; but they do know some Eichendorff, they come to see ballet shoes as magical objects, they can write essays in which they phantasize about marriage customs of the Zulus, they get a large dose of the mystical geology found in Schubert's *Ansichten von der Nachtseite der Naturwissenschaft,* and there are some indications that they adopt Brunies' Freemasonry. They certainly do not learn his aversion to the Nazis.

Oskar Matzerath, the hero of Grass' first novel, *Die Blechtrommel,* is referred to as a third teacher: ["Brauxel and his co-authors have taken an example from someone who worked diligently all his life on lacquered tin" (117 / 106)]. This is no recommendation, for near the end of *Die Blechtrommel,* Oskar, having reached the fabled age of thirty, contemplates various problematic courses of action: ["I go out and play the Messiah they see in me; against my better judgment I make my drum stand for more than it can, I make a symbol out of it, found a sect, a party, or maybe only a lodge"].[16] Oskar has been guilty of making his drum into a symbol, of using art to promote mythical thinking, of setting himself up as a messiah; and the narrators of *Hundejahre* learn his skills well.

Walter Matern, for example, is described by Grass as an addicted disciple of ideologies: ["In the novel *Hundejahre* I believe I succeeded in portraying in the figure of Walter Matern a representative of German Idealism, one who finds the doctrine of salvation successively, and with great rapidity, in communism, National Socialism, Catholicism, and finally in an ideological antifascism"].[17] While living with his father, who can hear flour worms predicting Germany's economic future, Walter Matern develops his own economic/historical theories and speaks ["of history as a dialectical worm-process." Matern "disseminates Marx-fed worm myths, which are made to sustain the theory of necessary development" (507–508 / 428–29)]. This is clearly the ideological patterning of history, or the combination of myth and history Grass so vocally opposes.[18] And Matern is not alone in his beliefs.

Harry Liebenau is in love with barbarous Tulla, and, like Matern, also demonstrates a strong interest in mythical history. Liebenau is ["a knowledgeable young man, who read a hodge-podge of books on history and philosophy" (375 / 317)]. He is "ein Melancholiker," a category Grass describes along with "Utopist" in *Aus dem Tagebuch einer Schnecke* as being opposed to the rational attitude of doubt. In addition, Liebenau is ["a visionary, who lied a great deal, spoke softly, turned red when, believed this and that, and regarded the never-ending war as an extension of his schooling" (375 / 318)]. His list of heroes includes Hitler, whose mythical history brought the Nazis to power, and the historian Heinrich von Treitschke, whose ideologically slanted and anti-Semitic history of the early nineteenth century powerfully affected the historical consciousness of the German citizen. Martin Heidegger, whose concepts of *Geworfenheit, Sein,* and *Zeit* find their way into every facet of Liebenau's already hazy thought processes, is another hero. ["With the help of these models," it is said, "he succeeded in burying a real mound made of human bones under medieval allegories" (375 / 318).] He calls this pile of human bones at the Stutthof concentration camp a ["place of sacrifice, erected in order that purity might come-to-be in the luminous" (375 / 318)].

Liebenau is a fantast in love with barbarism and mythical histories and Matern is a violent Idealist; but what about Eddi Amsel, who, as Brauxel, heads the *Autorenkollektiv?*

Amsel has often been seen as the quintessential postwar writer who vigorously struggles to overcome Germany's past. John Reddick, for example, writes that where Matern attempts to mask reality, Amsel always sees clearly. Reddick even identifies Amsel at times with Grass himself.[19] But if we look at Amsel from the same perspective from which we have just observed Matern and Liebenau, we find a problematic figure.

In the account of Olschewski's teaching and Amsel's turn to mythology, mythical thinking is identified with a series of violent and mystical figures, including a black and pregnant German shepherd. Following this terrifying list comes the phrase ["Also Eduard Amsel" (68 / 64).] Later in the book, when Walter Matern is asked in the public discussion to name several ["important childhood experiences that left their mark on him" (602 / 505)] he begins with the names of three gods of Prussian mythology. He lists the same violent and mystical figures we saw before, and again ends with ["also Eddi Amsel" (604 / 506).]

Eddi Amsel, the artist whose work could lend support to a rational acceptance of historical contradictions, instead intensifies Matern's mythical thinking. His mythical scarecrows frighten away birds; but some are birds themselves and strengthen the superstition of the villagers. During the Nazi period his mechanical figures reinterpret history on the basis of Nazi myths and Romantic heroes. His scarecrow ballet has some promise, but he agrees to change it to fit Nazi taste. Eddi also sponsors miller Matern in his economic divination. As Brauxel, he predicts the end of the world astrologically and dabbles in numerology. And most telling of all, he takes over the care of Pluto in the end, leaving the black dog [(SS-black, priest-black, Amsel-black")] to guard his factory.

Eddi Amsel, Harry Liebenau, Walter Matern — the three narrators of *Hundejahre*, victims during the dog years, are also responsible for the dog years. The relation of these three would-be *Vergangenheitsbewältiger* [conquerors of the past] to the past is manifest by the *Erkenntnisbrille* [spectacles of recognition] used during the public discussion of Matern's guilt. This ubiquitous postwar symbol for the overcoming of the past is produced in *Hundejahre* by Brauxel and Company. ["Jena-trained opticians" (548 / 461)] act as consultants for the glasses. Jena is not only famous for lenses, of course, but also for German Romanticism. The glasses' secret ingredient is mica, collected by "Romantic" Oswald Brunies. Looking through the glasses one can indeed see the horrors of the past; but the Romantic lenses distort the view, and the viewers demonize Hitler and Matern, having no insight into their own guilt.

Thus, the glasses made to overcome the past are themselves products of the past. Postwar writers (or at least *Hundejahre's* postwar narrators), seeking to overcome Romantic thinking, use tools forged by the Romantics. Mythical histories are replaced by more mythical histories. Eddi Amsel is a black bird attempting to scare off black birds. Walter Matern attacks fascism with fascist methods. And Harry Liebenau tries and convicts Matern as a Nazi while himself praying to the black German shepherd. Or, as it says in the novel, ["There's a worm in the worm" (491 / 414).]

Hundejahre, then, is not a Romantic/mythical/occult novel, it is a realistic novel about Romanticism, myth, and the supernatural. On the one hand, the ["Morning Shifts," "Love Letters," and "Materniads"] written by Amsel, Liebenau, and Matern are mythical interpretations of a segment of twentieth-century history, interpretations of a sequence of events in which all three narrators have vested interests. And the three accounts, beyond any nominal [overcoming of the past] are an admitted attempt to establish a monument to "Romantic" Oswald Brunies.[20]

On the other hand, however, the novel *Hundejahre* is about its narrators. We, as readers, must resist the tendency to think in their categories. We must recognize the accounts for what they are — confessions of misled, defensive, and representative minds. After recognizing the myths, Freemasonry, and numerology, we must then step back from the seemingly systematic but ultimately chaotic mass of supernatural and suprahistorical phenomena depicted and read the novel as a realistic account of a common and dangerous flight from reality. We must, as did Walter Benjamin for Goethe's *Wahlverwandtschaften*, "read these symbolic objects to the second power."[21]

Thus aware of the patterns and systems on which the narrator of the novel rely to overcome the contradictions of history they have experienced, we should return to Grass' statement: "I am even afraid of turning anti-ideology into an ideology. I just know what I want and don't want — the danger is when these things become a system." We have just worked through *Hundejahre*, pulling out passages which express sentiments similar to those Grass has expressed in interviews, and ironically, have woven them into a system. But ultimately, even this system which teaches us to distrust the novel's narrators and see their irrational methods of coping with reality as dangerous, is undercut.

For how do we know that the novel is about its untrustworthy narrators? Because they themselves have told us. They are the ones who describe the ["Marx-fed worm myths,"] they laugh at Oswald Brunies and his Romantic foibles, they describe each other and themselves as violent idealists, as mythical historians, as irrational artists. They themselves are aware of their untrustworthiness. Grass undercuts his narrators, but he also undercuts a systematic apperception of the narrators' unreliability. To fail to do this would be to demonize the narrators for their demonization of the Nazis. Grass is skeptical even of his own skepticism. And it is this thoroughgoing skepticism that he places in opposition to irrationalism of any sort. Or, as it says in *Hundejahre:*

> [The idea? Isn't it always pure? Even in the beginning not pure. Jesus Christ not pure. Marx Engels not pure. Ashes not pure. And the host not pure. No idea stays pure. Even the flowering of art isn't pure. (357 / 303)]

Notes

1. [Ed. note: Page references hereafter are given parenthetically and in double form. Page numbers before the slash refer to *Hundejahre* (Neuwied, Berlin: Luchterhand, 1963); numbers after the slash refer to *Dog Years*, trans. Ralph Manheim (New York: Fawcett Crest, 1966).]

2. *Revised Freemasonry Illustrated* (Chicago: Ezra A. Cook, 1919), p. 331.

3. The scenes in which Matern is initiated into the mysteries of this underground factory draw heavily on Masonic ritual. Each of the following details has its direct counterpart in Masonic initiation rites: Matern, referred to again and again as the ["Stranger to the mine"] (and thus in need of initiation), is led past a doorkeeper, receives instruction, signs a statement affirming his intention to go into the mine, must take off his clothing and exchange it for [a "mine outfit"], and descends in an elevator hung by a mystical cable while a bell is rung three and then five times. During the descent Brauxel instructs Matern as to the makeup, care, and importance of the cable. The lesson ends with the statement ["Light then"] as the elevator arrives and Matern is led into the mine.

For comparison of these actions with Freemasonic initiation rites compare *Revised Freemasonry Illustrated* or the account of Pierre's initiation into Freemasonry in *War and Peace.*

4. Of such criticism, Michael Harscheidt's *Günter Grass: Wort-Zahl-Gott* (Bonn: Bouvier Verlag, 1976), a 758-page numerological/theological interpretation, is the most conspicuous.

5. In *Der Bürger und seine Stimme: Reden, Aufsätze, Kommentare* (Darmstadt und Neuwied: Hermann Luchterhand Verlag, 1974), p. 89.

6. *New York Times,* Sunday, December 17, 1978, Book Review Section, p. 14.

7. "Unser Grundübel ist der Idealismus," *Der Spiegel,* August 11, 1969, p. 94.

8. *Structural Anthropology* (New York: Basic Books, Inc., 1963), pp. 207, 229.

9. *Structural Anthropology,* p. 209.

10. It is somewhat surprising that such congruence between seemingly radically opposed positions exists. Grass approaches Lévi-Strauss' position even more closely in a later novel. After making his point about the dangers inherent in mythical thinking in *Hundejahre, Aus dem Tagebuch einer Schnecke,* and even in *Der Butt,* Grass, in the latter work, appropriates large portions of Lévi-Strauss' *The Raw and the Cooked* to develop a myth of cooking as an antidote to the *Weltgeist* / flounder. For further details see my "The Raw and the Cooked: Claude Lévi-Strauss and Günter Grass," in [*"The Fisherman und His Wife": Günter Grass's 'The Flounder' in Critical Perspective,* ed. Siegfried Mews (New York: AMS Press, 1983), 107–20].

11. *The Philosophy of Symbolic Forms, Volume Two: Mythical Thought,* tr. by Ralph Manheim (New Haven and London: Yale University Press, 1975), p. 235.

12. *The Myth of the State* (New Haven: Yale University Press, 1971), p. 278.

13. Cf. also the statement by Mircea Eliade on Marxism, myth, and history: "It is indeed significant that Marx turns to his own account the Judaeo-Christian eschatological hope of an *absolute (end to) History;* in that he parts company from the other historical philosophers (Croce, for instance, and Ortega y Gasset), for whom the tensions of history are implicit in the human condition, and therefore can never be completely abolished." *Myth and Reality* (New York: Harper and Row, 1968), p. 184.

14. "Green Years for Grass," *Life,* June 4, 1965, p. 56.

15. In *Der Zauberberg,* when Naphta tells Hans that Settembrini is a Freemason, he gives a detailed account of the history of Freemasonry, an institution with a rational, Enlightenment beginning and a subsequent turn to alchemy and various other Romantic irrationalities. Brunies embodies both sides of Freemasonry, but the synthesis of the two, as would be expected here, tips heavily toward the irrational.

16. Frankfurt am Main and Hamburg: Fischer Bücherei, 1962; p. 490. [Ed. note: *The Tin Drum,* trans. Ralph Manheim (New York: Vintage Books, 1964), p. 585.]

17. "Unser Grundübel ist der Idealismus," p. 94.

18. The narratively serious but ultimately satirical worm dialectic has an analogue in Störtebeker's use of Heideggerian language in speaking of and to rats: ["The rat withdraws itself by unconcealing itself into the ratty. So the rat errates the ratty, illuminating it with errancy. For the ratty has come-to-be in the errancy where the rat errs and so fosters error. That is the essential area of all history" (367 / 311)].

19. *The "Danzig Trilogy" of Günter Grass* (New York and London: Harcourt Brace Jovanovich, 1975), pp. 239–66.

20. ["But to him, . . . Dr. Oswald Brunies, . . . — a monument will be erected to him" (108 / 100).]

21. *Marxism and Form: Twentieth-Century Dialectical Theories of Literature* (Princeton: Princeton University Press, 1974), pp. 66–67. The context of the quoted passage follows: "It is the originality of Benjamin to have cut across the sterile opposition between the arbitrary interpretations of the symbol on the one hand, and the blank failure to see what it means on the other: *Elective Affinities* is to be read not as a novel by a symbolic writer, but as a novel *about* symbolism. If objects of a symbolic nature loom large in this work, it is not because they were chosen to underline the theme of adultery in some decorative manner, but rather because the real underlying subject is precisely the surrender to the power of symbols of people who have lost their autonomy as human beings. 'When people sink to this level, even the life of apparently lifeless things grows strong. Gundolf quite rightly underlined the crucial role of objects in this story. Yet the intrusion of the thinglike into human life is precisely a criterion of the mythical universe.' We are required to read these symbolic objects to the second power: not so much directly to decipher in them a one-to-one meaning, as to sense that of which the very fact of symbolism is itself symptomatic." This passage, as has been shown here, can be applied almost word for word to *Hundejahre.* And it should be noted, finally, that in *Die Blechtrommel,* along with *Rasputin und die Frauen,* Oskar reads *Wahlverwandtschaften* [*Elective Affinities*].

Günter Grass's Rehearsal Play
Lore Metzger*

The English translation of Günter Grass's updated *Coriolanus, The Plebeians Rehearse the Uprising* appears in a format widely used in modern editions of Shakespeare's history plays: the text preceded by a critical essay and followed by extracts from sources. In place of a selection from Plutarch or Holinshed, the volume includes a documentary report of the East German uprising of June 17, 1953; and instead of a preface by a Frank Kermode, Grass provides his own delightfully parodic contribution to *Stoffgeschichte*, "The Prehistory and Posthistory of the Tragedy of *Coriolanus* from Livy and Plutarch via Shakespeare down to Brecht and Myself." This trifocal arrangement points up Grass's free borrowing from literary and historical sources in a virtuoso display of montage and reportage. Having in his early works, such as *The Tin Drum*, emulated the imaginative plenitude of a *Moby-Dick*, Grass in *The Plebeians* finds his challenge in working with minimum invention and maximum manipulation of material culled from Shakespeare's *Coriolanus*, Brecht's adaptation of and commentary on Shakespeare's play, biographical information about Brecht and the Berlin Ensemble, Brecht's plays and poems, and eyewitness reports as well as other documents on the East German uprising. In his Shakespeare lecture that ends with a sketch of his own *Coriolanus*, Grass defends the "theft of literary property," as practiced by Shakespeare and Brecht: "all subject matter is free; let other owners fence in their property, the real estate of the mind is fair game for all." And he quotes Brecht's remark, "Obviously the basis of just about every great age in literature is the force and innocence of its plagiarism."[1]

In learning the art of plagiarism from Brecht, Grass also mastered Brecht's dialectical dramaturgic method in order to reveal, among other things, the paradox and pathos inherent in Brecht's aesthetic and political choices. Brecht's dialectical method suited Grass perfectly because it aimed at tracing the uncertainties, inconsistencies, and fluctuations of both individuals and social processes. Brecht argued for the theatrical application of dialectical materialism which "regards nothing as existing except in so far as it changes, in other words is in disharmony with itself." To illustrate, Brecht suggested imagining "a man standing in a valley and making a speech in which he occasionally changes his views or simply utters sentences which contradict one another, so that the accompanying echo forces them into confrontation."[2]

Günter Grass adopts precisely such shifting views, such confrontations of contradictory echoes, as he dramatizes his protagonist's dilemma of choosing between long-range artistic goals and immediate political action as well as the workers' dilemma of choosing between limited

*Reprinted from *Wisconsin Studies in Contemporary Literature* 14 (1973):197–212, by permission of *Wisconsin Studies in Contemporary Literature* and the author.

rhetorical protest and sweeping revolutionary engagement. These motifs reverberate with multiple echoes. We hear Grass's own voice echoing contrapuntally over Brecht's in exposing the Marxist artist's bittersweet profession; we hear the tone of tragedy echoing over the comic mode of the rehearsal play; we hear the dark note of human and humane failure jarringly echo over the optimistic Marxist affirmation of inevitable social change and evitable human suffering. As Grass rehearses his interacting antitheses, he eludes both chaos and synthesis; instead of Hegelian simplifications, he exhibits a sober view of the choices open to intellectuals and artists committed to improving society. He shows us the gaiety and agony of a provocative dramatist committed to rational, liberating transformation of society, confronting an irrational, liberating revolutionary action. The choices open to him and to the revolutionaries are fraught with compromised ideals and inescapable guilt.

Grass has modeled his artist (simply called "Boss" in a parodic echo of Brecht's use of American gangster cliché) not on Brecht the bold iconoclast but rather on the prestigious theater director presiding over his own company in a state-subsidized theater, the privileged trustee of his own dramaturgical tradition. Turning his ironic scrutiny equally on the Brechtian artist and on the workers' uprising, Grass concentrates on his protagonist's action and inaction on June 17, 1953. On the day of the East German workers' revolt, the theater Boss's chief action consists of rehearsing *Coriolanus*, experimenting with changes to bring into greater prominence the revolutionary struggle in which Coriolanus was to confront "class-conscious enemies."[3] While the first scene of Shakespeare's play is taking shape on the stage, the Brechtian rehearsal, which includes much debate of every detail of the Roman street scene, obliquely points to the workers' revolt concurrently taking shape offstage in the streets of Berlin, as in the Boss's remark: "We want to rehearse the revolution and the plebeians are late! Symbolism? No. Sloppiness" (14 / 12).

The unstated but clearly implied parallel between Roman plebeians and German workers evolves further in the highly compressed discussion of Menenius' parable of the state. The Boss is doubtful about the logical consistency of allowing the incipient plebeian revolt against Coriolanus to be quelled by Menenius' "Bauch- und Gliederstory" [story of the belly and the members], a mere nurse's tale that would convince no modern worker:

> [And this parable propped up by crutches / calls itself classical and
> world-renowned. / Try telling it to welders and mechanics, / try telling
> it to cable winders now! (12 / 10)]

Not only do these comments hint at attempts by East German party spokesmen to pacify the workers who were uncertain of their next move in fighting the exorbitant production norms, but the Boss's comments on whether the belly in Shakespeare's parable means the state or the nobility ("There was a time when all the body's members / Rebell'd against the belly . . ." [11 / 9], also raises the question whether the belly that fattens itself on "lard and beans" is to be equated with the Communist Party bosses. And it raises the further question: are the theater Boss and his associates to be identified with these privileged party bureaucrats who bleed the people?

Into this rehearsal, rich in innuendo, actors cast in plebeian roles bring word of an infectious mass protest action filling the streets outside the theater. From here on the parallel actions of stage representation and offstage uprising are explicit and are dramatized contrapuntally. The workers' uprising is not however presented directly on the stage but is represented, reported, and reenacted by delegations of striking workers who enter the Boss's theater world to appeal to him to draft a manifesto to lend their cause the authority of his words. This fictitious confrontation of striking workers and the Berlin Ensemble constitutes the main action of Grass's play, into which he assimilates a mass of factual details about Brecht and about the uprising.[4] Grass himself provides an inimitable synopsis of this action, pinpointing his ironic juxtaposition of the theater Boss and the striking workers on the *Coriolanus* rehearsal stage:

> In my play the Boss does not refuse out of hand to write the statement the workers hope for. He agrees to compose it as soon as the masons and carpenters have shown him exactly what happened at the beginning of the workers' revolt; he wishes to derive benefit from current events for his production of *Coriolan*, for his uprising of the plebeians. The construction workers talk about Ulbricht and Grotewohl; he talks about the tribunes Sicinius and Brutus. The workers discuss the increased norms; he stresses the importance of Sicilian grain deliveries for Rome. The workers quote him; he quotes Shakespeare. The workers invoke the authority of Marx; he invokes the authority of Livy. The workers try to win him over to their revolt; he uses the workers for the staging of his plebeian uprising. The workers are undecided about their future atti-tude; he, the theater Boss, is sure of his thesis: in his play the plebeians are victorious, while on the stage of his theater, which mirrors the revolt of the construction workers, the workers' revolt collapses.[5]

In an intricate serio-comic game, Grass has plotted his moves with utter economy: past and present, biography and fiction, plagiarism and invention, example and parody, reflect each other and reflect on each other. Grass exhibits his multiple perspectives, his mirror images of rehearsed scenarios and unrehearsed events, through the economical device of rehearsal conventions. The rehearsal structure organizes his chaotic wealth of allusive material into a visible microcosm. By strictly observing the unities of time and place — a reversal of Brecht's practice — Grass keeps the play focused on the rehearsal motif. All of the action takes place on the rehearsal stage, the *Coriolanus* set whose chief prop is a tailor's dummy draped with Coriolanus' costume. In the Royal Shake-speare Company's production,[6] the stage on the stage was marked off by a

large white circle; from outside the circle the god-like theater Boss—
superbly acted by Emrys James—supervised the actions in the microcosm
of his creation. All of the action of Grass's play is contained within the
timespan of the rehearsal, full of Pirandellian interruptions, of the first
scene of *Coriolanus*. This circumscription of time and place allows the
play's satiric point to come into sharp focus: neither the fictional plebeian
revolution nor the actual uprising of East German workers gets beyond Act
I, scene 1!

Both actions are abortive rehearsals, short-lived experiments. The
term *Probe*, suggestive of both these meanings, reverberates through
Grass's play that is constructed out of a series of intersecting tryouts—the
Ensemble rehearsing the opening scene of *Coriolanus*, the Boss rehearsing
workers and actors in a protest march, the workers staging the theater
Boss's hanging, everyone trying out vast resources of invective, the workers'
heroine eulogizing the workers' hero—all these impromptu scenes are
viewed and reviewed on the rehearsal stage. As in all rehearsal plays from
Molière's *L'Impromptu de Versailles* to Weiss's *Marat/Sade* dramatic action
appears as improvisation.[7] Whether tinkering with Menenius' parable of
the stage or with "reeducating" the tribunes, Grass's theater director
dissolves the fixed text into fluid scenes.

In the theatrical principles he imputes to his omnipotent theater
director, Grass fully exploits the happy coincidence between the improvi-
satorial rehearsal tradition and Brecht's amplification of this tradition into
his own theory and practice. Among Brecht's numerous statements of his
position, the most succinct is his description of "a new technique of
acting":

> When he [the actor] appears on the stage, besides what he actually is
> doing he will at all essential points discover, specify, imply what he is
> not doing; that is to say he will act in such a way that the alternative
> emerges as clearly as possible, that his acting allows the other possibili-
> ties to be inferred and only represents one out of the possible variants.
> He will say for instance "You'll pay for that," and not say "I forgive
> you". . . . Whatever he doesn't do must be contained and conserved in
> what he does. In this way every sentence and every gesture signifies a
> decision; the character remains under observation and is tested.[8]

By exhibiting alternative decisions and solutions, Brecht hoped to stimulate the spectator's active critical judgment rather than to anesthetize him
into willing suspension of disbelief. "Disbelief can move mountains," said
Brecht.[9] Above all he wanted his audience to disbelieve that human misery
was inevitable; he sought to probe rather than ennoble the ways of the
world in an age that included two world wars. "I see the world in a
mellow light: it is God's excrement," was the young Brecht's Swiftian
comment.[10] And he believed that the modern artist must work like a
Baconian scientist rather than like a visionary prophet in order to awaken
the public to the excremental realities of human existence.

Grass transfers to his protagonist Brecht's self-image of the poet as craftsman rather than as *vates*, a technician who freely displays the techniques by which he seeks to probe the social fabric in the laboratory of his theater. Grass's theater Boss punctuates his rehearsal with instructions to his lighting technician—"Kowalski more light"—and like the hero of *Krapp's Last Tape*, he employs a tape recorder to listen to instant replays. As he points out when he has taped an unrehearsed exchange of invective between construction workers and himself with which he hopes to enrich his production of *Coriolanus*: "The masses will be dispersed;/this taped material however will remain" (62 / 62). Grass satirically extends the Boss's detached examination of alternative dramatic choices to moral and political issues that intrude upon his theater world. When the striking construction workers interrupt his rehearsal, he approaches their decisions and indecisions with the same detached skepticism with which he weighs the dramatic possibilities of transforming Shakespeare's opportunistic tribunes into revolutionary leaders.

Both in his rehearsal of the opening scene of *Coriolanus* and in his interrogation of the workers on the opening scene of their uprising, the Boss wants the participants to view their own roles as spectators of themselves, reporting their actions dispassionately like eyewitnesses.[11] As he examines the presented material critically, he highlights some scenes with satiric formulations before proceeding to fresh perspectives. When, for example, actors and construction workers, plebeians and proletarians, as he says, tangle in a heated fistfight, he stops the action, restages it more plastically [("like statues, like Laocoön")] and wishing it could be cast in bronze, he improvises an inscription for his *tableau vivant*:

[Ah, could we only cast you all in bronze, / place you on a pedestal, with this inscription: / Not shunning pain or charley horse / Well, what does socialism do? Behold—it conquers! (40 / 38)]

Thus the Boss asserts his directorial freedom in relation to workers and actors alike, projecting and controlling alternative choices in the isolated frames of improvised tableaus, divesting actions of their emotional immediacy, and freeing them from irreversible consequences.

Given his stand that the unrehearsed life is not worth living, the Boss sets up a loaded contest between art and life: "I'd like to know who in the end brings home better marks—real life or my theater" (26 / 25). From the Boss's point of view the revolutionary events outside his theater, indecisively taking shape in the streets, are absurdly ineffectual and meaningful only as source material for his play in which the outcome is certain: his plebeians will be victorious. Having mockingly directed actors and workers in a protest demonstration on his rehearsal stage, he comments: "By showing what should not take place, we can make clear what the revolution demands" (50 / 49). From the workers' point of view, the playacting is inconsequential tomfoolery while the real action is out in the streets, where their colleagues are marching in ever-lengthening columns; in the streets rage is boiling over while in the theater mere dust is being stirred up, as the Boss's leading lady (modeled on Helene Weigel) puts the case for moving from the theater into the streets.[12]

In the course of the contest between rehearsed and unrehearsed actions, between the theater Boss and the construction workers, both sides prove recalcitrant to efforts at conversion. The workers cooperate only up to a point to lend contemporary authenticity to the Boss's staging of Roman street scenes and then they depart from the script and almost hang the director in a bit of Brechtian gallows humor. On the other hand, the Boss appears to cooperate with the workers up to a point—despite his mockery—producing an ambivalent manifesto for them; yet he shies away from any decisive commitment to the workers' revolution. While he is accused of seeking to recast masons into actors, he complains that everyone is intent upon molding him into a saber-rattling hero. That is, workers and actors alike seek to cast him as Coriolanus, the warrior-hero who singlemindedly serves his country by his sword. Although the Boss continually parodies this role, remaining impervious to appeals to put his talents in the service of the revolution while everyone around him is hypnotically pulled into the rows of marching, chanting workers, ultimately even he, the skeptical ironist, is for a moment seduced by the echo of his own voice. A Brechtian Saint Joan (nameless in Grass's play, identified merely as a hairdresser)[13] takes the center of the stage to eulogize her "rain-drenched hero," a mini-Coriolanus, wounded and bleeding, who has braved police bullets to cut down the Communist flag at the Brandenburg Gate. Like the Roman Volumnia, the Berlin hairdresser glories in battle scars, in heroic action, even heroic death.

For a brief moment, the Boss is, like Coriolanus, swayed by a woman's emotional appeal against his own convictions; he is tempted by the role she offers him, to join her, his heroine, in the street, mounting the barricades, annihilating tanks. But this romantic dream remains in the rehearsal stage, a mere preview, since before it can be carried out, Russian tanks have crushed the revolt, and martial law has been declared. And for the first time since the masons interrupted his rehearsal, the Boss discovers not the bungling absurdity but the deep pathos of the aborted revolt; his mockery turns into lyrical soliloquy as he reviews his seemingly well-justified aloofness as guilty betrayal:

> [Benighted children pray to a dove: / "Come Holy Spirit, visit us" / Come, my dove, come reason. / Come, Holy Spirit, you the first atheist, / don't bother about stairs—take the emergency door; / ply me with hard stage props. / I, knowing, cunning, cool, alone / joined in for almost a poem long. / . . . / The Holy Spirit breathed. / I took it for a draft, / cried: who intrudes! (91–92 / 94–95).]

He rewinds the tape of the rehearsal session but he cannot wipe out the workers' voices echoing in his mind, the voice of the old socialist, for example, who had said to him: "You can't stand aside and watch. You have to pay" (67 / 70).

In playing out the contest between inartistic revolution in the street and artistic revolution on the stage to the bitter end, Grass's chief satiric target — though by no means the only target — is the aesthetic detachment of the artist-spectator witnessing an emotionally charged unaesthetic calamity. The Boss's dramaturgical method of exploiting the workers' clumsy revolutionary moves for updating his plebeians is savagely parodied toward the end of the play after the uprising has collapsed in bloodshed. One of the Boss's assistants, who had joined the workers in the streets battling against tanks while the Boss solved the problem of how to reinforce the Roman tribunes, proposes to explore the brutal scenes he has witnessed as material for a new stage production. He wields the Boss's ironic rhetoric to taunt the Boss: ["Source material! Material for three plays and one adaptation! Boss: You were absolutely right. Your theory was vindicated: we can work, adapt, rehearse, and keep our goddamn cool" (94 / 96)].

He brushes aside his colleague's reminder that men were killed out in the street as irrelevant to the job at hand, the sifting and testing of all the newly gathered material. There are technical problems to be solved: Can the cross section of a Soviet tank form the setting for a play? Can the demolition of tanks be shown on the open stage? In this bitter parody of Brecht's method, Grass exposes the modern artist's guilty uneasiness over converting the horrendous events of our time into an evening's entertainment. Is it morally justifiable to dramatize the inexpressible brutality of concentration camps? While Brecht believed that he could use the theater to demonstrate the "resistible" power of such facts as Hitler's tyranny, Grass makes no such claims. His Brecht surrogate in the end refrains from reshaping the failed revolt into a didactic play (Lehrstück). (Grass, however, is more Brechtian than his Brecht and completes the political transformation of Coriolanus into a didactic play in The Plebeians Rehearse the Uprising.)

"Irony and radicalism," Thomas Mann once wrote, "this is an alternative and an Either-Or. An intelligent man has the choice (if he has it) to be either ironical or radical."[14] If Günter Grass ironically exposes the culpability of a great ironist, he also uses that ironist to express his equally ironic view of the radical alternative. On any June seventeenth the alternative to the Brechtian detached, rational scrutiny of principles and actions is the blind yielding to contagious anger and violence. Repeatedly Grass stresses the contrast between the theater Boss's knowing suspension of a decision on how and to what extent he will participate in the workers' uprising and the workers' unknowing, undirected, precipitate mass action. The Boss is Grass's spokesman when he ridicules the workers for their failure to project the reactions they may set in motion by their strike and their demonstration. They play it all by ear. Against their shortsighted improvised revolt, milling about the streets without a plan, Grass sets the farseeing director's practical questions: Have you taken over the radio station and issued a call for a general strike? Will the police look the other way? Have you assured the Soviet Government that you will keep to socialism? And what if tanks move in? (29 / 28–29).

The expert theoretician has quickly taken in the entire situation—its disastrous neglect of foresight. (The questions have gained additional pertinence since they were written through the events in Prague in 1968 and in Gdańsk in 1970.) In the Boss's ironic eyes the workers' rebellion is a poor show, the exact analogue to the indecisive revolt of the plebeians in Shakespeare's *Coriolanus*, which he seeks to change. "I know his thesis," says his assistant; "No muddleheaded revolters but conscious revolutionaries is what he wants" (9 / 6). The Boss believes in revolution executed with the immaculate craftsmanship of art. Grass thus plays off Brechtian art, which aimed at long-range enlightenment and transformation of society, against unenlightened short-range upheaval; rationally directed, reversible speculations against irrational, planless, irreversible deeds. Grass's satiric rehearsal declines to provide us with comfortable choices, neat alternatives.

The multidirectional impact of Grass's satire is well-illustrated in the ironic manifesto the Boss composes for the workers' delegation, which while gently mocking the workers also sharply impugns the Stalinist East German government. Once more Grass resorts to the rehearsal motif. On his *Coriolanus* set, with Roman tribunes intermingling with German strike leaders, the Boss dictates his pronouncement—["my contribution"]—addressed to Ulbricht:

> [Comrade Secretary, you must not shoot; / this folk festival is not worth the bloodshed. / The citizens only want to test / whether the streets are wide enough / in case it really comes to a revolt. / Then they'll obediently go home to mother / to gobble twelve potato pancakes. (72–73)]

So far the workers are the satiric target. Impersonating Coriolanus, the Boss mocks them for being pusillanimous, merely staging a tryout for revolution, caring more about their stomachs than about political principles. But halfway through his manifesto comes the ironic turn:

> [But this much, Comrade is established: / For an unparalleled revolt / the streets, the squares, do terribly suffice! / . . . And if your people do not suit you, / then elect yourself some other that suit you better. (72–73 / 73)]

Here the target is Ulbricht, the oppressive representative of an oppressive regime. And here Grass reverses the previous implications of the rehearsal metaphor. If June 17 were to be viewed as an isolated, impromptu holiday from work it would be no threat to the totalitarian state. But when seen as a rehearsal, the anomalous incident becomes an ominous preparation for a more carefully staged future general strike.

While Brecht in fact did not write a comparable document, Grass borrows the last lines of his fictitious manifesto from Brecht's poem "Die Lösung" (The Solution).[15] He alludes to the title in the Boss's remark that he is offering the suspicious workers a "solution" that really ought to be transmitted to the government. Brecht's own modest proposal of how the government might deal with the people who it claimed had betrayed the government's trust was widely circulated in East and West Berlin shortly after the June uprising. Brecht neither acknowledged nor disclaimed his authorship, typical of the delicate course he steered between angry provocation and spineless approbation of the government that financed his theater.

If the workers do not rehearse knowingly enough and the Boss rehearses all too knowingly, the East German government represses all unauthorized rehearsal. Grass clearly suggests these contrasts earlier in the play in relation to the Boss's speech affirming that all activities need to be rehearsed:

> [Listen: in bed, the pleasure of love, / later baptism, troublesome death, / war, peace—all have to be rehearsed. / The rabbit chase, football games, / even chaos must be rehearsed; / chance, hiccups, magic tricks, / the saint must rehearse miracles, / the plebeians' uprising must be rehearsed. (59–60 / 60)]

Here the Boss's position that all the world's a stage on which all parts must be rehearsed becomes a political argument. The Boss's speech is directed at his Communist rival, a strict party-liner, who suggests that what is being rehearsed in the Boss's theater is a putsch—which is of course partly true. To him the uprising is the work of western agents, provocateurs, much as in the Polish uprising in 1970 when government functionaries attributed all unrest to "anarchist hooligans." Presumably workers never rebel against a workers' state. And the party mouthpiece has his own notion of dramatic decorum: What good is theater, he asks, when the people disregard direction and act on their own? (59 / 59). Although the striking workers' delegates interpret the Boss's ironic detachment from their cause as a sign of his solidarity with the party bosses, Grass here clearly distinguishes the Brechtian from the Stalinist orientation toward art and society, pointing to both through the rehearsal analogue. He sets the antitotalitarian emphasis of Brecht's method of critical experimentation with all ideas and activities against the Stalinist method, advocated by Ulbricht's spokesman, which prescribes unalterable official formulas for everything from brewing beer to writing plays.

Nevertheless the Brechtian Boss remains a figure sufficiently contradictory and ambivalent so that his behavior can be arbitrarily interpreted, much as the uprising could prove grist for all propagandistic mills. The Boss's leading lady, who adjusts convictions as readily as makeup, plays the sibyl predicting Brecht's fate: ["And legends will spread around you: actually he was against. Rather for, actually. That's what he said but his heart was — where actually? Everyone will see you as he pleases: a cynical opportunist; a common brand of idealist; he thought only about his theater; he wrote and thought for the people. Which people?" (104 / 107)].

The Boss finally abandons his playful conversion of the workers' actions into stage effects for *Coriolanus*; he abandons, too, his godlike invulnerability and analyzes the all too human role he has played: ["Shall I write: congratulations to the commendable murderers of the people? Or congratulations to the ignorant survivors of a feeble uprising? And what congratulations will reach the dead? — I, capable of only small, embarrassed words, remained a spectator. Masons, railroad workers, welders and cable winders remained alone" (104 / 108)]. With equal sharpness, his "farseeing eye" now takes the measure of the future consequences of this event which intruded upon his theater. He foresees the "face of hypocrisy" of West Germany, mouthing slogans of freedom, distorting the workers' cause into anti-Communist propaganda, turning horror into holiday. And he foresees the East ruthlessly incarcerating the leaders of the uprising and distributing a heavy burden of guilt: ["Here, however, the penitentiaries will disgorge the wreckage of this uprising. Denunciation will make the rounds. It will address and mail many packages of guilt. Our package has already arrived" (105 / 108)].

Thus Grass adds to his satiric rehearsal a tragic perspective. He gave his play the subtitle "A German Tragedy" (*ein deutsches Trauerspiel*), leaving it an open question whether he claimed to have written a tragedy or whether plebeians rehearsing an uprising is a tragic game Germans play. The tragic sense of inevitable suffering dawns on the protagonist only retrospectively, only after the event. Having recognized the full implications of his rehearsal of invulnerable aesthetic solutions while, concurrently, vulnerable men and women paid for their revolutionary attempt with terror, imprisonment, and death, the Boss retires from the theater world. The day's progress has called in doubt his convictions on art and moral responsibility. Where only a few hours earlier, he says, he stood on solid ground, he now finds gaping cracks. Whereas earlier he had commanded a large arsenal of invective, he now lacks a single term that would take the measure of the principal actors on this great stage of fools. He abdicates his playcraft, like Prospero relinquishing his power of enchantment. He is not deposed but deposes himself.[16]

As he sweeps the stage clear of the *Coriolanus* props and theater staff, he and the audience are left confronting an empty world, unilluminated and unformulated. In this emptiness the Boss's final words reverberate, much as the workers' accusations resound in the Boss's own mind: ["Hereafter to live with voices in my ear: You. You. I'll tell you what you are. Do you know what you are? You are, you, you are. . . . Ignorant ones, you ignorant ones! Guilt-ridden, I accuse you" (107 / 111)]. Grass has here plundered the last section of one of Brecht's confessional lyrics that expressed his private guilt about the uprising:

> [Last night in a dream I saw fingers pointing at me / As at a leper. They were gnarled by work and / They were broken. / "Ignorant ones," cried I / Guilt-ridden. (*Gedichte,* VII, 11)]

Günter Grass's adaptation of these lines enlarges the circle of guilt to encompass not only Brecht but all "ignorant survivors" of the seventeenth of June.

Notes

1. Günter Grass, "The Prehistory and Posthistory of the Tragedy of *Coriolanus*. . . ," in *The Plebeians Rehearse the Uprising,* trans. Ralph Manheim (New York: Harcourt, Brace & World, 1966), p. viii.

2. "A Short Organum for the Theatre," in *Brecht on Theatre,* trans. John Willett (New York: Hill & Wang, 1964), pp. 193, 191.

3. *Die Plebejer proben den Aufstand* (Berlin: Luchterhand, 1966), p. 8. All subsequent references to the text of Grass's play are to this edition, cited by page number since the lines are not numbered. The translations are my own and are intended to be as faithful to the German as possible, without any attempt at approximating Grass's rhythms. His terse idiom is as difficult to render adequately as is Brecht's language. [Ed. note: Page references are given in the text in parentheses and in double form. Numbers before the slash refer to the German text; numbers after the slash refer the reader, for purposes of comparison, to Ralph Manheim's translation (see fn. 1).]

4. The workers' report of all the developments on June 17 abounds in specific details and quotations Grass borrows from the compilation of eyewitness accounts by Joachim Leithäuser, *Der Aufstand im Juni, ein dokumentarischer Bericht* (Berlin: Grunewald, 1954).

5. "The Prehistory," in *The Plebeians,* p. xxxv.

6. The Royal Shakespeare Company performed *The Plebeians Rehearse the Uprising* in its London season of 1970. Apart from a few student productions in England and America, the play had not been performed in an English version previous to the London premiere on July 21, 1970. Although both the German premiere of January 15, 1966, in Berlin and the London production were widely reviewed and vigorously debated by theater critics, I know of only one detailed analysis of Grass's play, James Redmond's "Günter Grass and 'Der Fall Brecht,' " *Modern Language Quarterly,* 32 (Dec. 1971), 387–400. Redmond illuminatingly traces parallels between Grass's own dilemma and Brecht's—the dilemma of the modern artist of the Left who seeks to preserve his political independence and artistic integrity.

7. On the rehearsal tradition see Robert J. Nelson, *Play Within a Play. The Dramatist's Conception of His Art: Shakespeare to Anouilh* (New Haven: Yale Univ. Press, 1958); Anne Righter, *Shakespeare and the Idea of the Play* (London: Chatto & Windus, 1962). A number of dramatists have found the rehearsal play or the play within a play congenial to a wide range of themes in recent works. See, e.g., Anouilh's *Pauvre Bites, ou, le dîner de têtes,* Beckett's *Krapp's Last Tape,* and Heller's *We Bombed in New Haven.* Combining the rehearsal play with historical documentary, the closest analogue to Grass's play is Weiss's *Die*

Verfolgung und Ermordung Jean Paul Marats dargestellt durch die Schauspieltruppe des Hospizes zu Charenton unter Anleitung des Herrn de Sade.

8. "Short Description of a New Technique of Acting which Produces an Alienation Effect," in *Brecht on Theatre*, p. 137.

9. "A Short Organum for the Theatre," in *Brecht on Theater*, p. 189.

10. *Baal*, quoted in Martin Esslin, *Bertolt Brecht: A Choice of Evils* (1959; rpt. London: Mercury Books, 1965), p. 228.

11. Cf. Brecht's interesting discussion of training actors to report what their roles call for as if they were eyewitnesses ("The Street Scene: A Basic Model for an Epic Theatre," in *Brecht on Theatre*, pp.212-29).

12. Da draussen kocht die Wut sich Suppen, / Und hier bewegt man Bühnenstaub. . . . (p. 20) (Out there rage boils over like soup / And here we stir up stage dust. . . .)

13. The Boss's dramaturgical expert recognizes the hairdresser as a Brechtian character—life presumably imitating art—and remarks, "She could have been written by you, Boss," to which the Boss replies, "I almost fear she was" (89 / 91). She provides an interesting example of Grass's highly compressed allusions: she not only recalls Brecht's Joan of *Die heilige Johanna der Schlachthöfe* but through her elevated iambic pentameter recalls as well Schiller's Joan of *Die Jungfrau von Orleans*, whom Brecht parodied. In her enthusiasm for martyrdom she also recalls the Brechtian heroine to whom she approvingly refers, the mute halfwit Kattrin of *Mutter Courage* who sacrifices her life in order to warn the defenders of Halle of an impending attack during the Thirty Years War. In his program notes, Brecht had juxtaposed a picture of Kattrin with that of a photograph of a Frenchwoman who had thrown herself in front of a train carrying arms to the war in Vietnam. Grass similarly illuminates the present through allusive juxtapositions.

14. *Betrachtungen eines Unpolitischen*, quoted in Erich Heller, *The Ironic German: A Study of Thomas Mann* (1958; rpt. Cleveland/New York: Meridian, 1961), p. 231.

15. Brecht's poem was published posthumously in *Gedichte* (Frankfurt am Main: Suhrkamp, 1960–65), VII, 9. In deliberately prosaic language Brecht mimics Communist propaganda; he speaks of leaflets distributed after the uprising, proclaiming . . . "that the people / Had forfeited the government's trust / Which only redoubled efforts / Could regain. Would it in that case / Not be simpler if the government / Dissolved the people and / Elected another?"

16. The question of deposing Brecht as the most powerful, most prestigious theater director-author of his time is emphasized toward the end of the play as Kosanke remarks threateningly to the Boss: "And you too are replaceable" (p. 103). Earlier in the play, Grass had slyly applied the possibility of a personality cult to Brecht by hinting at parallels with Coriolanus. Brecht himself, in his notes on *Coriolanus*, insisted on the central importance of examining the social consequences of the hero's belief in his own indispensability. ("Das Vergnügen des Helden," *Gesammelte Werke*, ed. Elisabeth Hauptmann [Frankfurt am Main: Suhrkamp, 1967], VII, 1252-53.) Grass borrowed freely from Brecht's notes for his opening scene of the *Plebeians*, in which Brecht's reinterpretation of Coriolanus is discussed: "The Boss wants to show that Coriolanus is replaceable" (p. 8). In the course of this discussion Grass hints at ironic parallels between Coriolanus' pride and Brecht's.

The Motif of Failure and the Act of Narrating in Günter Grass's *Örtlich betäubt*

James C. Bruce*

The motif of failure and the act of narrating are among the many thematic elements of Günter Grass's fiction. As regards the motif of failure, the existences of central characters in the first three of Grass's major narrative works are significantly marked by frustration and failure. In the novel *Die Blechtrommel* (Neuwied, 1959), Oskar Matzerath ultimately fails in his attempt to overcome the problems and difficulties of his adult existence.[1] In the novella *Katz und Maus* (Neuwied, 1961), the existence of the adolescent main character, Joachim Mahlke, who has been decorated for military heroism in World War II, becomes completely disorganized when he is thwarted in his desire to address an audience of students at his former *Gymnasium*, ostensibly to tell them of the forces that guided him in the performances of his heroic deeds.[2] In the novel *Hundejahre* (Neuwied, 1963), Walter Matern, one of the two central characters, is a generally unsteady and unsuccessful man.[3] As regards the act of narrating, each of these works has a narrator or narrators — the three books of *Hundejahre* are narrated by three different persons — who are obviously conscious of their roles as writers and tellers of a story. Each of their narratives, which is either in form or in essence a first-person narrative,[4] contains some reference to the technique of beginning the story.[5] In *Die Blechtrommel* and in the first book of *Hundejahre*, the narrators Oskar Matzerath and Brauxel (i.e., Eddi Amsel, the other central character of *Hundejahre*) refer on occasion to certain techniques they use to help them reconstruct the particularities of their past for the narratives.[6] In the course of their writing, therefore, Grass's narrators write about their writing. Thus, alongside the various other elements that comprise the content of these works, their content also explicitly concerns the very medium of art that the works themselves represent. Like the earlier works, Grass's most recent novel, *Örtlich betäubt* [*Local Anaesthetic*],[7] also contains the motif of failure and presents the figure of a narrator who is manifestly conscious of his role as a writer and teller of a story. The narrator is also the central character of the novel, and his life, like that of Oskar, Mahlke, and Matern, is significantly marked by frustration and failure. In his narrative, moreover, he not only gives information about the actual process of his writing, or preparing to write, the story of his present, but also tells about the *telling* of an oral story about his ostensible past.

The novel derives its title from the local anesthetic administered to

*Reprinted from *Modern Fiction Studies* 17 (1971):45–60, by permission of *Modern Fiction Studies* and the author. © Purdue Research Foundation, West Lafayette, Indiana 47907.

the narrator-hero, the forty-year-old West Berlin German teacher Eberhard Starusch, by his dentist during treatments in partial correction of a painful congenital malocclusion. Starusch gives a detailed account of these treatments, which occur in two sets of visits to the dentist's office during the latter part of January and the earlier part of February 1967, separated by an interval of about two weeks. As he gives this account, he tells us the story he spun for the dentist about his alleged engagement to the cement heiress Sieglinde Krings, the daughter of former Field Marshall Ferdinand Krings, between 1954 and 1956, while he was ostensibly employed as an industrial engineer at the Krings cement factory in Andernach. We are told of the triangle that arose when the electrician Heinz Schlottau began enjoying the amatory favors of Starusch's fiancée and of Starusch's decision to abandon engineering and turn to the study of German after ending his engagement to Sieglinde. Investigating Starusch's story of his past love life, the dentist finds that there was no Krings factory in the Andernach area, though the Tubag cement factory is located there, and that according to the [employment office] in Andernach, Starusch was not an industrial engineer at the time of his alleged engagement, but merely a student who worked for Tubag during vacations in 1954 and 1955. But though the dentist confronts Starusch with this evidence, Starusch refuses to concede that his story is untrue.

In the course of telling us the story he told the dentist about his ostensible past, he tells us a story about his actual present. This story concerns (a) his relationship to his seventeen-year-old student Philipp Scherbaum, whom he tries to dissuade from the planned burning of Scherbaum's pet dog as a public protest against the use of napalm in Viet Nam, (b) his relationship to Scherbaum's seventeen-year-old girl friend, the revolutionary-minded Veronika Lewand, also Starusch's student, who tries to seduce Starusch in an effort to get him to stop interfering with her boy friend's plan, and finally (c) his relationship to his thirty-nine-year-old colleague, the music teacher Irmgard Seifert, to whom he ultimately becomes engaged. The novel thus comprises a three-fold story, with the account of the dental treatments serving as a framework for the tale of Starusch's ostensible former engagement and the story of his present relationships. Although Starusch tries, in the account of both his past and his present, to put forth an image of himself as he would have himself be, he cannot altogether conceal his truer image as largely a failure, a man who suffers from the pain of a disappointing life and seeks to anesthetize himself against this pain by means of fanciful fictions.

One of Starusch's main failings is a certain inability to carry things through to their proper end, a shortcoming that is especially evident in his references to his unfinished manuscript about the World War II military figure General Schörner, which he regularly calls ["the beginnings,"] and to other unfinished work on the desk in his apartment.[8] This shortcoming is perhaps also reflected in the structure of the concluding section of the third and final part of the narrative. Except for this section, Starusch wrote his narrative in May 1967, about three months after his last dental treatment and some two months after his proposal to Irmgard Seifert.[9] The first sentence of the concluding section, a brief section of eleven sentences, was likewise written at that time. The remaining sentences, however, were not written until some two years after the last treatment, hence about in February 1969. While the first sentence tells what Starusch found on his desk when he came home from that treatment—his unfinished Schörner manuscript—the other sentences, separated from the first by a dash, describe the situation of various characters two years later. Irmgard Seifert is "still engaged," as he puts it, a circumstance that indicates that he has not yet carried his engagement through to its proper end in marriage. The sudden jump of almost two years in the course of the concluding section and the fact that the third part of the narrative is disproportionately shorter than the other two parts suggest that Starusch did not carry his narrative all the way through to its "proper" end at the time when he was originally writing it, but that he stopped at a certain point and simply tacked on an ending two years later. Ironically, the mention of the Schörner manuscript here contains a specific reference to perseverance, a quality that Starusch himself considerably lacks: ["On my desk I found my beginning: the gesture of fighting to the finish—or the Schörner case" (358 / 255)].

Another of Starusch's problems is that of sexual inadequacy. Shortly before he decided to propose to Irmgard Seifert, he tried unsuccessfully to engage in sexual intercourse with this willing woman: [" 'I admit, Doc, that after two hours of strenuous effort that first attempt to include sex in relations with Irmgard Seifert proved a failure. And yet, when we were smoking again, she said: "It won't prevent me from loving you. We must be patient with one another" ' " (332 / 237)]. Besides this explicit instance of impotence with Irmgard, it is intimated that Starusch also proved inadequate when he succumbed to the enticement of his student Veronika Lewand. In his first account of the seduction he quotes Veronika as saying: [" 'C'mon, Old Hardy! Or can't you make it?' " (291 / 208).] But in a later reference to the incident he changes the question to a statement and quotes her as saying: [" 'Aw, come on, Old Hardy! You probably can't. . .' " (326 / 232).] Moreover, he attributes his impotence with Irmgard to visions of Veronika and Sieglinde plotting against him (332 / 237). Since the dentist exposes Starusch's story of his engagement as largely, if not altogether, imaginary,[10] the reference to Sieglinde's plotting against him on the occasion with Irmgard suggests that he has long been haunted by the question of his sexual adequacy, despite his claim of having had intercourse not only with Sieglinde (141 / 112), but also with her two friends, Inge and Hilde (109 / 81).

Starusch is seldom any more successful in other endeavors than in amatory matters. His attempt to pass himself off to the dentist as a sometime brilliant engineer is exposed by the dentist's investigations. He tries to represent himself to the dentist also as a radical revolutionary, but is forced to recant his advocacy of violence when the dentist threatens to treat his teeth without anesthetic if he does not recant (134–37 / 98–100). Since Starusch finds it necessary to invent a fanciful story about his past, a story of failure for all his efforts to glorify himself, his past life must have been deeply disappointing indeed, as he himself indicates in referring to the "Sieglinde" story as a "Lamento" (14 / 13).

As a seventeen-year-old during World War II, Starusch was the leader of a gang of juvenile delinquents known as the "Dusters" (15–16 / 14).[11] He romanticizes his youthful delinquency into a form of anti-Nazi resistance (16 / 14), however, and constantly tries to hold himself up as a model for Scherbaum. While he does thereby make an impression on the youth, it is not the intended one, for when Scherbaum finally abandons his planned demonstration, he does so not because of Starusch's positive efforts at dissuasion, but because he decides he does not want to go around later as a forty-year-old with the deeds of a seventeen-year-old, as Starusch is doing (307 / 219).

In his student Scherbaum, Starusch would like to see a reflection of himself as both a would-be radical and a failure. In telling the dentist of unsuccessfully trying to persuade Scherbaum to assume the editorship of the school newspaper, he falsely imputes anarchism to Scherbaum (16 / 14). Scherbaum refuses to assume the editorship not because of radicalism, however, but simply because he feels that student co-responsibility should imply student co-determination (8 / 9). Similarly, Scherbaum's plan to burn his pet is not anarchistic, but merely sacrificial. He contemplates sacrificing the dog because he feels that Berliners, who seem to care more about dogs than about people, will be more moved by that type of demonstration than by some other act (174 / 125, 230 / 136). While Scherbaum is much opposed to Chancellor Kiesinger because of Kiesinger's former affiliation with the Nazi party, there is nothing anarchistic about his opposition, as is shown by the fact that after Scherbaum finally does take over the editorship (though not because of Starusch's persuasion), he yields to the objections of other members of the editorial staff to his wish to satirize Kiesinger in his first article (325 / 232). Rather than being an anarchist or a radical, as Starusch tries to suggest, Scherbaum is merely a young man deeply concerned about current affairs like many others of his generation. He specifically disclaims any anarchistic intentions (269 / 192), and Starusch himself says, at one point, that not even Scherbaum's friendship with Veronika could radicalize him (211–12 / 152).

Wishing to see Scherbaum as a failure like himself, Starusch intimates that a projected comic-strip adaptation of Schiller's play *Die Räuber* [*The Robbers*] by Scherbaum and Veronika will not materialize because Scherbaum has no patience, but only ideas (47 / 36). When Starusch learns from the dentist that Scherbaum has given up the idea of burning the dog and has decided to take over the editorship of the paper and, further, that he has also decided to have his teeth corrected — like Starusch, Scherbaum also has a faulty occlusion, but his is not congenital — Starusch maintains that Scherbaum will fail to see the treatments through to the end and that he will moreover prove a disappointment with the paper (308 / 220). Starusch bases his assumptions on what he calls Scherbaum's proven lack of staying power: ["No staying power. He's just proved it" (308 / 220).] The "proof" of deficient staying power to which Starusch alludes is Scherbaum's decision to give up the idea of burning the dog. The aspersions about Scherbaum's perseverance and potential editorship, which refer to the very things Starusch has been ostensibly trying to get Scherbaum to do, reveal Starusch's annoyance at the prospect of Scherbaum's taking resolute action. Accordingly, they betray Starusch's malicious desire to see his own failings reflected in his student.

Starusch's nature as a failure is mirrored in the condition of his teeth. The tartar that builds up on his teeth is described by the dentist as an accumulation of hatred resulting from past failures and producing in turn a latent store of violence (40 / 31). Under the influence of the local anesthetic during the treatments and the palliative Arantil prescribed to alleviate the pain that lingers in his teeth after each treatment, Starusch engages in the wildest flights of fancy, in which he often imagines himself causing the death of his ostensible former fiancée either through outright murder or by less direct means. The temporary obviation of the pain in Starusch's teeth thus causes latent thoughts of violence occasioned by past frustration to surface in his consciousness and vent themselves innocuously in homicidal fictions.

With the partial correction of the condition of his teeth, an improvement in his nature seems also to occur. He is able to proceed much farther with his writing of his narrative, which was begun after the completion of his dental work, than he had been able to do earlier with his Schörner manuscript and other unfinished work. After his dental work has been completed, he is also able to bring himself to propose to Irmgard Seifert and thus, as he ambiguously puts it, to have contact with her in a way that seemed relatively satisfactory to both of them: ["Three weeks after my dental treatment, three weeks after, my bite corrected, I tried to ascertain certain other changes in myself — I managed for the first time to have intercourse with Irmgard Seifert in a manner that seemed relatively satisfactory to both of us — three weeks after the dentist's intervention . . . I proposed to Irmgard Seifert" (339 / 242)]. The idea of proposing to her occurred to him as he was undergoing his final treatment (342 / 244) and was winding up the story of his ostensible engagement. With the improvement of his dental condition, he progresses, as it were, from an ostensible engagement to Sieglinde to an actual one to Irmgard. Two years, more or less, after his engagement to Irmgard, however, he still has not married her, and it seems unlikely that he ever will, for, after all, his dental condition has been only partially corrected. Just as his malocclusion, being congenital, cannot be altogether corrected, so his nature as a failure is unlikely to be completely overcome. At the end of the novel, two years after his treatments, his teeth are acting up again, causing Starusch to observe that there will always be new pains: ["Nothing lasts. There will always be new pain" (358 / 255).] He will continue to be something of a disappointment.

In telling the dentist of his ostensible engagement to Sieglinde, Starusch, inspired by the television that the dentist has in his office to divert patients during their treatments, spins his story as though he were staging a television production. He speaks, for instance, of the ["little production" (13 / 12)] as he is working up to the "Sieglinde" story proper, discusses technical aspects of his "production," and even asks the dentist's opinion about the handling of a scene (48 / 37). Thus the motif of narration, the act of narrating as an element of the content in *Örtlich betäubt*, is in part developed imaginally in association with another form of literary art, the drama.[12] In spinning the story for the dentist, Starusch is not only engaged in one kind of creativity, but is quite conscious of being so engaged and makes that consciousness especially evident by presenting this particular creative activity in terms of the conceiving of a television play. In his written narrative, he shows himself recording notes, from time to time, that contain material that ultimately becomes part of the story line of the written narrative, as over against the oral narrative, which is itself of course told about and retold in the written one. The first of these notes, recorded late at night after a party at which Starusch had seen Irmgard after the second dental treatment, contains the words: ["Let's see what keeps silent in the suitcase" (67 / 51)], and concerns Irmgard, who has been tormented by feelings of guilt caused by her recent discovery, in a trunk at her mother's house, of some pro-Nazi letters she had written during World War II. Elevated, by means of Arantil tablets, out of a self-pitying engrossment in the "Sieglinde" story that persists even away from the dentist's office, Starusch, on the morning after the recording of the first note, expresses the feeling that he has cast off defeat: ["Thanks to Arantil . . . I was free from pain and inspired by the side effects as I wrote: Our defeats lie behind us. Now let us reflect and gain" (72 / 54)]. He thereupon decides to apply his "self-interrogation" — like the reference to defeat, an allusion to the "Sieglinde" story — to the "private case" of Irmgard: ["But then two tablets helped me to deliver my Sunday soul-searching to a female colleague's private problems . . . for if Irmgard Seifert hadn't found those letters, she would be happier" (72 / 54–55)]. In this elevated mood, he records a further note about Irmgard's mother's house and Irmgard's apartment (73 / 55). Since he has been inspired to spin an oral story to the dentist and has already continued that tale through two treatments, his act of recording notes about Irmgard and about such things as her apartment and her mother's house and his allusions to the "Sieglinde" story in connection with these notes suggest that he has now been motivated to try his hand at another kind of creativity and undertake a written narrative and that he has in mind writing about Irmgard.

In the interval between the two sets of dental treatments, as he becomes increasingly involved with Scherbaum, who approached him about the planned burning of the dog right after the completion of the first set of treatments, Starusch begins recording notes about him, adding these notes to those he has been accumulating about Irmgard. Thus he observes, after reporting a telephone conversation with the dentist in which the dentist inquired about his supply of Arantil, that he not only had Arantil, but also notes piled on notes. It would seem, therefore, that in the course of his involvement with Scherbaum, which leads to a series of other involvements, his intended story grows more and more into a story of these entanglements. To write about Scherbaum, he must include Veronika Lewand, with whom he has become involved through Scherbaum, and the dentist, whom he has brought into contact with Scherbaum.[13] Through Starusch, Irmgard, who is also Scherbaum's teacher, is drawn into the Scherbaum matter. At first repelled by Scherbaum's plan, Irmgard subsequently comes to view it as a potential redemptive act for the failings of herself and her generation (268 / 192), so that in attempting to dissuade Scherbaum from his plan, Starusch must deal not only with Scherbaum and Veronika, but also with Irmgard, who is likewise on Scherbaum's side.[14] When Scherbaum gives up his plan, Irmgard loses interest in him, and shortly after this the romance develops between her and Starusch. With all these entanglements, Starusch's intended written story accordingly becomes a lamentation about himself, an account of past and present failures.

An explicit linkage of the failure motif and the act of narrating occurs when Starusch, recounting an episode in which he was glancing at stories in an illustrated magazine in the dentist's anteroom while waiting for a heavy dose of anesthetic to take effect, observes that failures and rejects invent enemies and stories in which the invented enemies are killed: ["Failures and rejects. . . . They invent enemies and histories in which their invented enemies actually occur and are liquidated" (96 / 72)]. This observation, which aptly describes the homicidal fictions invented by Starusch under the narcotizing influence of the anesthetic or the pain-killing Arantil, follows a statement in which Starusch wonders what might have happened if Hitler, who desired to become a painter, had not failed to gain admission to the Vienna Academy of Art. The motif of narration is also combined with the motif of painting again in the account of the final dental treatment. Having grown tired of the "Sieglinde" story, the dentist refuses to hear anything more about a triangle involving Starusch, Sieglinde, and Schlottau. Starusch thereupon tells him about a seventeenth-century Danzig painter named Anton Möller, whom a supposed love triangle helped to achieve an allegorical painting about sin and salvation, and likens himself and his "Sieglinde" story to Möller and Möller's painting (347–50 / 247–49). Thus it is suggested not only that Starusch himself is to be viewed, at least in part, as an artist figure, but also that his creator, the twentieth-century, Danzig-born author Günter Grass, has intended *Örtlich betäubt* to be in part an allegory about "sin" and "salvation" in the creative life.

The nature of Starusch's creativity leads toward a possible partial interpretation of this allegory. Starusch's creativity is characterized by a talent for free invention and a dualism between the use of vicarious, imagined experience, on the one hand, and the use of actual experience and lived reality, on the other hand. The tale that Starusch tells orally to the dentist is an extemporized narrative that especially exhibits his talent for free invention on the basis of imagined experience. As over against the extemporized oral tale, his written narrative is an account of his lived reality. Since his talent for free invention, a talent that is heightened by the anesthetic and the Arantil, is also part of his reality, he writes of his own reality when he recounts the telling of the oral story and when he records the wild, obvious flights of fancy in which he imagines himself causing Sieglinde's death.

In comparing himself with the painter Möller, Starusch claims to have made three artistic "compromises" in his "Sieglinde" story, just as Möller did in his painting, namely, (a) that he changed to Krings the surname of the unspecified figure whom he used as the prototype for Sieglinde's father, while retaining the forename Ferdinand, (b) that he disguised Sieglinde by placing her and her father in the milieu of the cement industry, and (e) that he discreetly concealed an affair involving the married dentist and the dentist's female assistant by never mentioning them by name.[15] These "compromises" suggest that three factors in particular, besides the dentist's television set, led Starusch to begin to extemporize the tale of his ostensible former engagement: (1) an intention, not yet fulfilled, to write a historical essay about General Schörner, (2) a painful memory of a frustrated passion, and (3) a seemingly unwarranted suspicion of an affair between the dentist and the dentist's female assistant. The reference to changing the last name of Krings's prototype while keeping the first name and the striking parallels between Krings and the historical figure of Schörner point clearly to Schörner as the prototype for Krings.[16] Similarities between Sieglinde and Monika Lindrath, the daughter of the dentist in Andernach of whom Starusch's dentist inquired about Starusch's alleged engagement, suggest that Monika is the prototype for Sieglinde.[17] If Starusch had a frustrated passion for Monika during his student days, as evidence seems to indicate, then in placing Sieglinde and her father in the milieu of the cement industry around Andernach, Starusch has put them at the place where his unrequited passion for

Monika occurred.[18] The suspicion of an affair between the dentist and the assistant, for which Starusch offers no substantiation, appears to be simply a figment of Starusch's imagination. If Monika Lindrath is indeed the object of Starusch's former passion, then it seems likely that on his first visit to the dentist's office the presence of the assistant brings to his mind Monika, a dentist's daughter, and quickens the memory of his passion for her, the pain of which has lain freshly-preserved in the deepfreeze of his mind, as it were, to be thawed out and used at an appropriate time.[19] It seems further likely that Starusch, in an erotic fantasy, imagines the dentist as his competitor for the Monika-figure suggested by the assistant and, inspired by the imposing electrical equipment in the office,[20] derives the figure of the electrician Schlottau for a fancied amatory triangle.[21] From the recollection of a painful experience in his past, a recollection quickened, in likelihood, by the presence of the dentist's assistant, and from the long-pestering thought of his unfinished work on the Schörner manuscript[22] — from the lived reality, that is, of a specific frustration in the past and a still unrealized hope of a particular success in the present — Starusch proceeds to extemporize a fanciful web of vicarious experience in the form of a story about a brilliant engineering career prematurely terminated by a disappointment in love.

The dualism of imagined and lived experience in Starusch's creativity is reminiscent of the dualistic typology of modern poets set forth by Grass in his essay "Das Gelegenheitsgedicht" ["The Occasional Poem"][23] and suggests for Örtlich betäubt as an allegorical novel about artistry an interpretation in terms of this typology. In his essay Grass distinguishes between poets who produce poems by experimenting with the "raw material" of language as in a laboratory, whom he calls ["Laboratory poets"], and those whose poems are occasioned by actual personal experience, whom he calls ["occasional poets"].[24] The ["laboratory poet"], as Grass describes him, lacks a muse and puts together and hashes up whatever he pleases, experimenting constantly with whatever combinations of elements suggest themselves, while the ["occasional poet"], who has a muse and is dependent on it, not only has to have his poems occasioned by lived reality, but works his poems out on the basis of things which he has himself witnessed or lived through or of which he has firsthand knowledge.[25] For the ["occasional poet"], Grass indicates, the experiencing of pain is often necessary to please the muse that furthers his inspiration, while the ["laboratory poet"] simply works in comfort and painlessness. In Grass's aesthetic theory, imagination plays an important role, of course, but he is against the use of imagination irrespective of one's actual, first-hand experience, as is often the case with the ["laboratory poet"]. Such a use of the imagination is, for Grass, an aesthetic shortcoming, signifying a lack of disciplined artistry required for the highest creative treatment of lived, as against merely vicarious, experience.[26]

In terms of the ["laboratory/occasional poet"] dualism, Starusch may be viewed as mainly a ["laboratory poet"] type of narrator who has something of the ["occasional poet"] in him. Like the ["laboratory poet"] he develops his "Sieglinde" story largely on the basis of vicarious experience and experiments with whatever combination of elements his imagination brings to mind. As opposed to the ["occasional poet"], his creativity is especially associated with the alleviation of pain, rather than with the experiencing of it.[27] He is led to spin his "Sieglinde" story precisely in the dentist's office, where he has gone for relief from pain. The obviation of pain through the local anesthetic and Arantil causes his creative faculties to thrive. Only under the influence of Arantil is it possible for him to record the notes about Irmgard and Scherbaum. By the time of the actual writing of his narrative, however, he is free of the pain in his teeth and therefore no longer needs Arantil.[28] But while the act of creating, in Starusch's case, is associated with the alleviation of pain, what he creates concerns his own experiencing of pain. To this extent he has something of the ["occasional poet"] in him.

Insofar as Starusch is a ["laboratory poet"], he is devoid of a muse. The element of ["occasional poet"] in him suggests, however, that although he at first lacks a muse, he desires one and that in this desire he invents one for himself in the figure of Sieglinde until, while the improvement in his nature signified by the improvement in his teeth, hence with the increment of the ["occasional poet"] element in him, he is able to cultivate an actual one, of a sort, in Irmgard. But in contrast to the decidedly spirited and determined Sieglinde, with whom as just an imaginary fiancée Starusch could not manage,[29] Irmgard is bland and indecisive. Yet even with so vapid a figure as Irmgard, Starusch is capable of a relationship that is only "relatively satisfying," as he said of his engagement to her. Though somewhat improved, Starusch is still, as it were, an artist incapable of altogether satisfactory intercourse with a muse, even an insipid one. Just as Starusch's malocclusion is congenital and therefore cannot be completely corrected, so as an artist figure he is inherently a ["laboratory poet"] type who will never become completely [an "occasional poet"]. He will always represent something less than complete aesthetic success.

In *Örtlich betäubt*, as in earlier works, Grass has combined a treatment of the problem of creativity, specifically the motif of the act of narrating, with a treatment of social, political, and moral questions. The figure of Starusch as a teacher of German and "therefore history," as Starusch describes himself (16 / 14), serves as a vehicle for treating such topical matters as activism, protest, the *engagement* of contemporary youth, radicalism and revolution as against moderateness and evolution, the Viet Nam War, and the "generation gap." The figure of Starusch as the spinner of a fanciful tale about his past and the writer of a narrative about both his actual present and his fictionalized past serves as a vehicle for treating the theme of creativity. A complex work of many significances,

Grass's latest work presents a hero who is by and large a disappointment. As a pedagogue, he is unsuccessful in influencing his favorite student and indeed only causes the young man to wish not to be like him. As the imaginary lover of a fictitious fiancée, he invents a competitor to rationalize the ever-present spectre of inadequacy that haunts him even in his fancy. As the betrothed of a real fiancée, he is unable, in the course of nearly two years, to bring his engagement to its logical end in marriage. In his attempts to present would-be versions of himself to his dentist he is frustrated. As the writer of a planned historical work, he cannot seem to get beyond the beginning of it. And as an artist figure, he represents largely that type whose mode of creativity Grass considers to be fundamentally flawed. He is indeed a man for whom, as he himself says, there will always be new pains.

Örtlich betäubt poses a question similar to that which Robert H. Spaethling sees in *Katz und Maus*, the question of the "function, value, and moral effectiveness of an art which appears to be inextricably bound to the inadequacies of its time with little hope that it will morally or aesthetically improve the artist or his time."[30] This question, which in Spaethling's view is answered indirectly in *Katz und Maus* by the very act of writing the novella and directly in *Hundejahre*, "where the act of narrating is seen with grim but hopeful irony as an act of sheer self-preservation,"[31] is also answered in Grass's latest novel. If *Hundejahre* holds forth a grim but ironic hope, this hope appears more positive in *Örtlich betäubt*, for Starusch undergoes an improvement. Here the act of narrating implies the necessity of ultimately facing up to the truth about oneself and one's time and exposing one's lived realities and the realities on one's time in all their paradoxes, contradictions, absurdities, and insufficiencies. As a "laboratory" artist in a "laboratory" age, the modern technological era, Starusch is a modern writer. But in this age of the laboratory, an age in which astonishing technological advancements have been accompanied by an appalling dehumanization of the spirit, an art that tends merely to experiment with itself and fails to ground itself constantly in the lived realities, as over against wishful fictions, is likely but to continue the moral and spiritual questionability of the times. This is an implication of the ["laboratory/occasional poet"] dualism in Grass's aesthetic theory.

Starusch is able to face up to the reality of his lived, as against his merely imagined, experience only to the extent that the pain of that reality is removed by a correction of the source of the pain. While pain-killing agents may bring relief for the time being, they do not remove the source of the pain. Although the local anesthetic and the Arantil stimulate Starusch's creativity, they do so largely in the direction of ideas of violence. Thus they represent potentially destructive forces and promote in Starusch the paradox of a destructive creativity. Constructiveness, however, is represented by a correction at the source of the pain. The paradox of a destructive creativity is also the great paradox of modern technology, hence one of the great problems of the age. In one sense creative, technology has become more and more damaging to the very existence it is purported to serve and is a significant source of the distress of the contemporary human condition. To insensitize man to the distress of his present state, to induce in him artificially a euphoric state of mind about his circumstances, is not only to open the door to the potential activation of destructive forces, but also to promote the false idea that this destructiveness, while it may be in some sense creative, is at the same time necessarily constructive. As for Starusch, so for modern man in general the way to constructiveness is through the correction of his distress at its source. Whether the sources of distress in the contemporary human condition can be sufficiently corrected at all and whether man can ultimately rescue and restore his sorely damaged humane values in the present era are open questions. But certainly as long as he insensitizes himself to the distress of his existence through the local anesthetic of narcotizing ideologies or the palliative of moral, social, and political delusions, and until he consciously realizes and completely exposes the underlying problems, the ambivalences, ambiguities, and shortcomings of his time, there is little likelihood of an effective salvation. Herein lie the potential constructiveness of the act of narrating in the present age and the possibility of a positive function, value, and moral effectiveness, to borrow Spaethling's formulation, of an art that appears to be bound to the inadequacies of the time. This is perhaps the major import of the combined motifs of failure and creativity in *Örtlich betäubt*.

Notes

1. Having escaped the responsibilities of growing up by means of an ostensibly selfwilled infantilism that arrested his physical growth at the level of a three-year-old for almost eighteen years, and having protected himself, especially by means of a tin drum, the object inseparably associated with his infantilism, against any unwanted encroachment of the adult world upon his personal existence, Oskar finally resumes his physical growth, again ostensibly through an act of conscious willing, and endeavors to come to terms with adulthood as an adult. Forced to abandon his hope of a bourgeois existence, he does well in terms of the material circumstances of his adulthood, but in terms of his inner self, his inability to cope with his adult existence culminates in his incarceration in a mental hospital, an incarceration that he himself contrives, for a crime of which he is innocent. Through this incarceration he accomplishes for a short time what he had achieved earlier through his prolonged infantilism, namely, protection from the world at large, but the failure to cope with adulthood that is signified by his incarceration is ironically paralleled, at the end of the novel, by the frustration of his desire to remain withdrawn from the world at large, as the discovery of the real culprit in the crime for which Oskar has been committed is about to occasion his release from the institution and his re-exposure to the world from which he had managed to escape.

2. Denied the opportunity to speak to the students, he subsequently deserts from his military unit — he is still in the service — and goes to hide out in the sunken minesweeper in the Gulf of Danzig that had been the scene of much of his activity in earlier days. He dives

156 Critical Essays on Günter Grass

down into the ship and never reappears, presumably meeting his end there at the age of eighteen.

3. Insofar as Matern has a primary vocation, it is perhaps acting, but he has trouble holding any position, either as an actor or in various other endeavors, for an appreciable length of time. In a futile search for an absolute doctrine of political salvation, he looks in turn to Communism, Nazism, Catholicism, and ideological anti-fascism, as Grass himself points out in a letter to a friend published under the title "Unser Grundübel ist der Idealismus" in *Der Spiegel*, 23, No. 33 (August 11, 1969), 94. After World War II Matern tries to pass himself off as an anti-fascist victim of Hitlerism and sets out to take revenge on former members of the storm-trooper unit to which he himself once belonged. In his intended "settling of accounts" with these figures, however, he is largely frustrated, and his acts of revenge are often reduced to pointless acts of sheer destructiveness. In spite of his claim of having been an anti-fascist during the Nazi years, he is ultimately exposed as having been akin to Hitler.

4. In *Hundejahre*, which consists of three narratives, only the second one, ["Love Letters"], written in the form of a series of letters from Harry Libenau to his cousin Tulla Pokriefke, is a first-person narrative in both form and content. In the first book of the novel, ["Morning Shifts"], Eddi Amsel, writing under the name of Brauxel, consistently refers to himself in the third person. In the third book, ["Materniads"], written by Matern, Matern likewise refers to himself consistently in the same way, except for the final paragraph of the book, in which he switches to the first person pronoun: ["And this man and that man — who now will call them Brauxel and Matern? — I and he, we stride . . ." (*Hundejahre*, 682 / *Dog Years*, 569)]. Since the narrators of the first and third books are writing about themselves — they are the two central characters of the novel — their stories, though related in the third person, are essentially first-person narratives.

5. In the first chapter of *Die Blechtrommel*, several paragraphs after the initial paragraph, Oskar discusses certain technical problems of writing a novel and explains how he will begin his story, which, to be sure, has already begun. In the first chapter of *Katz und Maus*, after an opening paragraph that begins in the middle of a sentence, the narrator Pilenz, who tells the story of Joachim Mahlke, indicates how he will proceed with the beginning of his story. The opening paragraph of ["Morning Shifts"] in *Hundejahre* contains a discussion of who should begin the narrative and how it should begin. In the first ["Love Letter"], Harry Liebenau explains that he has been advised to begin with his cousin's forename, as at the beginning of a letter. The second paragraph of the first ["Materniad"] opens with the observation that to begin is to choose, and the idea of choosing is developed for two more paragraphs.

6. For Oskar, in his hospital bed, drumming on a tin drum is his special device for calling forth the desired images and reconstructing the desired scenes out of his past: ["If I didn't have my drum, which, when handled adroitly and patiently, remembers all the incidentals that I need to get the essential down on paper, and if I didn't have the permission of the management to drum on it three or four hours a day, I'd be a poor bastard with nothing to say for my grandparents" (*Blechtrommel*, 22 / *The Tin Drum*, 25)]. Brauxel, who takes the Vistula as the point of departure for his narrative, forms an outline of that river on his desktop with cigarette stumps and ashes to help him reconstruct the particularities of his past: ["The present writer . . . has mapped out the course of the Vistula before and after regulation on an empty desk top" (*Hundejahre*, 7–8 / *Dog Years*, 12)].

7. [Ed. note: Page references are given in the text parenthetically and in double form. Numbers before the slash refer to *Örtlich betäubt* (Neuwied: Luchterhand, 1969); numbers after the slash refer to *Local Anaesthetic*, trans. Ralph Manheim (New York: Fawcett Crest, 1970)].

8. [311 / 222: "Get my beginnings going or resume my Forster studies"].

9. The time of Starusch's writing is revealed as follows, in a reference to Sieglinde's

father's actions at the end of the war: ["Reckoning back from today, exactly twenty-two years ago . . . on May 8, 1945 . . ." (59–60 / 45)]. The time of the proposal to Irmgard Seifert is given as follows: ["Three weeks after [the last] dental treatment . . . early in March, on the fourth to be precise, I proposed to Irmgard Seifert" (339 / 242)].

10. In investigating Starusch's story of his ostensible engagement, the dentist learns from a colleague in Andernach, a Dr. Lindrath, that Lindrath's daughter Monika, a pediatrician, vaguely recalls a student named Starusch (333–34 / 238). When Starusch refuses to concede that his story is not true, the dentist suggests that he may have been engaged to someone in Mayen instead of Andernach: ["Never mind. I'm willing to believe a Sieglinde existed, if not in Andernach perhaps in Mayen" (334 / 238)].

11. In his ["Dusters"] period, Starusch tells us, he was called Störtebeker (16 / 14) . Cf. the ["Dusters"] and the figure of Störtebeker in Die Blechtrommel.

12. Cf. the use of dramatic forms in Grass's two other novels. In Die Blechtrommel, part of the chapter ["Inspection of Concrete or Barbaric, Mystical, Bored"] is presented in the form of dramatic dialogue. A radio play comprises most of ["The Hundredth, Publicly Discussed Materniad"] in the third book of Hundejahre.

13. As Starusch becomes more and more involved with Scherbaum in the interval between the two sets of dental treatments, he repeatedly telephones the dentist for advice as to what to do about Scherbaum. Hearing so much about the young man, the dentist expresses a desire to meet him, and Starusch takes him to the dentist's office. Shortly after that Scherbaum disconcerts the dentist by telephoning him to ask for some anesthetic to give the dog so that the animal will not feel pain during its burning, which Scherbaum at this point still intends to carry out. Ultimately, Scherbaum becomes the dentist's patient and has his malocclusion corrected.

14. When Irmgard tries to encourage Scherbaum to go through with his plan as an act that will redeem the failures of herself and her generation, Scherbaum indicates that he not only does not know what she is talking about, but is not at all interested in what she may or may not have done when she was his age (268 / 192). In different ways, Starusch and Irmgard misunderstand their relationship to the younger generation. While Starusch tries to hold a romanticized image of his youth up as an example for Scherbaum, Irmgard tries to make Scherbaum an example for herself by romanticizing him as a potential redeemer. All they accomplish, however, is to make themselves look ridiculous.

15. Starusch's account of Möller's "compromises" may be summarized as follows: Commissioned by the city fathers of Danzig to do an allegorical painting of the Last Judgment, Möller used a voluptuous and well-known girl as a model for the naked figure of Sin, who was depicted in a boat leading other boats full of sinners to Hell. When Möller's fiancée, the daughter of the mayor of Danzig, saw the picture, she assumed Möller was having an affair with the model. The city fathers were also up in arms. Forced to make the all-too-recognizable likeness of Sin unidentifiable, Möller made his first "compromise" by painting the face of his fiancée onto the voluptuous body of the other girl. In the wake of the ensuing uproar over this scandalous representation of the mayor's daughter, he compromised further by painting a reflecting glass jar over his fiancée's face, thus distorting her features. He also painted the city fathers into the boat with the figure of Sin. But since he was not ready to have his fiancée and the city fathers go to Hell, he made a third compromise by painting himself in Hades holding the boat back and looking out at the viewer of the picture as though to say that those people would be lost if it were not for him — the artist as savior, preserving sin for us and not giving up the triangle.

16. Like Krings's, Schörner's forename is Ferdinand, and like Krings, Schörner is referred to as a ["fight-to-the-finish general"] (51 / 39)]. From information that Starusch quotes from his manuscript at various points, we learn that Schörner was released from Soviet inprisonment and departed from the Soviet-occupied zone to West Germany in 1955 (268 / 192), that while he was returning home to Munich by train he was advised by the police to

leave the train in Freising rather than Munich, so as to avoid an impending demonstration by a group of veterans (305 / 217), and that at the time of Starusch's work on the manuscript, Schörner is in his seventies (286 / 204). Like Schörner, Krings, who would be in his seventies at the time of Starusch's writing (50 / 38), returns home in 1955 from Soviet imprisonment and is advised by the police to leave his train before he reaches his destination, in this instance Koblenz, so as to avoid an impending demonstration by a group of veterans (51–55 / 39–42; 63 / 46).

17. A pediatrician at the time of telling of the "Sieglinde" story, Monika would have been a medical student at the time of Starusch's alleged engagement to Sieglinde. Starusch claims that he induced Sieglinde to study medicine (35 / 28) and that she wanted to become a pediatrician (140 / 103). The last part of the name Sieglinde — Starusch regularly refers to her as Linde — is suggestive of the first part of the name Lindrath.

18. The dentist intimates that Starusch may have been enamored of Monika (334 / 238). While Starusch may have been attracted to her, he could not have made much of an impression on her, since she remembers him only vaguely. She apparently did not have any romantic feelings toward him.

19. Cf. the episode in which the image of a woman advertising a deepfreeze on television leads Starusch to imagine the woman as Sieglinde, then to envision Sieglinde lying naked and frosted at the very bottom of the deepfreeze under various frozen goods including Starusch's own "coagulated desires" and "bottled defeats," and finally to lament: ["Ah, how long-lasting she is in the cold smoke. Ah, how pain keeps fresh in the deep freezer" (37–38 / 30)].

20. Starusch is obviously fascinated by the dentist's electrical instruments, as on 22–23 / 19 where he refers to several of them while discussing the necessity of describing a simultaneity of a number of activities.

21. Although the names of the dentist and the assistant are never given, Starusch does refer to them as Schlottau and Sieglinde in the account of one of his treatments (156–58 / 114–15).

22. Starusch's first, obscure reference to the fragmentary manuscript as ["the exasperatingly thin portfolio inscribed in capitals with a working title" (39 / 30–31)], and his references to efforts to resume work on the manuscript from time to time in the course of the narrative indicate that this work has been preying on his mind for some time before his dental treatments.

23. *Akzente*, 8 (1961), 8–11.

24. Typical of Grass's practice of employing words in other than their most usual sense, the sometimes pejorative term "Gelegenheitsdichter" ["occasional poet"], which generally denotes a person who writes poems for special occasions, is tantamount here to the positive concept of *Erlebnisdichter* ["poet of lived experience"].

25. Cf. "Der Phantasie gegenüber," the third part of Grass's essay "Der Inhalt als Widerstand," *Akzente*, 8 (1961), 233–235, where Grass describes a poet in the process of writing a poem about a certain make of wire fence. The poet's imagination brings to his mind an electrically-charged barbed-wire fence, among other things, but he rejects this image because he has never seen a barbed-wire fence of the make in question. He admonishes his imagination to stick to what he has actually seen.

26. The concept of *Einfall*, or inspired idea, is important here. A given experience seeks expression through artistic forms, conceptions of which present themselves in the artist's mind as *Einfälle*. For the ["occasional poet"], which Grass considers himself to be ("Das Gelegenheitsgedicht," *Akzente*, 8 [1961], 9), the acceptable *Einfälle* must be concrete formulations of things of which the poet has actual, first-hand knowledge. Of himself and his *Einfälle*, Grass has said: ["I work with the imagination, but I do not engage in experiments. Lots of things occur to me, some of them can be used, some not. I examine the whole thing very carefully in the context of linguistic usage, and it will then emerge that a particular,

purely fantastic notion can or cannot be realized (*realisieren*) in language"] ("Lyrik heute: Die Diskussion," *Akzente*, 8 [1961], 43). The term *realisieren* here means bringing the *Einfall* into line with lived reality. Thus, like the poet in the preceeding note, Grass tests his imaginative ideas against this reality and rejects those that do not pass the test.

27. Starusch cannot stand pain, though he claims to view it as a means of knowledge: ["I regard pain as an instrument of knowledge, even though I don't bear up very well under toothache and reach for Arantil at the slightest pang" (244–45 / 175)]. The Stoic motif, to which considerable attention is given in the novel, is thus in part a feature of the creativity theme.

28. In reporting the date of his proposal to Irmgard, which occurred some two months before the actual writing of his narrative, Starusch indicates that the proposal took place ["a few days after I had stopped taking Arantil" (339 / 242)].

29. Thus, for example, when Starusch, reacting to Sieglinde's affair with Schlottau, tells her that in retaliation he has enjoyed the favors of her two friends, she replies: ["I'm glad you've finally found something to keep you from meddling with Father and me" (109 / 81)].

30. "Günter Grass: 'Cat and Mouse,' " *Monatshefte*, 62 (Summer 1970), 162.

31. Spaethling, p. 162.

The Artist and Politics in Günter Grass' *Aus dem Tagebuch einer Schnecke*

A. L. Mason*

Günter Grass' *Aus dem Tagebuch einer Schnecke* [*From the Diary of a Snail*] presents an almost predictable development in the gradual refinement of his views about the artist and politics. Many facets of this latest work can be seen as a logical outgrowth of earlier fictional works which focus on artist-heroes and their relationships to society, as well as his essays concerning politics and the role of the artist in West Germany. Although this work appears, on the surface, to be predominantly a chronicle or diary of Grass' experiences campaigning for the SPD in 1969, and although it has generally been seen this way by reviewers and critics,[1] the fact that it is half-fictional and that Grass is clearly preoccupied with outlining his personal ideas about the function of the artist in West German society makes it necessary to consider this book as an extension of his previous work, as a presentation, in a new overtly autobiographical form of an artist-hero and an investigation of the interrelationship of politics and aesthetics.

That the book is an extension of his previous depictions, in fiction and essays, of artist-heroes is clear from its development of three images for artists that Grass has most committed himself to in recent years: the artist

*Reprinted from the *Germanic Review* 51 (1976): 105–20, by permission of Heldref Publications and the author.

as bourgeois; the artist as man with a split identity, as writer and as citizen; and the artist as Enlightenment man. These three images have come to the forefront of Grass' work as he has turned to the problem of the artist and his position in postwar democratic society; unlike the portrayal of Oskar and Amsel in *Die Blechtrommel* and *Hundejahre* respectively, a portrayal of artist figures who in complicated ways embodied and parodied Romantic-Nazi thought about the artist and his position in society, these images are attempts to develop an explicitly post-Nazi and democratic conception of the artist in an increasingly self-conscious, didactic manner.

Both the entire framework of *Tagebuch* and the image which Grass projects of himself as writer-campaigner relating stories about the campaign to his family are quite consistent with his previous attempts in essays, interviews, and fictional works to break down artificial, outmoded barriers between the artist and the public. In his novels and essays such as "Die Ballerina" ["The Ballerina"] and "Vom mangelnden Selbstvertrauen der schreibenden Hofnarren" ["On the Lacking Self-Confidence of Court Fools who Write"] Grass has repeatedly criticized the traditional view of the artist as special idol, as a projection of the nineteenth century "Geniekult" [cult of genius], and has attempted to modernize that image by dissolving the traditional dialectic between the artist and bourgeois man in German literature. For him, there is no such dichotomy: the artist is also the bourgeois citizen, and to try to view him as part of an elite is to once again fall prey to the false and artificial categories of the German Romantic tradition or, more politically apt, to regress to the dangerous glorification of the artist and "artistic, elitist" German which characterized propaganda of the Nazi era.[2] Elsewhere, Grass makes his position clear:

> [For the writer's place is *in* society, and not above or outside society. So
> away with all spiritual pride and recalcitrant elitism! You utopians and
> sectarians in your beautiful sheltered edifices: Step outside the door! Get
> your knees and your foreheads bloodied by our reality! Genius dwells no
> longer in blissful madness, but in our own sober consumer society. The
> saints have become pragmatists.][3]

Thus, while Grass does refer to his fame in *Tagebuch*, he is at pains to stress the negative aspects of it, how it has isolated him from people;[4] moreover, the whole idea behind the book, that of campaigning and addressing himself to the public, is an attempt to abolish this sort of isolation. Further, the structural device of addressing himself to his children (and of extending this metaphorically to "other people's children" [346 / 292]), underscores the image of himself not as famous artist but rather as bourgeois family man. By interspersing anecdotes about his family life with stories about his experiences on the campaign trail, fictional accounts of the Nazi era, and thoughts about German literary and intellectual tradition, Grass forces the reader continually to consider him as bourgeois citizen rather than aloof artist. Indeed, the small details and anecdotes about his family life are among the livelier and most memorable passages in the book: the sketch of Laura who can think of nothing but painting dream horses (95 / 79), Grass' absorption with Anna, working out her ballets far away on the beach (210 / 176), Bruno's parody of his father's campaign speeches (142 / 119), or the description of Anna in the audience at a rally (242 / 206). Occasionally, the remarks of his children function ironically, further deflating any pretension the artist may have about being spetial or even particularly influential: a good example is Laura's comment:

[Whatcha writing now? Do you always have to? You writing about horses or my bunnies? Or is it still the same old SPD? Couldn't you just stop? (269 / 227)]

That the writer should not be elevated above common reality is something that Grass has long stressed. This is evident when we look at one of his earliest meditations on the artist, "Die Ballerina." In "Die Ballerina," the image of the controlled, classical, yet bourgeois ballerina is contrasted with the more avant garde, but superficial "expressive dancer":

[The ballerina knits wool socks for her little brother, the ballerina talks nonsense, the ballerina has got engaged just a while ago. . . . The ballerina puts on her glasses, she's a little short-sighted, and leafs through a magazine. . . . The enemy and the deadly serious opposite of the ballerina is the expressive dancer. While the ballerina moves her body according to fixed rules and smiles while she is doing it . . . the expressive dancer dances with her complicated soul. . . .][5]

Nowhere before, however, has Grass developed this image of the bourgeois artist so fully as in *Tagebuch*, and nowhere has he expressed this attitude in a more realistic, plain style, in contrast to the "high-riding style" of the German idealistic tradition (52 / 44).

The second image of the artist which Grass is concerned with, that of the artist as a man with a split identity, both a writer and a citizen, is both an extension of his criticism of the notion of the artist as a specially gifted person, elevated above common reality, and an attempt to redefine the idea of social *engagement* by artists in a postwar, democratic context. At the end of "Vom mangelnden Selbstvertrauen der schreibenden Hofnarren" ["On the Lacking Self-Confidence of Court Fools who Write"] the delicate balance of his position is summarized:

[Let's be clear: the poem knows no compromises; we, however, live by compromises. Whoever can tolerate this tension productively is a fool and changes the world.][6]

The artist must be both a writer and a citizen who works within the system for political reforms. Grass' two roles appear side by side in

Tagebuch; passages about his action as campaigner and political reformer within the system are interspersed with fictional stories about Danzig during the Third Reich. The fact that the fictional parts of the work are not overtly didactic, whereas the other parts of the work have a didactic tone, further underscores the dual role which Grass sees himself as playing. What is different than his previous works is the direct blending of non-fictional didactic commentary with fiction. Grass' concern for the fate of the individuals during the Nazi era is no longer hidden behind numerous masks. To be sure Zweifel's quasi-artistic activities, the endless story-tellings and dramatic productions, which he performs in order to avoid Nazi persecution, resemble, in many ways, the attitudes and actions of Oskar and Amsel; all three protagonists use art or quasi-artistic entertainment as a means of masking their identity and eluding Nazi terror. Oskar eventually joins a propaganda troupe which tours Germany, and Amsel changes his identity and becomes director of a ballet company in Berlin. Similarly, Zweifel ["Doubt"] is forced to relate ever new stories and improvise dramatic productions in order to entertain his host, thereby discouraging Stomma from turning him over to the Gestapo. Unlike Oskar and Amsel, however, Zweifel's attitude is not ambivalent vis-à-vis the historical-political situation; unlike Oskar and Amsel, he is never partially in collusion with the Nazis and, instead, remains literally underground, surviving as best he can.[7] Nor is the sly skeptical entertainer any longer the narrator as in *Die Blechtrommel* and *Hundejahre*; nor in this latest work is there a narrator who is still at least partially entrenched in fascist fantasies of power and attempting to liberate himself through dialogue as in *örtlich betäubt*. Instead, in *Tagebuch*, Grass presents the artist as working to define more clearly than before a philosophy of action and theory of art which is distinguished from both right-wing and left-wing extremism and which is no longer based on slyness and evasiveness. In addition, the novel's two voices, the voice of nonfictional didacticism and that of fictional storytelling, show a new interdependence within this work: Grass makes it clear that his continuing preoccupation with stories about the Nazi period in Danzig actually serve as the impetus for his activity as engaged artist in postwar Germany: recent German history, he tells us, is the reason for his present-day political involvement:

> [I owned to the almost-socialist monks that I was busy telling you in a roundabout way how things came to be as they are, why I have to be away from home so much, and how many defeats Doubt had to swallow before he began to consider flight. (145 / 121)]

Here Grass' two roles, that of political strategist of present-day German politics and that of storyteller of the fictional past, become functionally inseparable.

The third image for the artist-hero projected in earlier work and further developed in *Tagebuch* is Grass' notion of the artist as Enlightenment man; in recent essays, Grass has associated traditional values of the Enlightenment with his own role in modern society. In "Des Kaisers neue Kleider" ["The Emperor's New Clothes"], a campaign speech for the 1965 election, Grass sums up the intended effect of his speech:

[My attempt to illuminate the dark corners of our everyday political doings, with the help of the Danish teller of tales Hans Christian Andersen, was intended as a statement of faith in the German tradition of Enlightenment, a tradition often renounced, but one continually renewed in the face of terror and violence.][8]

In *Tagebuch* the function of the artist as Enlightenment man, as educator, as humanist, as advocate of tolerance and reason, opposed to terror, is evident both in the structure and content. Structurally, Grass, as narrator, relates stories about the campaign and historical events to his children and thereby to "other people's children" in a tone which frequently tends to be pedagogical and prescriptive rather than narrative; there are numerous passages which reflect Grass' didactic tendency, which, on the whole, is more obvious and direct than in his earlier works:

[Let's try to be broadminded. The violent and the righteous are hard of hearing. Only this much, children: don't be too righteous. People might be afraid of your righteousness; it might put them to flight . . . (31 / 26)].

The infantile tone of the children's questions and remarks does not, however, as it does in *Die Blechtrommel*, function consistently to underscore violence and terror through understatement and contrast; more often, it serves to keep the narrative on a concrete level with few flights into abstractions or, in some instances, to point up the limits of language: how silence is the only sincere response to painful basic questions, in contrast to Grass' endless speeches on the campaign trail.[9] Further, Grass' preoccupation with Dürer as a humanist who gradually extracted himself from the tightly structured ideology of the medieval world amplifies his own self-image as neo-Enlightenment man. As in his earlier works, Grass states in *Tagebuch* his basic distrust of all ideologies, the need for tolerance, and his continuing opposition to idealism; for example, he puts the matter bluntly when he says:

[Or in discussions, when the sons of the bourgeoisie start exculpating themselves by trying to redeem the world with a microphone. When grimly I try to pull the weeds of German idealism, which spring up again as inexorably as rib grass. How they persist in pursuing a cause — even the cause of socialism — for its own sake. . . . (39–40 / 33)]

It should be apparent from the above discussion that in *Tagebuch* Grass is quite concerned with art and the function of the artist, not only with politics or autobiographical episodes. Indeed, the book culminates in two major parallels between art and politics, both of which are significant for an understanding of Grass' theory and works. These two principal parallels between art and politics are closely linked with the two dominant motifs: the snail and Dürer's "Melencolia I": both these motifs culminate in the appended speech, "Vom Stillstand im Fortschritt" ["On Stasis in Progress"], given at the Dürer centennial in Nuremberg. Indeed, most of the themes and leitmotifs introduced and developed throughout the work are recapitulated and woven together in the speech which functions as both a structural and thematic summary of the book. In addition, it is meant to have a sobering effect, to "weigh down" the end of the book, thereby undercutting the notion that the 1969 campaign victory for the SPD meant instant utopia; the speech, placed as it is at the end of the book and regarded by Grass as the final result of his meditations on art and politics (["This lecture comes at the end of a snail's balance sheet" (347 / 292]), makes it clear that Grass thinks of that victory merely as provisional and limited progress. The two major parallels between art and politics help to illuminate the general structure of this book.

First, Grass' concept of stasis in progress, associated with the snail motif, becomes, in the course of the book, both a theory of socio-political practice and of artistic expression; both applications of this image require considerable discussion.

In politics, Grass' principle of stasis in progress is the antithesis of both radical right-wing and left-wing politics and, of course, closely connected with the notion of limited progress which Grass associates with the SPD. It is clearly opposed to any absolutism, revolutionary action, or ritualized protest (191 / 160) on the part of student radicals or fellow writers. Grass clearly contrasts his mundane, day-to-day campaigning with the political actions of more radical writers such as Enzensberger:

> [These reformists! Look what fun Enzensberger is having: hops off to Cuba without a care in the world while you knock yourself out trying to drum up enthusiasm for the activation of pensions for war victims. . . . (88 / 73)][10]

At the same time, Grass' principle of stasis in progress is clearly in opposition to supporters of the status quo, particularly the power elite of the corporate structure; and it is, moreover, precisely because he is opposed to the conservative structure that Grass attempts to counter the utopian idea of rapid progress, for such utopian ideals merely serve to strengthen the status quo by making small, but meaningful changes more difficult:

> [From time immemorial, the dead weight of things as they are has been played off against progress as the possibility of change. For wherever progress is frustrated by premature aims or utopian flights from reality, wherever its advances are so slight as to be ludicrous, the conservative who 'knew it all along' triumphs. His melancholy gestures signify that

nothing can be changed, that all human effort is vain, that an imponderable fate rules: human existence as doom. (349 / 293–94)]

It is evident, then, that in his political theorizings Grass is attempting to undercut all categorical opposition between stasis and progress and, more generally, any tendency to see either art or politics in terms of absolute polarities. The fact that Grass, by means of his principle of stasis in progress, attempts to eliminate this sort of dialectical thinking should come as no surprise. His opposition to dialectical tradition is an important part of many of his earlier fictional and non-fictional works. This general tendency is, for example, obvious in Oskar's parodies of pseudo-polarities in *Die Blechtrommel* and is characteristic of such essays as "Konflikte," "Über Ja und Nein," and "Das Gelegenheitsgedicht" ["Conflicts," "On Yes and No," and "The Occasional Poem"].[11]

In terms of the literary structure of *Tagebuch*, the image of stasis in progress is also of crucial importance. Most obviously, it is reflected in the way the writing alternates between something at least provisionally progressive (Grass' notion of the SPD) and something regressive (his preoccupation with the history of the Nazi era); the use of the diary form, however, when seen in conjunction with Grass' political ideas, suggests a number of subtler, more interesting ways in which form and content are interconnected in *Tagebuch*. Perhaps the most general of these parallels is the meandering style which reflects Grass' aversion to goal-directed, ideological social and political action and his emphasis instead on slow social reform in contrast to student radicals with their utopian demands and mottos from Marcuse:

> [Be patient. My entries come to me on the road. Since in my thoughts, words, and deeds I am categorically earth-bound and even aboard a Super 111 am at best an unauthentic flier, nothing, not even an election campaign, can speed me or any part of me up. . . . I mean to speak to you by (roundabout) bypaths: sometimes offended and enraged, often withdrawn and hard to pin down, occasionally brimful of lies, until everything becomes plausible. Certain things I should like to pass over in circumspect silence. I anticipate a part of the part, whereas another part will turn up only later and partially. And, so, if my sentence twists, turns, and only gradually tapers to a point, don't fidget and don't bite your nails. Hardly anything, believe me, is more depressing than going straight to the goal. We have time. Yes, indeed: quite a lot of it. (13 / 9)]

Thus, Grass is well aware of the ways in which the structure and style of *Tagebuch* function to emphasize his own social and political philosophy. In addition, these same methods characterize his manner during the campaign, his actions in situations which called for a straight-forward approach. In describing his reactions to discussion with groups on the campaign trail, Grass remarks:

[My answers were short or long-winded, quotably sarcastic or embarrassed and evasive. (On demand, I told anecdotes: the things that happen to you on a trip.) (96 / 80)]

Even a goal such as winning the election for Brandt and the SPD is seen as merely a provisional goal and Grass is at pains to counter the image of the frenetic campaign schedule with the slow, rambling pace of his "diary." The fact that the book was written after the campaign victory further underscores the idea that Grass regards that victory as only a temporary goal; only twice in the book does he speak directly of a victory, once at the beginning when he refers to the election of Heinemann as President and once briefly near the end when he mentions the importance of Brandt's election, which for him confirms the possibility of change through the system. Instead, the emphasis is almost exclusively on the importance of the process and of a ["wee little beginning" (35 / 29)] rather than absolutes.[12]

Similarly, Grass' polemic against dogmatism, implicit in his image of stasis in progress, is related to many stylistic and structural devices. He is well aware of the ways in which language can be manipulated for political ends through the use of labels and political symbols; prejudice begins with dogmatism. Both Zweifel in his cellar and Grass on the campaign trail stress the dangers of approaching politics and society from the standpoint of an absolute system and, instead, view reality in terms of multiplicity. Zweifel writes in his diary:

["There is no system, because there are several. Even snails hesitate to take themselves in an absolute sense." (210 / 177)]

And this reflects Grass' own approach to politics:

[My speech that I write in Nouzov is titled "Of Limited Possibilities."
. . . I oppose skepticism to faith. I contest the permanent and unchanging. My disgust at the absolute and suchlike thumbscrews. Why I'm opposed to the claims of the 'one and only truth' and in favor of multiplicity. (170 / 141–42)]

Thus, it is evident that many peculiarities of Grass' style in *Tagebuch* derive basically from this skepticism and multiplicity. Despite Grass' frequently pedagogical and polemical tone, one is aware of an attempt to be undogmatic stylistically, an unwillingness to name things directly, a necessity for seeing things from multiple viewpoints, and a distrust of simplistic one-to-one symbols and allegories. The most obvious examples are, of course, the metaphor of the snail and Grass' many-sided reflections on Dürer's "Melencolia I." The book, however, literally abounds in patterns and leitmotifs.[13] Behind this multiplicity of meaning is one of the book's central stylistic and conceptual paradoxes: Grass is trying to argue clearly and didactically for unclarity, anti-ideological thought, and multiplicity. His self-image as political revisionist and neo-Enlightenment man requires that, on the one hand, he teach and make his position thereby clear, and that on the other hand, he does not thereby foreclose discussion, either through ideological absolutism, too strong an arrogation of authority as polemicist, or too monolithic and logical a form of rhetoric. This paradox is expressed most clearly when Grass argues that the writer's function is to resist ideas and thus to write against suction, a precept which is everywhere reflected in the book's style: ["(A writer, children, is someone who writes against suction)" (290 / 244)]. On the one hand, this comment is couched in the most simple and naively didactic form imaginable; on the other hand, its message is explicitly anti-ideological.

The second major way in which Grass' views on art parallel his political views in *Tagebuch* is revealed by his use of Dürer's "Melencolia" and is linked with his self-image as revisionist. To be sure, this is no new self-image; in his 1968 essay "Über Ja und Nein" ["On Yes and No"], for example, Grass states his position in terms which also foreshadow his principle of stasis in progress:

> ["Stand or fall" was once a catch phrase; but occasionally I like to sit, indecisively, full of doubts, irresolutely — I am a revisionist. This insult, laden with consequences, crying out for rebuttal, has no effect on me. There is no form of society which would never need incessant revision. There is no reform without revision of what already is. A Yes that consists of many Nos.][14]

In *Tagebuch* Dürer's "Melencolia" is a focal point for Grass' portrayal of himself as a revisionist. On the socio-political level, Grass introduces the engraving as a means of criticizing the excesses and faults of both Western and communist society and politics. On the one hand, he uses the engraving to point up the boredom and passivity of capitalistic consumer society of the West with its dehumanizing technology, its problem of leisure, with its surfeit of products and its emphasis on capitalistic gains:

> [By the conveyor belt the Melencolia of rationalized production finds her everyday expression: a state of mind guaranteed by the legal wage scale. No self-doubting erudition. No dire astrological constellation, no predetermined, inscrutable fate. . . . No inventors or subtle perfectors, let alone stockholders or directors, but girls and women sit wingless and as though sexless at the conveyor belt for eight hours a day. . . . A silent Melencolia reduced to silence by the noise of production. . . . What utopia might provide a counterworld to the melancholy-producing conveyor belt? (343–44 / 289)]

Similarly, just as Grass exposes compulsive consumption in capitalist countries and its consequences, ["surfeit and disgust" (365 / 308)], so he criticizes communist dicatorships and the neo-Marxist New Left for utopian rigidity of dogma and a surfeit of ideology:

> [The young people of the ideological dictatorships, so joyful in photographs, know a different kind of surfeit. It springs from the duties

imposed by revolutionary phraseology, from a directed will, no longer
free to make decisions, from a decreed socialism, in which the concept
of freedom has ceased to be anything but an ornament of scholastic
casuistry. Like Saturn in his day, the revolution has marked its children
with melancholy. (365–66 / 308)]

At the same time, however, that the engraving suggests the excesses
and ideological rigidity of both Western consumer society and communist
society, it is used to express the polar opposites of these criticisms. It
expresses as well a positive analysis, the formulation of what Grass calls,
inverting the usual value judgment of the term, a revisionist resistance to
such rigidity and surfeit; Grass then goes on to show how such resistance
or spirit of revisionism is either branded as sick or suppressed by both
societies. He associates melancholy with a growing spirit of resistance in
Western society to the rigid conservative order which classifies the masses
as ignorant and denies them the right to be melancholy, that is, to reject
the existing order and its conventions (349 / 294). Conservative capitalistic
society with its power elite suppresses rejection or rebellion by branding
the attitude of melancholic dissatisfaction with society sick or suspect:

[Melancholy arouses suspicion the moment it ceases to be the privilege
of an elite and colors social attitudes. Suspicion of melancholy as a
preliminary to interdiction of melancholy has always been based on the
identification of melancholy with disease. (349 / 294)]

Thus, Western society maintains the status quo by disparaging those who
actively question its manifestations and goals.

Grass again criticizes communist society for similar reasons; just as
Western society regards melancholy as a sickness in order to retain the
status quo, so in communist society the feeling which melancholy represents, revisionism, lack of goal-directed action, resistance and skepticism,
is suppressed as a political threat to socialism; communism has become
inflexible and enslaved by its own conceptions of utopia:

[On the other hand, where the utopia of communism first became
reality and has learned to exert power, it has become enslaved by its own
conceptions of happiness. Since Lenin, punishment has been imposed
for offences that go by the name of skepticism and nihilism. Revealingly
enough, intellectuals in recent years have been punished for critical
attitudes by internment in psychiatric clinics: in the strictly ordered
home of communist socialism Melancholy as Utopia's sister is under
house arrest. (356 / 300)][15]

It is apparent, therefore, that Grass not only employs Dürer's engraving and the concept of melancholy to criticize the extreme of both
capitalistic and communistic society and ideologies but also uses it as a
representation of a third view linked with his own principle of stasis in
progress: it represents for him the self-critical thought, skepticism, slow
reevaluation of society, and compromise of extremes which must contin-

ually take place if any progress is to follow. This is, for Grass, the essence of the notion of stasis in progress; it is what is lacking in the politics of both Western and communist countries. "Melencolia" represents the self-critical, patient, non-ideological, non-revolutionary attitude of resignation which must precede the acceptance of small seemingly insignificant provisional goals; this is the only sort of progress possible:

> [Our Melencolia sits brooding between ideologies and stunted reforms, impoverished amid inertia. Tired, disgusted by long-drawn-out snail processes, dejected amid timetables, she, too, like Dürer's Melencolia, props up her head and clenches her fist, because in hermaphrodite fashion stasis in progress begets and gives birth to progress from stasis. In a moment she will rise to her feet, reform some bungled reform, appoint a provisional goal, set some important deadlines. . . . (355–56 / 299)]

Just as Grass focuses on Dürer's "Melencolia" to criticize the extremes of capitalistic and communistic political and social practice, so he also uses the engraving to polemicize against both European literary tradition and Marxist literary theory. Grass' criticism of Marxist literary theory, like his criticism of communist society in general, stems primarily from what Grass sees as a narrow view of the function of literature; although it is clear from the way in which he analyzes Dürer's art that Grass is attempting to bridge the gap between art and everyday reality by reinterpreting "Melencolia" in light of present-day political and social realities, he, like Martin Walser, rejects the literary standards of socialist realism and, more specifically, Lukács' categories of realism and bourgeois literature:[16]

> [At this point it would be easy to move a George Lukács into the picture in place of the nicked sword. How highhandedly he has relegated philosophers and theoreticians, to whom melancholy and resignation were neither alien nor forbidden, to a residence which he — who undoubtedly felt sure of his knowledge — called "Hotel Abyss" (358 / 301)]

At the same time, however, Grass uses Dürer to polemicize against the German literary tradition of viewing melancholy as a disease and sign of aloof genius. This polemic seems to be directed against the nineteenth-century [cult of genius] in general and against his predecessor Thomas Mann in particular. Although Grass never mentions Mann in *Tagebuch*, several themes of Grass' work are reminiscent of Mann; Grass' analysis of the contemporary political situation juxtaposed with the fictional accounts of the Nazi era, his references to Dürer's art in light of German philosophy and history, and his interweaving of the problems of culture with the problematic situation of contemporary German politics recall Mann's preoccupation with similar themes in *Doktor Faustus*. For both Grass and Mann, Dürer's "Melencolia" becomes a focal point for meditation on the nature of art and German politics. Grass is clearly aware of the ways in which Mann draws parallels between art and politics in *Doktor Faustus;* a short comparison between their views of Dürer's "Melencolia" shows that Grass is consciously reinterpreting German literary tradition as well as evaluating trends in recent German history and politics.

In his 1928 essay on Dürer, Mann clearly associates Dürer (together with Goethe, Schopenhauer, Nietzsche, and Wagner) with the essence of the German people, with a *Weltanschauung* which is heroic, self-sacrificial and daemonic:

> [Dürer, Goethe, Schopenhauer, Nietzsche, Wagner—there, one might say, in one "passage" with two marginal notes, you have everything all together at once, the whole complex of fate and constellations, a world, the German world with its ambitiously theatrical self-portrayal and final magical-intellectualized dissolution. . . . For beside the great juggler and conjuror stands the seer and conqueror, the myth itself beside the theatricalizer of myth, he, hero and victim, herald of a new, higher humanity.][17]

In the earlier essays as well as in *Doktor Faustus*, Mann associates Dürer with, as Bergsten puts it, "the romantic germ of illness and death which was planted in the period of Germany's transition from the Catholic Middle Ages to the Lutheran Reformation, its deadly fruit was the Second World War."[18] Mann links Dürer, as well as Nietzsche, with attitudes which he later associates with Nazism:

> [The spiritual prerequisites and origins of the ethical tragedy of [Nietzsche's] life, however—this immortal European drama of self-control, self-conquest, self-crucifixion, with its spiritual suicide, as heart-rending and brain-rending climax—where else are they to be found than in the Protestantism of the pastor's son from Naumburg, in that nordic-German, bourgeois-Dürerean-moralistic sphere of "Knight, Death, and Devil" that remains through all his voyages the spiritual home of his soul?][19]

Dürer is, then, for Mann, a representative of the medieval German atmosphere of ["passion, the odor of the crypt, sympathy for suffering, Faustian Melencolia."][20] If we reflect on *Doktor Faustus*, we recall that the magic square of Dürer's "Melencolia" which hangs near Adrian's piano is associated with the dissolution of reason into the daemonic and the seduction of superstition and mysticism, both in art and politics. Further, the Devil is associated with the promise of genius, inspiration, the daemonic, the apocalyptic and Dürer's "Melencolia"; in the dialogue between the Devil and Adrian, in which they discuss the problematic stagnation of art and the need for a "breakthrough" in art and politics, Adrian remarks:

> ["You have an extraordinary fondness for Dürer—first 'How I shall freeze for lack of sun' and now Melencolia's hourglass. Is the magic square next?"][21]

Thus, in *Doktor Faustus,* Dürer's "Melencolia," as work of art and psychological state, expresses two sides of the same problem: the notion of culture in a state of stagnation and crisis, and, at the same time, the necessary elements for a new "breakthrough": anti-bourgeois genius and inspiration coupled with disease, aestheticism and the daemonic coupled with barbarism. On the political level these tendencies are shown to be the foundation of Nazism; on the artistic level they are depicted as leading to hero-worship of the anti-bourgeois artist and to art which has an irrationalistic and daemonic bias.

It is precisely these qualities and ideas which Grass repudiates in his references to Dürer's "Melencolia" in *Tagebuch;* he is clearly concerned with reinterpreting Mann's associations with the engraving, as well as the political and artistic implications of Mann's views:

> [True, where melancholy has taken demonic forms, it has been accepted as a professional quirk of genius. When benighted genius proclaimed the rule of barbarism and the monstrous forces of the irrational were unleashed, this melancholy, interpreted as creative madness, could count on the applause of aesthetes and the sacred awe of the public at large. Melancholy has been a privilege granted to "solitary eminences"; as a social attitude, however, it has seldom been legalized. (358–59 / 302)]

Whereas Mann associates Dürer with the psychological brooding nature of the Germans, Grass links the work throughout *Tagebuch* with the persecuted Zweifel; while Mann focuses on the engraving from a negative point of view — as an allegorical representation of pre-Nazi Germany, the decline of the arts, the general pessimism and skepticism of the age which tended toward the daemonic as an escape from cultural and political despair — Grass now disparages the connection between "Melencolia," disease, and genius and, although the engraving still mirrors the skepticism of the postwar era, this state of mind is no longer something which indicates crisis or eccentricity. On the contrary, Grass sees skepticism and contemplation not as an expression of ultimate stagnation and lack of progress, but rather as the basis for slow progress, as stasis in progress:

> [Saturn still rules; but his reign is no longer exclusively disastrous, for it secures the area of melancholy as a place of contemplation. (348 / 293)]

Rather than being a suspicious eccentricity, melancholy is closer to healthy skepticism and resignation which, according to Grass, provides the basis for progress: it is merely the dark side of utopia. By reinterpreting "Melencolia" Grass makes it clear that he rejects extremism, eccentricity, and revolutionary claims in both art and politics. While for Mann "Melencolia" is linked with the notion of "breakthrough," for Grass it expresses revisionism: the acceptance of melancholy as a social reality is the first step toward tolerance and realistic change.[22] Thus, it is evident that the way in which Grass updates Dürer's work is closely related to his most basic ideas about art and politics; *Tagebuch* represents Grass' most recent revision of German literary and political tradition:

> [While writing—for my own and other people's children—a book in which progress is measured by snail standards, I also described what makes the heart heavy. I have tried to put in a good word for melancholy. I have shown its modern variations, in order that we may use it as the social reality it is, and no longer as suspicious eccentricity. (368 / 309–10)]

The above discussion should make clear the plethora of ways in which *Tagebuch* is both more than a simple campaign document in thematic emphasis and more than a diary in the way it is evidently crafted, the way in which its style is not just transparent or "polished" but also closely interconnected with the ideas and the didactic impulse of the book. Does this mean, then, that a reader may go so far as to take the book as fiction rather than reportage, as written by a literary persona rather than the historical personality of Günter Grass? The book seems to me to intentionally prohibit a decision between these alternatives. On the one hand, the fact that the diary was written retrospectively, was carefully crafted, and represents a highly self-conscious form of self-presentation indicates that one should respond to it as fiction; on the other hand, the fact that it is written about contemporary public events and by an author who is himself a well-known public figure forces one to respond to it as nonfiction. The book resists genre classification, something that is no doubt related to Grass' political and moral aversion to nineteenth and twentieth-century aestheticism, its glorification of the artist and its demands for a "pure" work of art. Moreover, it seems to be an extension of the kind of writing Grass has been doing for some time now: an experimentation with genre that will allow him to try to unify the diverse aspects of his (increasingly more diverse) artistic and intellectual interests and social activities. He is working to find an inclusive form that will not be final, but which will be as "in-process" as he now feels himself and his society to be, a form that will incorporate his storyteller's gifts, his moral and political insights, his impulse to be a polemicist, his family life and public roles, his scholarly-parodic-moralistic understanding of German literature, intellectual history, and history. In *örtlich betäubt* he wrote what was partly a novel, partly a didactic parable, partly fiction, partly topical; it was still unified by means of a wholly fictional complex plot. With *Tagebuch*, he has tried an additional splintering of form, one that attempts to be still more complicated, unified, and "in-process." The attempt to write a novel that is "in-process" is, of course, related to Grass' political thought as it has been discussed in this article. The basis for it is Grass' posture of skepticism, his skepticism about all absolutes and systems. Even his own principle of stasis in progress is not a fixed dictum; in a statement that could describe his present experiments with literary form, he stresses the process of evolving his theory: ["Still indeterminate, I am gradually evolving into the snail principle" (76 / 63).]

Notes

1. See, for examples, the reviews in *Literatur und Kritik* (February 1974), and in *Der Spiegel*, August 21, 1972. Exceptions are articles by Fritz J. Raddatz, "Der Weltgeist als berittene Schnecke," in Jurgensen, ed., *Grass Kritik* (Bern, 1973), 191–197, who sees the book as a self-portrait which emphasizes Grass' "Einsamkelt," and Manfred Jurgensen, *Über Günter Grass* (Bern, 1974), who briefly discusses the structure of *Tagebuch* and several of the major themes and images in the context of Grass' other literary works.

2. Elsewhere I have discussed Grass' view of the artist in relationship to recent German history and German literary tradition more thoroughly than is possible here. See my book *The Skeptical Muse: Günter Grass' Conception of the Artist* (Bern, 1974).

3. Grass, "Des Kaisers neue Kleider," *Über das Selbstverständliche* (Neuwied, 1969), pp. 44–45.

4. 90/76. [Ed. note: Further page references are given parenthetically in the text, in double form. Numbers before the slash refer to *Aus dem Tagebuch einer Schnecke* (Neuwied: Luchterhand, 1972); numbers after the slash refer to *From the Diary of a Snail*, trans. Ralph Manheim (New York: Harcourt Brace Jovanovich, 1973).]

5. Grass, *Die Ballerina* (Berlin, 1963). pp. 6–7. Originally published in *Akzente*, VI (1956), 528ff.

6. Grass, "Vom mangelnden Selbstvertrauen der schreibenden Hofnarren unter Berücksichtigung nicht vorhandener Höfe," *Über meinen Lehrer Döblin und andere Vorträge* (Berlin, 1968), p. 72.

7. For a more detailed discussion of the complicated relationship between Grass' major protagonists and the Nazi political situation see my article "Günter Grass and the Artist in History," *Contemporary Literature*, XIV (Summer 1973), pp. 347–362.

8. Mention of Grass' ideas of education and Enlightenment as they appear in *Tagebuch* is made by Kurt Lothar Tank, "Deutsche Politik im literarischen Werk von Günter Grass," in Manfred Jurgensen, ed., *Grass Kritik* (Bern, 1973), 167–189, and by Manfred Jurgensen, *Über Günter Grass* (Bern, 1974).

9. For example, Grass notes the impossibility of answering such questions as the following about the concentration camps of the Nazi era: ["Exactly how many were they? How did they count them?" (16 / 11)].

10. Criticism of radical left-wing writers for their lack of concrete involvement in the politics of Germany is also characteristic of Grass' 1965 campaign speeches; in "Über das Selbstverständliche," Grass comments ["They are more likely to be moved to compose a lengthy heroic epic on Fidel Castro . . . than to have it occur to them to speak out against lies in their own country by writing a simple statement of support for Willy Brandt"] (*Über das Selbstverständliche*, p. 76).

11. "Konflikte" and "Über Ja und Nein" are collected in *Über das Selbstverständliche* (Neuwied, 1969); "Das Gelegenheitsgedicht oder—es ist immer noch, frei nach Picasso, verboten, mit dem Piloten zu sprechen," appears in the collection *Über meinen Lehrer Döblin und andere Vorträge* (Berlin, 1968).

12. This idea is frequently expressed through the metaphor of cooking ["My plans are simmering on a low flame. For the present I'm busy preventing. And aiming at small gains" (39 / 33)].

13. The structure of the book reflects a careful counterpart of themes and leitmotifs. Some examples are: family details (Laura's wish for a horse, Raoul's wish for a record player),

news items (Apollo 11 on the moon), motifs from German philosophy (Hegel's *Weltgeist* and Schopenhauer's Will), themes connected with present-day politics (Maoist students, the black of the CDU as opposed to Grass' "grey" skepticism), personal motifs (Grass' cooking), etc. This list is by no means exhaustive; tracing the development of all the prominent themes and motifs would undoubtedly result in the conclusion that *Tagebuch* is constructed more along the lines of a novel than a diary. One further example, the motif of collecting, will illustrate how consciously these themes are developed. As details about the characters are revealed, it becomes apparent that many of them are in some way involved with collecting something: Zweifel collects snails and, like Grass, stories, Lisbeth endures her narrow world by collecting cemeteries; Grass collects sea creatures when on vacation, Stomma collects bike accessories and Augst collects memberships and mushrooms. Further, it is evident that these details are not just arbitrary; they are consciously connected to a number of the book's major concerns: boredom and the search for order in an impersonal, alienated world of disembodied objects and melancholy [". . . collecting is an active manifestation of Melancholy" (254 / 216)].

14. Grass, "Über Ja und Nein," *Über das Selbstverständliche*, pp. 198–199.

15. Grass' critique of communist society has been sharply influenced by the Soviet invasion of Czechoslovakia. This is evident in earlier speeches and essays such as "Die Prager Lektion" and "Über Ja und Nein" as well as in *Tagebuch* where he uses the invasion as a Soviet counter-example to America's involvement in Vietnam. Terrorism and exploitation are common to both communist and Western countries: ["Soon the occupation of Czechoslovakia will be explained . . . as a tragic but (alas!) for reasons of security necessary event. What the United States government (in Vietnam) calls 'pacification,' the Soviet government calls 'normalization.' (Rewritten crimes that have found their rewrite men)" (168 / 140)].

16. See Walser's critique of Lukács in his essay "Wie und wovon handelt Literatur," *Wie und Wovon handelt Literatur* (Frankfurt, 1973), 119–138. Although Walser and Grass have different views of the characteristics and function of art, they both attempt to define the function of art and the artist in dialectic with Marxist criticism and both regard the tendency on the part of Marxist critics to create and use a system of categories as unacceptable. . . .

17. Thomas Mann, "Dürer," *Gesammelte Werke*, X (Oldenburg, 1960), p. 231.

18. Gunilla Bergsten, *Thomas Mann's Doctor Faustus* (Chicago, 1969), p. 129.

19. Mann, "Dürer," p. 231.

20. *Ibid.*, p. 231. See also Bergsten, p. 45.

21. Mann, *Gesammelte Werke*, VI (Oldenburg, 1960), p. 303.

22. This represents a shift in emphasis from Grass' previous use of melancholy as an allegorical expression for the socio-political situation of Germany in his earlier essay "Die melancholische Koalition" ["The Melancholy Coalition"]. In that essay, the idea of melancholy reflects the negative state of German society under Kiesinger as well as Grass' dissatisfaction with the SPD's role in the [Great Coalition]: ["The allegory of Melancholy offered itself to me. And because this cabinet is not equipped to radiate the notion of democratic power, it will, almost as a substitute, broadcast instead, on the federal level, its own most obvious common denominator, melancholy"] (*Über das Selbstverständliche*, p. 104.)

"Here Comes Everybody": An Appraisal of Narrative Technique in Günter Grass's *Der Butt*

Osman Durrani*

When it became known that Günter Grass was about to publish a novel entitled *Der Butt* [*The Flounder*], a German anglers' magazine is said to have put in an urgent and earnest request for a review copy.[1] If this story is true, it must represent the first in a long series of misunderstandings on the part of the book's would-be reviewers, many of whom have been less than lukewarm in their response to the work. Hellmuth Karasek, one of *Der Spiegel's* literary editors, remembered among other things for his apodictic line "Brecht is dead"[2] greeted the new novel with an echo of one of Ibsen's family dramas: "Nora — ein Suppenheim."[3] The reference to *A Doll's House*, where, in the claustrophobic world of *fin-de-siècle* high society, Nora, apparently extravagant and thoroughly materialistic, triumphs morally over her conventionally decent husband, seems to imply an overriding interest in the author's marriage as it is glimpsed in the novel, and that at the expense of the many other themes which Grass has brought together in it. So Karasek's verdict reflects his concentration on the domestic bickering that goes on in some parts of the novel, and he concludes that the historical sections of the book do not adequately counterbalance the theme of marital discord:

> [It is obvious . . . that he is attempting, with great expenditure of words and noise, to thrust forward his yesterdays in place of the present day; as in his novel *Der Butt*, written after a long pause, where the whole of good old Kashubia is trotted out to cover up a present-day tummyache: problems with women, irritations of marriage.]

Having thus given pride of place in his assessment to the ["present-day tummyache"], Mr. Karasek fails to see any point in the diverse ideologies which the work communicates to its readers, and ends up berating Grass for his schoolboyish primitivism in much the same way as early reviewers of *Die Blechtrommel* had done:

> [Grass, who, with apparent impassivity, cooks up ideologies into a bubbling brew in his great stewpot, still manages (out of epic necessity?) to broadcast the comfortable stable smells and kitchen odors of the good old days, where a fat arse, a thundering fart, a satisfied belch have more to say than any argument.]

This is Grass as *Der Spiegel* would like to see him — still very much the *enfant terrible* of the early 1960s. Its rival among the German weeklies,

*Reprinted from *Modern Language Review* 75 (1980): 810–22, by permission of *Modern Language Review* and the author.

Die Zeit, provided a much more detailed introduction to the new novel, and, in addition to a review by Rolf Michaelis, threw in a schematic plan ["The Bones of the Flounder"] and a short interview with the author ["Nowadays I Prefer to Lie in Print"][4]. While there is praise for some of the early sections of the novel, Grass is sternly rebuked for the eighth and ninth "months" (["Father's Day"] and Maria Kuczorra). Rolf Michaelis seems to regard the two ladies Billy and Maria as unnecessary extras which Grass, as an overambitious chef, wilfully insists on stirring into the already indigestible broth he has prepared for his readers (it will be noted that almost all the reviewers find it convenient to substitute culinary vocabulary for literary terminology). ["Grass is just repeating himself here"], we are told; and ["Father's Day"] is criticized for Grass's ["cramped employment of 'filmic' techniques"]. Finally: ["What is an intensifying reiteration for the first seven chapters turns in the last two—to stay with the culinary jargon of the book—to unappetizing dishwater"]. Amazingly, Mr. Michaelis seems to ignore the obvious fact that the last two sections hold the novel together by providing the vital link-up between the past and the present: not only do they complete the "story"; they also enable us to discern the point of the historical episodes.

Anglo-Saxon attitudes, as enshrined in the columns of the *Times Literary Supplement, The Observer,* and the *New York Review of Books* were no less hostile to the new arrival when the book appeared in English translation on both sides of the Atlantic fifteen months after its German début. There is a suggestion that our reviewers would have preferred not a tasty *pot-pourri,* but instead some nasty, though perhaps necessary medicine. Anthony Burgess believes that while Grass is "not a novelist" he may still, in a sense, be "good for the Germans," and ends up regretting that so many of the recipes are attuned to German rather than Mediterranean relish: *"The Flounder* is not a wine and garlic book but a beer and dill one."[5] Which is a little odd, when you consider the amount of garlic which Grass uses in his recipes!

Inevitably one man's poison is another man's relish, and it is hardly surprising that Nigel Dennis of the *New York Review of Books* should, by contrast with two of his predecessors, single out the recipes and the ["Father's Day"] section as being, along with the Calcutta episode, the only claims to distinction which the novel possesses.[6] For the rest, he is content to disinter some very antiquated ammunition:

> The coarse, permissive words that overwhelm the sentences much as the author's vast mustache overwhelms his face [there is a cartoon to illustrate this point] do nothing to revitalize a language struck dumb by the Nazis.

It is, of course, a little strange that Mr. Dennis, having shuddered at the permissiveness of the language, should have enjoyed ["Father's Day"] at least to the point of being able to say "This story would have made a fine short novel — in the hands of another writer." He then adds insult to injury when he suggests that Ralph Manheim's translation of the novel into American is actually an improvement on the original: "Here, as elsewhere in the novel, Mr Manheim uses a cooler hand and chooses his words from a harder vocabulary." Neal Ascherson of *The Observer* is no less unsympathetic. Applying one of those remarkable metaphors so often passed off as axiomatic value-judgements in the Sunday press, he claims that, in *The Flounder*, "some inner bit of elastic seems to have snapped . . . In the theme of *The Flounder*, Grass isn't sure of his own feelings."[7]

Finally, another oddity in the form of a spoof review appeared in *Die Welt* on 31 December 1977. Here it is claimed that Grass had just published yet another 700-page novel (*Der undichte Sarg*) [*The Leaking Coffin*], in which this time the story of Snow White and the Seven Dwarfs provides the leitmotif in an anti-feminist polemic by the ["Pasha From Danzig"]

> [But in Grass's case, understandably, the seven dwarfs move into the center of the action. His passion for Lilliputians is well known, and here he is able to wallow in the description of no less than seven little Kashubian tin drummers all at once and their doings in the forests of the Vistula delta.]

Here again, the suggestion is that we have heard it all before: the fairy-tale *montage*, the misshapen anti-heroes, the nostalgia for the lower reaches of the Vistula. One would be tempted to commiserate with the maligned novelist, were it not for the common front formed against the reviewers by the general public on the one hand and the academics on the other, who for once show signs of uniting in an unexpected alliance. By purchasing 300,000 copies in its first year, the public have given adequate expression to their interest in and, one must assume, their approval of the book. Well within a year of its appearance, the first course on *Der Butt* had been organized at a German university, by Dr Bosse of Freiburg im Breisgau, who was to be heard lecturing on it every Monday from four to six p.m. during the summer semester of 1978. According to a published synopsis of the course, his students were expected to familiarize themselves with Conze's *Sozialgeschichte der Familie in der Neuzeit Europas*, and with Theweleit's two-volume study, *Männerphantasien*.[8]

It is not my present intention to approach the novel from a sociological angle. Instead, a literary analysis restricted to the narrative technique and the use of the *Butt* motif is to be attempted, after a few words about the dimensions of this extraordinary flatfish.

The 700 pages of Grass's novel encompass a time-span of approximately 4,000 years. To be more precise, time as narrated begins on 3 May 2211 B.C. and ends in September 1974. Within this ["temporal unit in the higher sense"] — to borrow an apt turn of phrase from Goethe[9] — there are eleven successive layers of time, beginning with the Stone Age and ending with eastern-European Communism. Each of these epochs provides the background to the biography of a principal female character, who, since she spends much of her time preparing meals, is accurately described as a "cook." Their stories are told, in the first person, by one or several of their male contemporaries. To compound the confusion created by this multiple perspective, all these narrators are presented as the figments of the creative intuition of a single central character, whom I propose to call the "author." While it would be tempting to identify the "author" with Günter Grass, the precise extent to which they can in fact be equated with one another is hard to establish. There are certainly some close parallels, but also many important differences. Grass apparently possesses a collection of valuable antique glasses, but these were not destroyed in the course of marital argument as recorded in *Der Butt*. But it would be futile to attempt to separate fact from fiction here, and to ascertain, among other things, whether the Grass household does in fact contain that fully automatic dishwasher with its twelve low-noise programmes.

The author is married to a lady by the name of Ilsebill, whom he impregnates in the first chapter of the book, which is divided into nine ["months"], and thus constitutes a kind of sympathetic pregnancy for its author. Each "month" contains some ten to fifteen subsections devoted variously to the eleven historical cooks, the progress of the above-mentioned pregnancy, and to the author's other preoccupations during his nine-month gestation: poetry, the trial of the eponymous flounder, and travel abroad. Only the eighth month, ["Father's Day"], is entirely single-stranded. The stories are offered as a diversion and frequently also as an irritant to the increasingly pregnant Ilsebill, though the book is dedicated to "Helene Grass," the name given to the daughter who duly emerges in the ninth month. It is therefore to the future that Grass presents his Gargantuan, amorphous offering: the history of the world as exemplified by eleven women, their husbands and lovers, their beds and their cooking-pots. Yet in all this diversity, the subject matter never actually gets out of control, since several form-giving devices are at work to create a semblance of unity. These include the omnipresent narrator who can and does pluralize himself at will, and the flounder, as he is called in the English version of the fairytale from which he was borrowed, ["Of the Fisherman and His Wife"].

As there always will be those who grumble that modern novelists spend too little time on story-telling and too much by far on playing confusing games with their readers (one of the principal objections latent in the reviews of *Der Butt*), a few general remarks on the novel are called for, especially on the relationship between the narrator and the plot. In a well-known passage of *Aspects of the Novel*, E. M. Forster has this to say about that vital ingredient, "story":

> Yes — oh dear yes — the novel tells a story . . . The primitive audience
> was an audience of shock-heads, gaping round the camp-fire, fatigued

with contending against the mammoth or the hairy rhinoceros, and only kept awake by suspense. What would happen next? The novelist droned on, and as soon as the audience guessed what happened next, they either fell asleep or killed him.[10]

In this view, the novelist can't win. He lulls his readers to sleep if he tells his story predictably, but if their expectations are *not* fulfilled, the critics will immediately reach for their cudgels. The novelist suffers from another handicap: his genre, the novel, had not yet been invented in Aristotle's time. So nobody, certainly nobody of Aristotle's stature, has ever drawn up a compelling list of dos and don'ts for the guidance of its authors. Worse still, there was nobody to disagree with, no authority against whom to pit one's brains while formulating an artistic credo—nobody whose stern precepts could be sublimely transcended by a Shakespeare, held up to ridicule by sundry *Stürmer und Dränger*, or outmanœuvred by Brecht's dialectics. Not for the novelist the joy of smashing conventions, such as Goethe must have felt when he wrote *Götz von Berlichingen*, or Brecht, when he warned his audiences ["Don't gape so romantically"], or Peter Handke, when he proclaimed ["Here we do not give unto the theater that which is the theater's"].

A degree of ambivalence, an open-ended quality, were necessary features of the novel from its earliest stages onwards. It is surely not fortuitous that the first European novel would have broken all the rules, had there in those days been any rules to break. This was *Gargantua and Pantagruel* by Rabelais, whose influence Grass has repeatedly acknowledged: wild, fantastic stuff, full of bizarre invention and yet at the same time both very erudite and highly critical of the way society was developing. It displays a peculiar, sprawling style which arises from the sheer mass of material that the novelist, in contrast to the dramatist, can allow himself to accumulate, and from his exuberance in piling episode upon episode without needing to worry unduly about how it is all going to end. It is this lure of the open-ended prose epic that imparts a distinctive quality to the novels of Rabelais and Grimmelshausen, Jean Paul, Döblin, and finally Grass himself. This, at any rate, is the context in which he has chosen to present himself to his public.[11]

One of the most significant decisions facing any writer of fiction is whether to avail himself of the first or the third person. The first-person narrator allows him more leeway in telling his story and at the same time commenting personally on the events, but this greater freedom is purchased at the expense of stretching his readers' credulity, especially on the old question of how the narrator could have managed so unswervingly to be in precisely the right place at exactly the right time. Most novelists using this perspective lay themselves open to criticism along these lines, and many ingenious devices have been tried in attempts to reconcile the limitations of the first-person narrator with the rewards of a freely-ranging narrative. Siegfried Lenz provides an illustration of their dilemma. In his novel *Deutschstunde* [*The German Lesson*], the narrator is a boy in his teens, Siggi, who is trying, in 1954, to reconstruct the events which he experienced as a young child during the war. The problem of how the young lad could have known about all the mysterious goings-on in his village is solved, perhaps rather pedantically, with Siggi forever assuring his readers that a given incident or conversation was witnessed through a keyhole, accidentally overheard through an open window, or otherwise observed from the shelter of some secret hiding-place. The result is less elegant, though more naturalistic, than Grass's invention of the "protean" three-year-old who figures in *Die Blechtrommel.*[12]

Attempts to adapt the limited narrator with his single perspective to the demands of a wide-ranging and variegated story are by no means peculiar to the twentieth century. The solution which Grass offers in *Der Butt* and which involves a pluralizing of the narrator was, in fact, not uncommon in the eighteenth century, the heyday of the epistolary novel, which takes the form of a compilation of letters written by different people. As such, it represents a fairly sophisticated experiment with perspective. By employing a succession of different narrators and thus an ever-changing point of view, many eighteenth-century novelists (Richardson, Laclos, Rousseau) were able not merely to enrich their novels by changes of style and incident, but to play off conflicting attitudes to their subject-matter, and sometimes come surprisingly close to questioning the very nature of truth. It is for this reason that Goethe makes *Werther* end, not with yet another letter from the unfortunate man, but with a sober account of Werther's death that is in complete contrast to his impassioned letters and makes it retrospectively impossible for the reader to regard them as embodying the whole truth of the matter.

Grass has long shared this concern about the function of the narrator, and his earliest experiments reveal a reluctance to use a conventional first-person narrator who is directly involved in the story he is telling. Before he wrote *Die Blechtrommel* he was planning an epic related by a recluse perched, in the manner of a saint, on a column high above the town which was to have provided the subject of the poem.[13] This idea was then scrapped in favour of the perspective of the child under the table, allowing Oskar Matzerath to unmask a ruthless and hypocritical adult world by investing it with his own carefully cultivated childish waywardness. In his next book, *Katz und Maus*, there are two centres of interest, Pilenz and Mahlke, and in *Hundejahre*, an *Autorenkollektiv* including several participant narrators, one of whom tends to interrupt the others with personal reflections and digressions of his own. From *Hundejahre* it is a relatively short step to *Der Butt*, where the narrator pluralizes himself to such an extent that he equates himself with almost every male character in the novel.

Inevitably, some confusion arises from the fact that the author introduces himself with the pronoun *Ich*, and then proceeds to apply the same pronoun to many of his characters. One may get round this ambiguity by distinguishing between the narrator-in-charge (the author who tells the stories) and his subjects, the "episodic" narrators, or simple *Ichs* within the stories. But in doing so, there is a risk of obscuring one of the central ideas of the work, which is the continuity and repetitiveness of history. This is reflected most clearly in the many similarities between narrators and author: their creative impulses, their attempts to behave rationally, their many conflicts with their emotional and unpredictable womenfolk. In the final chapter, the narrator and the author coalesce.[14]

The Stone-Age *Ich* ("Edek") begins his life as a simple fisherman, but is soon persuaded by the omniscient flounder to experiment with smelting metal. The women, represented by Aua of the three breasts, do not like the idea and take concerted industrial action to stop him. The medieval *Ich* (Albrecht Slichting) is involved in the affairs of the local swordsmiths' guild. His wife Dorothea suffers from migraine and, as a religious fanatic, effectively disrupts his life by compelling him to escort her on lengthy and exhausting pilgrimages. Sometimes, though, the roles are reversed. The nineteenth-century *Ich*, Otto Friedrich Stubbe, batters his wife when drunk and steals from the trade union kitty, while she, Lena, organizes the workers and compiles her "Proletarian Cookery Book." There is always a disharmonious element, even in the most docile relationships, such as that of Agnes Kurbiella and the duo Anton Möller / Martin Opitz. While serving them both with self-negating devotion, Agnes dreams of the Swedish soldier Axel who killed her parents and raped her when she was a child.

All these historical figures foreshadow and counterpoint the present-day author, whose Ilsebill is no less demanding than most of the earlier spouses, rebuking the author for his stories, extolling the ["low-noise dishwasher with twelve fully automatic cycles"] and planning her package holiday ["on the lesser Antilles"]. One could argue, as some of the reviewers have done, that Ilsebill and the author act out a variation on a theme which the book illustrates against different historical backcloths. But this would mean ignoring the gentle mood of resignation, the capacity for irony with which Grass endows his present-day author, and which distinguishes him from many of his antecedents. His somewhat schoolmasterly delight in giving away recipes, the baroque idyll in the ["gourd-vine arbor"] section, and the blatant irony with which the Vasco da Gama episode ends are vivid human touches which demarcate the author's *Erzählzeit* [narrative time] from his historical fictions. Take, for example, his trip to India in the third "month." Here, in the guise of Vasco da Gama (this to provide a link-up with Margarete Rusch, whose recipes rely on pepper from India), the author lands in Calcutta. He sees the shantytown, the temples, the poverty, the dreadful diseases. Finally he explodes in a great tirade against the misery he has seen. Yet his thoughts only underline his own impotence:

[Send a postcard with regards from Calcutta. See Calcutta and go on living. Meet your Damascus in Calcutta. As alive as Calcutta. Chop off your cock in Calcutta (in the temple of Kali, where young goats are sacrificed and a tree is hung with wishing stones that cry out for children, more and more children). (237 / 187–88)]

Then at last, having decided to transfer the United Nations to Calcutta, or to abolish the city altogether, he turns to himself and notes: ["In Calcutta, Vasco gained four and a half pounds" (238 / 188)].

Our survey of the many-faceted narrator would not be complete without a few words on the poems, which intertwine with the text and in which the author steps outside the framework of his stories and comments directly on his subject-matter. A telling example of his intentions is to be found in the short poem with the give-away title ["What I Write About" (14–16 / 8–9)] where it transpires that his underlying concern is similar to the theme of the fairytale about the flounder: ["I write about superabundance . . . in the midst of a mound of millet" (14 /8)]. Modern man is tunneling his way through a mountain of latter-day millet and choking in *Überfluß* ["superfluity"] — the word itself pinpoints cause and effect of many of today's problems: affluence and effluents. ["I write about breasts . . . I write about hunger . . . About nausea brought on by a heaped plate"]. Food is a substitute for the breast, brings comfort, allays unspecified fears. Hunger is the cause and effect of political developments (the potato in Prussia (sixth "month"); the famine in Bengal in 1942 (third "month")). But the modern world is replete; people long not for food but for new-fangled dishwashers, though, as Grass hints in his last stanza, the deep-freezes are just waiting for the juice to dry up as we cluster round a nearly empty table where the fishbones must inevitably stick in our throats. This image provides a suitable cue for an examination of the *Butt*-motif, a reworking of a traditional and trenchant indictment of vain acquisitiveness.

Like the fairytale *Von dem Machandelboom* (The Juniper Tree) which is used in *Die Blechtrommel*, the story of the *Butt* is of Pomeranian origin and therefore rooted in the Danzig hinterland.[15] Both tales were first recorded by the painter Philipp Otto Runge and sent to the publishers of *Des Knaben Wunderhorn* in 1806. *Von dem Fischer un syner Fru* appeared in 1812, and later in Grimm's celebrated collection, not without substantial changes. Another version is to be found among Runge's posthumous works, this time in a low German dialect, ["largely, though not completely, adapted to the dialect of Hamburg"].[16]

One day a fisherman, who lives with his wife in a dwelling described as a ["pisspot"], catches a flounder and sets it free when it reveals that it is an enchanted prince. His wife rebukes him for this and urges him to ask it to provide them with a little hut. Though apparently content to be where he is, the fisherman does as she suggests:

[". . . my wife says I should have wished for something; she doesn't want
to live in the pisspot any more and would like to have a little hut."—
"Well, off you go," says the flounder, "she's in it already."]

A week or two later, the wife, Ilsebill, remarks ["The hut is getting too
small for me"] and sends her husband off to ask for a castle. When this
proves unsatisfactory, she decides she must be king of the country as well,
and no sooner has she been made king than she wants to be the Emperor,
and as if that were not enough, she goes on to demand that she be made
Pope. Each time her dutiful husband goes down to the beach and repeats
his little ditty:

> [Mandje, Mandje, Timpe Thee!
> Flounder, flounder in the sea!
> My good wife, my Ilsebill,
> Isn't yet content like me!]

When her wishes have been fulfilled they retire to bed, and the man at last
goes to sleep with a certain degree of relief, for now that his wife is Pope,
there seems nothing left for her to aspire to. It is precisely this feeling of
having reached the end of the road that worries her now and causes her to
toss and turn all night long until dawn, when, seeing the sun rise, she
realizes that there is one thing left: ["I want to be like God"]. This gives
the poor man such a fright that he falls out of his bed. All his protests are
in vain, and she dispatches him to the sea-shore as she had done
previously:

["Well, what does she want now?" said the flounder. "Well," said the
man, "she wants to be just like God." "Off you go! She's sitting in the
pisspot again!" —And there they sit until this very day.]

This is the substratum that holds Grass's novel together by uniting the
principal ideological strands, which, viewed together, provide information
about the author's attitude to history:

1. The idea of progress. The fisherman's wife with her incessant
   demands brings about the creation of increasingly sophisticated material goods, as has happened over the past centuries. There is an
   apparent increase in the standard of living.
2. The idea of futility. The endless chain of demand, consumption,
   demand, is a process which, once started, cannot be stopped. The
   woman is trapped, her desires become gratuitous.
3. The idea of history as a cyclic process. The small cycles determined by human greed are themselves contained within a larger
   cycle. The level of consumption becomes so outrageous that the
   whole process is terminated by a "big bang."
4. The interaction of the sexes as part of this historical process.
   Their apparent polarity (the reluctant husband versus the appetitive
   wife) provides the battleground on which the issue of social progress
   is fought out. Eventually Ilsebill wants not just greater wealth or
   comfort, but to be a man (king, emperor, Pope). She betrays not

only her husband, but her own sex as well: this extreme aspiration anticipates the events of ["Father's Day"].

This story was not chosen for arbitrary reasons — it is evidently a variation on the Paradise Lost theme, and there are parallels in *Macbeth* and in folk tales from most corners of the world (see Bolte and Polivka, I, 142–48). It would be wrong to follow the majority of the reviewers and regard it as the anti-feminist backbone of the book, the more so as Grass actually provides an alternative version in ["The Other Truth" (438 / 345)] Here it is claimed that Runge had two versions dictated to him by an old woman on the island of Oehe. In the second of the two it is the man who went back and asked for more — bridges, houses, and towers, carriages pulled along by invisible forces, ships that travelled under water. When he has all these things, despite protest from his wife, he says: ["And now I want to be able to fly"] and then ["I want and I want to be able to fly to Heaven"], whereupon the bridges and towers collapse, the dykes burst and the dirigibles fall apart. A new ice-age comes about, and the story ends with the unfortunate couple cowering somewhere amongst the ice: ["And there they still sit under the ice until this very day"]. Runge, confused by the contradiction, asked his informant which was the authentic one. But she gave an equivocal reply, ["The one and the other together"], and waddled off to the market-place to sell her sheep's cheese. The whole episode is one of Grass's brilliant inventions. An animated discussion takes place between the leading Romantics (Clemens Brentano, Achim von Arnim, the brothers Grimm, and Bettina Brentano) on the question of which version to include in the proposed collection of German folk-tales. For various reasons, partly because the second version might be misunderstood as an attack on Napoleon, partly because Brentano insists, for reasons of his own, that the woman in the first version represents ["the essential woman"], it is decided to suppress the second variant, rather against Runge's better judgement. [" 'It is obviously the case,' said the painter a trifle bitterly, 'that we humans are prepared to tolerate always only the one truth and not the others as well' "]. This is surely the trap that Grass is trying to avoid in *Der Butt*, by presenting not one or two, but several dozen different points of view, and allowing pro- and anti-feminist arguments to stand side by side. When Neal Ascherson says "Grass isn't sure of his own feelings" (see note 7), one might counter: "Of course Grass isn't sure of his own feelings about women. If he were, he would love them or leave them: he wouldn't turn them into literature." After all, even *Anna Karenina* presents the reader with three separate and irreconcilable statements about marriage.

The dangers of aligning oneself wholeheartedly with one or the other sex are in any case illustrated by the career of the flounder, the relentless advocate of ["male affairs"]. Gradually, under his influence, society changes from a matriarchal system, presided over by Aua, to one in which men strive to reach their fullest potential. But as time goes by he becomes dischanted with his protégés, who misunderstand and bowdlerize his suggestions, and bore him with their petty worries. So he resolves to switch his allegiance to women instead:

["Nothing can be expected of you daddies any more. Nothing but dodges and gimmicks. Now," he said as though in leave-taking, "I'll just have to pay a little attention to the Ilsebills." (47 / 35)]

But the chosen sex of the Ilsebills, as represented by three rather neurotic lesbian activists, Siggi, Fränki, and Mäxchen, refuse to listen to his advice, and instead put him on trial before an all-female tribunal (das Feminal) for discrediting the feminist cause. The resulting show trial may be read as a comment on some of the excesses of the emancipation movements of the early 1970s. But it is also more lighthearted and more serious than that. It reminds the reader of a carnival rather than of a court case (as when seven principal splinter groups are formed with names like Buttpartei, Frauenkollektiv Ilsebill, Feministische Initiativgruppe 7. August; compare also the reactions of the gutter press, the popular demand for recipes mentioned at the trial, ["mushrooms à la Aua"], etc., and the lurid graffiti illustrating key motifs from the trial which begin to appear all round the town). But the proceedings also incorporate a large number of details reminiscent of political developments of the recent past: election rallies, demonstrations, protest meetings. There are some parallels with the trial of the Baader-Meinhof group in a specially-equipped court at Stuttgart — the protective enclosure needed to ensure the flounder's safety recalls security precautions there, as does the scrutiny of authorized observers.

Repeatedly, the thirty-three members of the Feminal disagree among themselves as to how the trial is to be conducted. Caucuses are formed, secret understandings are reached, new seating arrangements demanded:

[Throwing ideological scruples to the winds, the left-wing majority, consisting of four different factions, had suddenly (and only because the Flounder had three times used the word "evolution") allied itself with the radical-democratic Federation of Women, and voted in favor not only of prefixing the title "Advisory Council" with the word "revolution-ary" (which decision was carried by a bare majority) but also of the proposed new seating arrangements. (112–13 / 89)]

It all sounds very familiar, not just from the doings of the political fringe, but from the very heart of democracy, from parliamentary organization itself: ["Accordingly as the Revolutionary Advisory Council voted, the chairs to the left or right increased or decreased" (113 / 89)].

One of the peculiarities of the trial is that affinities exist between members of the Feminal and characters described in the historical sections of the book. There is a resemblance between the president of the tribunal, Dr Ursula Schönherr, and Aua (p. 65). Helga Paasch is described as ["the image of my Wigga"] in a reference to the Iron-Age ["wurzel mother" (87

/ 68)]. The effect is to draw attention to an underlying persistence of human character traits which may easily be blurred by superficial cultural differences. Grass takes these correspondences to amusing and sometimes preposterous extremes:

> [And the latter-day Mestwina — this, too, must be mentioned — also had the glazed and empty look that had betrayed my then Mestwina when she had sopped up too much fermented mare's milk. (115 / 90)].

Some conclusions will be drawn from these astonishing correspondences in the light of the intertwining of themes in the novel, our next and final topic.

Throughout the text, Grass describes his female characters as ["cooks"], and pride of place is given to the meals which they prepare. He frequently depicts their concoctions with such relish that the reader is tempted to believe that this is done for its own sake. Nigel Dennis writes (see note 6):

> Certainly his recipes for cooking eels, fish, birds and pigs are inspiring enough to make any man insist that the woman's place is in the kitchen. And how wonderful it is to find recipes that are not hazy, as they so often are in cookbooks.

At the same time it is clear that a relationship exists between the food and the fate of the eater. The image of the "Köchin" ["cook"] thereby acquires a sinister dimension, and reminds us of "die schwarze Köchin" ["the black cook," the Black Witch] in *Die Blechtrommel*. Not only is man, according to Feuerbach and other materialists, the result of his own diet, but woman, by supplying his food, gains control over his destiny and over the collective destiny of the community. From the start, we see her exploiting this power. The neolithic shaman Aua keeps her men in a state of placid subservience by breast-feeding them. Her successor, Wigga, starts off a migration which will topple the Roman Empire by supplying palatable cereals to a handful of disgruntled Goths, thus encouraging them to strike camp and begin a long search for tastier sustenance. Mestwina is able to temper the zealous Bishop Adalbert's missionary fervour by stirring an aphrodisiac additive into his soup, with amazing and instantaneous consequences: ["Time and time again the ascetic penetrated her flesh with his by now utterly unrepentant gimlet" (107 / 84)]. A new synthesis is effected between the spirit and the flesh [("he exhausted himself inside her, all the while mumbling his Church Latin, as though he had discovered a new way of pouring out the Holy Spirit")], and the result is explicable in Hegelian terms. The bishop's passionate evangelizing is halted, and pagan rituals come to be amalgamated with the new religion as it is introduced into northern Europe. In many of the subsequent cases Grass shows women taking advantage of their ability to affect the course of history, sometimes on a local level, as happens when Sophie Rotzoll poisons the governor of Danzig at the time of the Napoleonic Wars, sometimes indeed with far-reaching consequences for the future of the nation, witness Amanda Woyke's restless exertions to see the potato established as the staple diet of rural Prussia.

Just as history does not follow a linear course, the recipes do not steadily improve — here, as in other fields of human endeavour, there are many ups and downs. Some of the tastiest-sounding morsels were served up in the sixteenth century by the Rabelaisian ["Fat Gret"], while the most recent cook, if she deserves that title, works in a drab canteen in the Lenin Docks of Gdańsk. But for all his gourmet's interest in herbs and spices, Grass is principally concerned to demonstrate his characters' involvement in human affairs through their control of what goes into the cooking-pot.

The further we have delved into the entrails of *Der Butt*, the greater has been our awareness of the author's concern to interlink the various layers of his narrative. The omnipresent author is only one of his methods, but an effective one, since it reinforces the impression that all the various narrator-*ichs* share a family resemblance. They are, for the most part, artists or artisans. Aua's Edek describes himself as a ["baltic Daedalus" (122 / 97)], carves wood, and makes pots. Dorothea's husband is a swordsmith. Agnes Kurbiella devotes herself equally to two artists, the painter Anton Möller and the poet Martin Opitz. These many alternative personae of the author, with their often obvious limitations and faults, give some continuity to the work and persuade the reader to draw his own comparisons between the successive epochs to which he is being introduced. As we have observed, the women of the *Feminal* are presented, however ironically, as reincarnations of the historical cooks. Several of the other figures are related to one another across the centuries. Ulla Witzlaff is descended from the old peasant woman who told Runge the story of the flounder. Billy, the tragic victim of the motor-bike spivs, is the great-granddaughter of Lena Stubbe. Isolated events and entire philosophic systems are shown to repeat themselves; the flounder is forever drawing parallels between different levels of time. St. Augustine and Ernest Bloch are compared on page 182 / 145, Zeus and Karl Marx on page 188 / 150. Recipes for cheese and for herrings, taken from different epochs, demonstrate continuity in matters of culinary taste (73–75 / 56–58; 200 / 160). The famines of 1317 and 1520 are viewed in the light of Europe in 1945 and present-day India (222 / 175). History is surveyed panoramically and interpreted as a never-ending succession of fads and philosophies, of intrigues and deceptions, with which men and women strive to make their lives bearable. Ultimately, it is a cyclic process, and the reader, represented in the first instance by the never-content Ilsebill, is invited to view the present in terms of the past and to understand that our present whims and fancies are part of an unalterable psychological pattern. So the present-day Ilsebill's desire for exotic package holidays is deliberately compared to the Gothic Dorothea von Montau's passion for arduous pilgrimages. The excesses of the medieval flagellants remind Grass of modern, hashish-taking youth; their hymns, he reflects, must have sounded like today's pop music:

> [In those days flagellation was pretty much what pot smoking is today. Especially the High Gothic youth, among whom I could no longer number myself, sought out the warming stench of the bands of flagellants, the percussion rhythms that went with their litany, their terrifying descents into hell, group ecstasies, and collective illuminations. . . . Tramps and spongers, that's what they were! Who do you think brought us the plague! (149–50 / 118)]

The late-medieval guilds and the striking workers in Polish Gdańsk and Gdynia are also equated:

> [But if we consider the workers shot in Gdańsk in a political light, along with the executed ringleaders of the medieval artisans' uprising, then as now little was achieved: true, the Danzig particians dropped their plan of importing beer from Wismar, but they granted the guilds no voice in the city council or court of aldermen; and the demand of the shipyard workers for worker management went equally unheard. (152 / 120)]

Conflicts and wars are presented as extensions and continuations of one another; the Yom Kippur War is seen as a sequel to the Thirty Years' War (117–18 / 93). Each time, man tries to improve his lot, and is thwarted. The flounder's promises rarely benefit him. Grass is fatalistic, without being pessimistic. True, the recipes from the Polish workers' canteen are not an improvement on those of the preceding chapters. But the book ends with an acceptance, if not exactly a celebration of ["the Eternal Feminine"]. This is not to say that Grass solves the problem of feminism in the contemporary world. What the book demonstrates is that the issues which we regard as important today are not unique, as we are apt to imagine, and that seen in the context of the chequered and murky history through which the human race has passed, neither sex can claim any inherent superiority over the other—a sobering contribution to an often heated debate that has raged with particular virulence in Germany during the 1970s, and one that concerns everybody.

Notes

1. Fritz J. Raddatz, " 'Wirklicher bin ich in meinen Geschichten': *Der Butt* des Günter Grass—Erste Annäherung," *Merkur*, 31 (1977), 892. [Ed. note: Page references to *Der Butt* in this article are given in the text in parentheses and in double form. Numbers before the slash refer to *Der Butt* (Neuwied: Luchterhand, 1977); numbers after the slash refer to *The Flounder*, trans. Ralph Manheim (New York: Harcourt Brace Jovanovich, 1978).]

2. *Der Spiegel*, 27 February 1978, p. 216.

3. Hellmuth Karasek, "Nora—ein Suppenheim," *Der Spiegel*, 8 August 1977, pp. 103 f.

4. Rolf Michaelis, "Mit dem Kopf auch den Gaumen aufklären," *Die Zeit*, 12 August 1977, pp. 29 f.

5. Anthony Burgess, "A fish among feminists," *The Times Literary Supplement*, 13 October 1978, p. 1141.

6. Nigel Dennis, "The One That Got Away," *The New York Review of Books*, 23 November 1978, pp. 22–24.

7. Neal Ascherson, "A fish out of water," *The Observer*, 8 October 1978, p. 30.

8. *Kommentar zu den Lehrveranstaltungen des deutschen Seminars im Sommersemester 1978*, herausgegeben vom Lehrkörper des deutschen Seminars, Albert-Ludwigs-Universität (Freiburg i. Br., 1978).

9. Goethe used this formulation to describe the period of 3,000 years covered by Act III of *Faust II*, in a letter to Wilhelm von Humboldt, 22 October 1826.

10. E. M. Forster, *Aspects of the Novel* (London, 1927), pp. 41 f.

11. See especially "Über meinen Lehrer Döblin," *Akzente* 14 (1967), 290–309; and "Im Wettlauf mit den Utopien," *Die Zeit*, 16 June 1978, pp. 29–31

12. For a discussion of Oskar's "proteanism" in *Die Blechtrommel*, see John Reddick, *The "Danzig Trilogy" of Günter Grass* (London, 1975), pp. 58–86.

13. Günter Grass, "Rückblick auf *Die Blechtrommel* oder Der Autor als fragwürdiger Zeuge," in *Günter Grass: Materialienbuch*, edited by Rolf Geißler (Darmstadt and Neuwied, 1976), p. 80.

14. ["Finally the man, the *ich*-narrator, and the authorial *ich* stand there as one, and have lost the famous informational advantage of men, the flounder speaks first with the woman, Maria Kuczorra, then she comes back and turns out to be Ilsebill, the two of them talk, laugh, he doesn't understand a word, she passes him by, he runs after her — an open ending"]. ("Gespräche mit Günter Grass," *Text und Kritik* I / Ia [fifth edition, 1978], p. 30).

15. See Johannes Bolte and George Polivka, *Ammerkungen zu den Kinder- und Hausmärchen der Brüder Grimm* (1912, reprinted Hildesheim, 1963), 5 vols., I, 138.

16. Bolte and Polivka, I, 138. The following quotations are taken from the original Pomeranian version, "De Fischer un sine Fru," I, 138–42.

"Into the Orwell Decade": Günter Grass's Dystopian Trilogy

Judith Ryan*

In his recent novel *Kopfgeburten* [*Headbirths*] (1980) Günter Grass gives an ironic summary of his literary progress. "What am I getting myself into?" he asks, immediately supplying his own answer, "the present."[1] Looking back at his previous works, Grass takes stock of their reception at the time of their appearance. The "Danzig trilogy,"[2] written at the turn of another decade — from the fifties into the sixties — was received with acclaim because, as everyone knew, "we have to cope with the past. From a distance: Once upon a time." Almost ten years later, at

*Reprinted from *World Literature Today* 55 (1981): 564–67, by permission of *World Literature Today* and the author. © 1981 by the University of Oklahoma Press.

the turning of the next decade, there was some disappointment over *From the Diary of a Snail* (1972): "Pooh! How can you write so subjectively about the present. And so politically, too. We don't like Grass that way. That's not what we expect of him." *The Flounder* (1977) was a greater success, Grass claims, because the critics preferred him to keep to the past: "Obviously he has given up and retreated into the past. We like him better that way. He owed that to himself and to us." The new novel contains its own prognosis of prospective reviewers' commentary: "Of course!" Grass has the critics cry; "His contribution to the election campaign. He can't keep away from it. And what's all this about births? He's had enough children. He has nothing to say in this discussion. He'll never understand the social trend to childlessness. That's a topic for younger authors. He should remain in the past, with his 'once upon a time' " (*K*, 129–30). In response to all this, Grass claims that his own contribution to what he calls in his newest novel "the Orwell decade" is set in a different dimension of time that is unique to fiction: the "plufutureperfect."

This concept is the key not only to [*Kopfgeburten*], but also to its immediate predecessors *The Flounder* and *The Meeting at Telgte* (1979). In fact, I will be putting the thesis here that these three books comprise, in effect, Günter Grass's second major trilogy. The strange convolution of time, the "plufutureperfect" that links the three novels is at the same time the basis of their particular, "dystopian" form of social criticism. The three books have more in common than may at first be apparent. In one sense or another they are all flights of fancy, "born from the head"; they deal with problems of procreation, gestation and creation; they subscribe to a belief in the primacy of narrative, yet are uneasily spliced with fragments of reality that resist complete integration with the fiction; they explore at once boldly and playfully the relation between fictional and historical or "real" time. From the mythic beginning of *The Flounder* through the historical digression of *The Meeting at Telgte*, Grass moves with [*Kopfgeburten*] into a hypothetical near-future. In the course of 1979, while Grass was at work on [*Kopfgeburten*] the poet Nicolas Born died prematurely of cancer. But Grass imagines that with the new novel he can take his dead friend with him on a cerebral journey "into Orwell's decade." If *The Flounder* is Grass' rewriting of a tale from the Brothers Grimm, then [*Kopfgeburten*] is his updated version of Orwell's *Nineteen Eighty-Four*.

I stress the present relevance of Grass's latest trilogy because it is precisely this that has been overlooked in recent reviews of the English translation of its middle piece, *The Meeting at Telgte*. What are we to make of this "lifeless literary construct"[3] that very likely "may be Greek to non-Germans"?[4] *The Flounder* had taken a timely problem — women's liberation and its implications for men — and explored it through an ingenious combination of historical retrospective and the timelessness of fairy tale. To be sure, it was a rather querulous masculine version of the problem, but one way or another the issues treated were general enough to call forth recognition from the non-German reading public. *The Meeting at Telgte*, with its arcane references to seventeenth-century German literature, poses a different problem. But it would be ill-advised for us to ignore it just because it appears to be another one of Grass's periodic retreats into the "snail's shell." It should not be read merely as a "delectation for those whose idea of a good time is to curl up with an anthology of Baroque poetry, a biographical dictionary of writers, a handbook of literary terms and a history of the Thirty Years' War."[5] Perhaps the extensive glossary and notes appended to the English translation get in the way of the more immediate questions the novel raises.[6]

Of the American reviews, few credit the novel with addressing important issues. To be sure, one reviewer does admit that Grass, while voicing his suspicion of writers and writing, nonetheless finds in the end a word that counts, "and the word is honor."[7] And another critic perceives that "the novel fleshes out serious old questions about the place of literature in the lives of nations."[8] Seen this way, *The Meeting at Telgte* becomes an "elegy," an expression of "the dream of all poets that they will survive through their words and works, that they 'will mingle with eternity.' " With this we come much closer to the real meaning of *The Meeting at Telgte*. Yet again, it is more than just a melancholy reflection of the ineffectuality of poets.

It is important, as I have suggested, to bear in mind the novel's specifically German setting. This doesn't mean, though, that one needs to have any very precise knowledge of German Baroque literature or Group 47. While the book's events take place toward the end of the Thirty Years' War and refer, by a kind of loose allegory, to the post-World War II situation of German writers, the novel is nonetheless also a manifesto addressed to German writers as they enter the "Orwell decade." It raises questions, most specifically, about the role of literature in the two German states (Grass himself still thinks in terms of a "divided Germany") and about the extent to which writers can and should engage with political matters.

The pacifist manifesto of the Baroque poets — the document that binds them together in spite of their disputes over dactyls and loanwords — is destroyed in the final conflagration of the Bridge Tavern, where they have held their meeting: "And so, what would in any case not have been heard, remained unsaid" (*MT*, 131). But we know, of course, that two of the novel's most prominent figures remain figuratively alive and heard: the rascally Gelnhausen, later Grimmelshausen, lives on in his *Simplicissimus*, still a major work in the canon of the picaresque, as well as in his later metamorphosis into the Günter Grass of *The Tin Drum*; and Libushka, the keeper of the tavern, is Grimmelshausen's Mother Courage, who herself lives on in that paradoxical Brechtian figure who warns us against the "Great Capitulation" even while capitulating herself. In spite of all, literature does seem to have a certain staying power.

Thus Grass's critique of poetic impotence in 1647 and 1947 is at the same time a challenge to German writers of 1979 to continue to wrestle with important issues and not to give up the belief that literature can in some way influence people: "The poets alone, so said the appeal, still knew what deserved the name of German . . . ; they were the other, the true Germany" (*MT*, 67). I have shown elsewhere[9] that this reference to the "other Germany" is an allusion to the "two-Germanies" theory that was hotly debated by the German exile writers in America during the last phase of World War II. Applied to German writers at the close of the seventies, however, it also suggests that writing itself may be a truer expression of the "real Germany" than the ideological clamor of the "mancies" (Grass's patronizing word for feminists) and the "greenies" (ecologists). Both *The Flounder*'s historical excursion and the trip into the near future in [*Kopfgeburten*] are thus a kind of literary opposition to what Grass sees as current social fads. At the same time, however, the narrator of *The Flounder* recognizes that he is "far away" and "written off" (*F*, 453) simply by virtue of his being a writer, and the narrator of [*Kopfgeburten*] partially identifies with the physical decline of his fellow writer Nicolas Born. Is Grass's attempt to create a financial "plufutureperfect" doomed to failure?

We can perhaps best approach this question by comparing [*Kopfgeburten*] with Grass's earlier election-campaign novel *From the Diary of a Snail* (1972). Here Grass had worked with two narrative strands whose commentary on each other was largely implicit, though not very difficult to deduce. Interspersed with the author's account in letters to his children of his participation in the Willy Brandt campaign of 1969 is the story of Hermann Ott, known as Zweifel (doubt), who spends World War II hiding in a cellar and pursuing the rather slimy hobby of raising snails. Ott's story ends in the late fifties with his emigration from Poland together with wife and child. We have just a brief glimpse of his new life in West Germany, where he interrupts his quiet domesticity only to give occasional adult-education lectures on such topics as the medieval symbolism of snails or Lichtenberg and the French Revolution. The politicking narrator, for his part, concludes with the realization that "we've barely managed to win one election," thus situating himself on the one hand within the snaillike movement of history and expressing relief on the other hand that change has come by such normal means as the election process (*S*, 283). His ironic self-image as a snail malgré lui is completed by an analysis of the relation between melancholy and utopia in the concluding lecture "On Stasis in Progress," a meditation on Albrecht Dürer's engraving *Melancolia I*.[10] In the election year 1969, then, Grass had closed his novel with an apology for melancholy as the "dark side of utopia" (*S*, 310).

Progress is seen even more pessimistically in [*Kopfgeburten*]. Toward the end of the book, the narrator asks: "What has changed? Is the cat the only one to have had babies?" (*K*, 157). Instead of allowing his two time lines almost to meet, as he had at the end of *From the Diary of a Snail*, Grass breaks off the new stories, real and fictional, before the end of the campaign. The fact that he explicitly conceives — or claims, perhaps ironically, to conceive — the book as a potential filmscript makes this curtailment even more pronounced. The filmscript fantasy adds another dimension to [*Kopfgeburten*], linking it with the "Danzig Trilogy" by its assumption that this film too will be directed by Volker Schlöndorff, who made the movie of *The Tin Drum*. The writing of [*Kopfgeburten*] is simultaneous with the release of the *Tin Drum* movie, but the very notion that the realist director Schlöndorff could take on the experimental [*Kopfgeburten*] is bound to give the reader pause.

The new protagonists, Harm Peters and his wife Dörte, are said to have been deliberately characterized in a fashion that will not too severely restrict the potential film director. All that Grass specifies is their particular degree of hair-coloring (Harm's medium fair, Dörte's blond) and that the actors must be able to speak with an authentic Holstein accent (*K*, 130–31). The narrator repeatedly assures us that he cannot tell us anything about their physical defects — Harm's cross-eyes, Dörte's gappy teeth — because he wishes to give Schlöndorff a free hand in his choice of actors. The irony is, of course, that when confronted with the drastic restriction imposed by the dwarf Oskar in *The Tin Drum*, Schlöndorff was brilliantly able to resolve the difficulty by his selection of the growth-retarded child actor David Bennent. But Harm's and Dörte's defects are subtler than Oskar's, more characteristic of people as they really are. Doubtless, this is precisely Grass's point, just as he also leaves no doubt that this couple, however ordinary, is at the same time quite typically German.

During his trip to China the narrator is overcome by a horrendous vision of a Germany with the population of China, monstrously equipped, not with bicycles, but with automobiles (*K*, 38). In a grotesque and disquieting parallel to the Nazi search for Lebensraum, he imagines a German population explosion as a kind of "insurance policy against the void" (*K*, 39) — the corollary of his protagonists' fear of a "living space without people." He visualizes frantic Germans on a search for their own identity, desperately asking their "dwarfed neighbor countries": "Who are we? Where do we come from? What makes us German? And what the devil is 'Germany'?" (*K*, 39). The Peterses' indecision over having a child is a manifestation of two popular German trends: on the one hand, the warnings of mass magazines, in the wake of what was known as the "Pillenknick" (drop in the birth rate due to the use of oral contraceptives), that "the Germans are dying out" (the subtitle); and, on the other hand, the more recently voiced fear of world overpopulation. [*Kopfgeburten*] holds both of these possibilities, as it were, in suspension.

But the narrator knows that after the end of his film everything will go on as before. The apocalypse projected in the seventeenth century by the Baroque poet Andreas Gryphius and in the twentieth century by

Grass's fellow writer Nicolas Born will not come to pass: "We will conform, resist, compromise and secure ourselves. We will want to ship out, and we will want to reproduce: in the end (after the end of the film) even Dörte and Harm" (K, 152). Although the narrator sees his own efforts as a Sisyphean task, he also knows that he mustn't "ship out": "If I try," he says, "I'll just embark by the back door, from an only apparently different point, on the old contracts. My worn-out escape boots. Often I have to take a running start from far-off centuries in order to be present again. Once upon a time. It is once upon a time. It will have been once more. A meddling contemporary, I'm curious about the eighties" (K, 152).

It would be dangerous if we were to universalize this tale, as we have in effect the long-winded history of Germany that Grass gives us in The Flounder. More urgently even than in the Danzig novels, Grass's newest trilogy is an appeal to the Germans. Grass attacks both their division of time into a completely separated past and present and their alignment of writers into black-and-white ideological camps: "Willingly (or with regret) they drive their living writers into exile; they are diligent mourners and wreath-wavers for their dead poets. Survivors who take good care of the monuments, as long as the costs are not too great" (K, 153). Nonetheless, Grass maintains that "we writers can't be killed off," and proceeds to demonstrate it by drawing an elaborate set of correspondences between dead poets and living, between East German and West, in which he sees the younger writers as direct heirs to the older ones, and all of them as engaged in a continuing common task (ibid.). So he stresses anew his belief in the political importance of writing.

Literature, he claims, is the one thing that connects the two German states, "that overarching roof,"[11] our indivisible culture" (K, 154). His new task for the election campaign of 1979 thus comes to be an apology for art in the broadest sense, and he argues for a National Foundation that would unite the two Germanies (K, 155), a foundation that would be more than a mere "mausoleum," that would be a good solid building "even if you have to enter it by two doors" (K, 155). And yet—the ironic narrator knows that this too is just another idea "born from the head" (K, 156). At the same time, he seems to take perfectly seriously his notion that the public lecture he gives in China on "The Two German Literatures" or (its unwritten subtitle) "Germany—A Literary Concept" (K, 8) is in fact a meaningful contribution to the election campaign. One wonders if the supposed "literary concept" Germany is not, in reality, a delusion. In this Grass would seem politically somewhat naïve.

The novel itself is, of course, also meant as a contribution to the campaign. As contrasted with Orwell's Nineteen Eighty-Four, set almost forty years ahead of the date of its appearance, [Kopfgeburten] takes place in a future only a few months away from the time of writing. What needs to be attacked now is not the dramatic takeover of bureaucracy, but the creeping invasion of uncertainty, triviality and banality. The novel ends with a near-accident: a Turkish boy runs in front of the Peterses' car but remains luckily unharmed. The language teachers' VW is dusted down by the multitudinous offspring of Germany's foreign workers, whose inability to communicate with the Peterses is the subject of the novel's ironic last sentence. This minor private defeat of Dörte and Harm has its public counterpart in the defeat of one of their favorite causes, a suit brought against a construction firm by environmentalists. On their return from India, the Peterses see that construction has already begun: "The great self-activating, self-realizing Yes. . . . The Yes to progress, the Yes that keeps on building up anew. The Yes to the eighties. Big Brother's Yes, to which Orwell's No (even now uncontradicted) is a little bit, but not especially much of a nuisance" (*K*, 164).

But this has already been suggested by the dual meaning of the novel's title: on the one hand, it refers to its own cerebral fantasy—an idea, born like Aphrodite from the head of Zeus; on another level, it means simply a normal birth, a cephalic as opposed to a breech presentation—birth headfirst. The trouble with this apocalyptic descent of the normal is that it is unutterably boring. Orwell's nightmare of bureaucratic despotism has been reduced to the dithering of a featureless couple over whether to have a baby. Orwell's magnificent satiric invention Newspeak has been replaced by the pat clichés and cute phrases that serve this couple as a substitute for original thought. "Just let them come, the eighties," Grass has one character say. "That's in Orwell's hands!" replies Harm (*K*, 116). The author's implicit contention is that the "Orwell decade" has in fact come to Germany, though not in the guise in which it was expected. But the satire succumbs to its own butt: flatness and triviality. The very features that made *The Tin Drum* so suitable for film—plasticity of detail, depth of sociological, historical and political insight—are lacking in [*Kopfgeburten*], a "filmscript" doubtless destined to remain a stillbirth.

When I was recently required to attend a fancy-dress dinner attired as a character from a work that ought to be, but is not yet, on the syllabus of a certain General Literature course, my Oskar costume went uncontended. The new trilogy offers no such image. Even the flounder and his interlocutor's long string of female cooks remain abstractions. And the Schlöndorff film of *The Tin Drum* stopped at the very point that might have given Germany pause as it entered the eighties: before the novel's searing exposure of postwar Germany's repressions and corruption. One wonders whether Grass's recent fantasy binge is quite the right way for the grand master of postwar German letters to usher in the new decade. But as one of his long-standing followers, I hope nonetheless that the time has not yet come to put Grass out to pasture.

Notes

1. *Kopfgeburten oder Die Deutschen sterben aus*, Darmstadt, Luchterhand, 1980. Page references to this edition are indicated by the abbreviation *K*. Translations are my own.

2. *The Tin Drum* (1959), *Cat and Mouse* (1961), *Dog Years* (1963). The subtitle "The Danzig Trilogy" came into use after the appearance of the novels and has since been added to the German paperback editions.

3. Theodore Ziolkowski, *New York Times Book Review*, 17 May 1981, p. 22.

4. Robert Taylor, *Boston Globe*, 13 May, 1981, p. 33.

5. Ziolkowski, op. cit.

6. This is not meant as a criticism of Leonard Forster's afterword and excellent notes on German Baroque literature in the English translation by Ralph Manheim, *The Meeting at Telgte* (New York, Harcourt Brace Jovanovich, 1981). Quotations are taken from this edition, indicated by the abbreviation *MT*.

7. John Leonard, *New York Times*, 30 April 1981, p. C21.

8. Paul Gray, *Time*, 18 May 1981, p. 87.

9. "Beyond *The Flounder*: Narrative Dialectic in *The Meeting at Telgte*," in *The Fisherman and His Wife: Günter Grass's "The Flounder" in Critical Perspective*, Siegfried Mews, ed. (New York: AMS Press, 1983), pp. 39–53.

10. *From the Diary of a Snail*, Ralph Manheim, tr., New York, Harcourt Brace Jovanovich, 1973. References to this edition are indicated by the abbreviation S.

11. A reference to Simon Dach (*Dach* means "roof"), the central figure in the poets' conference at Telgte.

Chaos or Order? Günter Grass's *Kopfgeburten*

J. W. Rohlfs*

[We've learned in school that the present comes after the past and is followed by the future. But I work with a fourth tense, the paspresenture. That's why my form gets untidy. On my paper more is possible. Here only chaos forments order. Here even holes are contents. And loose threads are threads that have been left radically untied. (130 / 111–12)][1]

The aim of this essay is to explore, by looking at the role of the narrator and at the narrative structure of *Kopfgeburten* [*Headbirths*], the implications of the author's claim that the artistic order of the work arises from "chaos."

Writing in the latter half of 1979 and completing his first draft on New Year's Eve, Grass's first-person narrator projects the fiction of Harm and Dörte Peters's journey to Asia in the summer holidays of 1980, the year of parliamentary elections in West Germany. Almost defiantly, the narrator dismisses the order of a chronological succession of events in favour of simultaneity: ["Because, you see, I want everything to take place at once (on paper as in my head)" (106 / 90)]. He jumps back and forth in

*Reprinted from *Modern Language Review* 787 (1982): 886–93, by permission of *Modern Language Review* and the author.

time, transposing the future of his *erzählte Zeit* ["narrated time"] into the present tense of the *Erzählzeit* ["narrative time,"] and switches from speculation about the future of the Germans and of the human race in general to brief accounts of past events. Straining against the inevitability of linear narration,[2] the narrator persists in his attempts to simulate simultaneity.

By discarding chronology as a structural principle and proclaiming simultaneity in its place, Grass appears to attempt a re-creation of thought processes in the order in which they occur: frequently interrupted yet interrelated, straying from the present into past and future, but still, inevitably, in linear sequence. Despite breaks in the narrative sequence of *Kopfgeburten*, syntax and logical progression remain intact — there is no attempt to translate the associative rambling of the mind at pre-speech level into narration.

The central narrative strand is the fictional characters' journey to Asia. The few glimpses of exotic landscapes and mysterious cultures are not designed merely to add up to a colourful [travel description] in which the unknown lurks behind every corner. Dörte's religious revelation on Bali, ["I need something different, the force that comes from inside, no, from outside, all right, laugh, something supersensory, a divine power, whatever. . . ." (66 / 55)], is described as little more than a sudden attack of the irrational, which renders the Western [rational individual] inarticulate and ridiculous. Wherever the merely idyllic raises its head, Grass counteracts it with ironic deflation: ["Look around you, my dear Frau Peters. These gentle Balinese youths. The grace of their movements. Their playful, undemanding nature — all they want from anyone is a little money for gas" (118 / 100)]. On this organized journey in the age of mass tourism by jet the travellers have no time to immerse themselves in the mystic experience of an alien culture; the real gain for Grass's couple is that they learn more about themselves and their own deficient responses to the real problems facing the Third World. The reader of *Kopfgeburten* is offered much more than a travelogue in the conventional sense. He learns about the origins of the fiction, the stimuli that set the narrative process in motion — Grass's own impressions and experiences at home and abroad. As Harm and Dörte Peters emerge as fictional characters they in turn stimulate the author's responses. A dialectical structure develops: Third World and affluent society, narrator and fictional characters, are set against each other. It is precisely by means of this structure — which provides abundant scope for authorial reflection — that the fullest narrative account to date of the author's global concerns emerges in highly concrete terms. Instrumental in building up this account is a narrator who functions as authorial voice. In contrast to the narrator-figures of the Danzig trilogy, the first-person narrator has not been developed into a fully-fledged fictional character. Although occasionally projected on the fictive level, interacting with the fictional characters, he frequently appears to be the author's spokesman and has been endowed with a generous portion of autobiographical detail:

> [A dubious stroke of luck, my birth year of 1927, forbids me to condemn anyone. I was too young to be seriously put to the test (23 / 18).
> In the year 1927, I was born in Danzig. . . . My birth year says: I was too young to have been a Nazi, but old enough to be partially moulded as well by a system that, from 1933 to 1945, first astonished and then terrorized the world.][3]

In his dual function of storyteller and barely distanced reflector of authorial experience and opinion, Grass's narrator is a counterpart of the first-person narrator in *Aus dem Tagebuch einer Schnecke* (1972) [*From the Diary of a Snail*], the work to which *Kopfgeburten* is most closely related. Hanspeter Brode writes of *Aus dem Tagebuch einer Schnecke*:

> [This book can be understood as an exact documentation of the double function of the artist and the citizen Grass, specifically if one examines it quite objectively from the point of view of literary craft. Grass relates the problems of his practical, day-to-day political work, but he does this according to all the rules of the art of writing great narrative.][4]

In *Kopfgeburten* Grass again refuses to maintain an artistic distance from the public and political questions which concern him as a citizen, and instead puts a good deal of authorial weight behind the narrative voice. That this is a deliberate decision is made clear by the author himself:

> [The fact that first in the *Diary of a Snail* and now in a consequently developed version in *The Flounder* I introduced the authorial 'I' as a first-person narrator taking the place of a previously established fictive first-person narrator, as in *The Tin Drum* or *Dog Years*, and the fact that then in *The Flounder* I metamorphosed this authorial 'I' after a certain amount of time into a fictive 'I,' but one always corresponding closely to the authorial 'I' — that, in my opinion, is a new departure for me, and one that naturally generates different prose forms and different lyric forms.][5]

In as much as the *Autoren-Ich* ["authorial 'I' "] is a projection of the real author into the narrative and can claim to speak for the author, it differs from the entirely fictive *Erzähler-Ich* ["narrative 'I' "];[6] on the other hand even an *Autoren-Ich* clearly remains a persona created by the real author and may therefore bear fictive traits.

The narrative begins in the past tense with the narrator recounting impressions of a recent journey to China organized by the Goethe-Institut, a key experience which has triggered off the narrative impulse.[7] As can be expected, the past tense is employed in the narrator's recollections, in historical references, and in sketching in the background to the fictional characters. In *Kopfgeburten*, Grass openly dismisses the expectations of certain critics that the writer of fiction ought to look to the past for his subject matter:

[What am I letting myself in for? The present. In the fifties and early sixties, when I wrote extensively about the past, the critics shouted: Bravo! The past must be overcome. From a distance, that is! Once upon a time.

In the late sixties and early seventies, when I wrote about the present — the 1969 election campaign, for example — the critics shouted: Phooey! This undistanced involvement with the present! This blatant political position! That's not how we want him. That's not what we expect of him.

In the late seventies, when (again, extensively) I amalgamated the Stone Age and ensuing periods with the present, the critics cried out: At last! He has re-emerged. Clearly he has given up, he is escaping into the past. This is how we like him. He owed it to himself and us.

If now, shortly before the inception of the eighties, I am once again biting (undistanced) into the present — though Strauss is a relic of the fifties — the critics will shout (guess what?): Here it comes! His contribution to the election campaign. He just can't stop. (129–30 / 111)]

While Grass's *Autoren-Ich* apparently closes the gap between author and narrator, the distance between authorial comment and fiction is increased, not temporally, but by his declaring openly and repeatedly that Harm and Dörte Peters [("My teacher couple — this headbirth" (11 / 6))] are his brainchildren. The narrative process is prominently displayed as the reader is constantly encouraged to participate in their creation and evolution as fictional characters. As Grass maps out their progress at the desk, he mainly uses the present tense. Far from creating chaos or confusion, this use of the present tense on the levels both of [narrative time] and of [narrated time] appears perfectly convincing. Indeed there are sound structural reasons for it. First, the temporal distance between these levels is less than a year — they are both embraced by Grass's [narrative present] in the wider sense. The temporal proximity of the narrator at the time of writing to fictional characters allows Grass to stress their involvement in the same contemporary issues. Secondly, the use of the present tense on both levels facilitates an 'exchange' of points of view between the generations as if an actual discussion had taken place. Moreover, the immediacy thus achieved increases the likelihood that the reader will be drawn into the issues: *Kopfgeburten* was written to be published in 1980, before the parliamentary elections. Harm and Dörte Peters represent the post-war generation that has emerged from the years of student unrest to take up positions of responsibility. ["He is in his middle, she in her early thirties. . . . Both are indefatigably self-reflecting veterans of the student protest movement" (11 / 6)]. They are representative of this generation in their willingness to commit themselves politically to achieve change:

[Our teacher couple from Itzehoe — which is near Brokdorf — are politically, personally, and generally cut out for the Central European 'Ontheonehand-on-theotherhand" parlor game. She belongs to the FDP

(Free Democrats); he lectures about the Third World at SPD (Social Democratic) meetings. Both say, "On the one hand, the environmentalists are right; on the other, they'll get Strauss elected." (15 / 10)]

The fact that change and progress, even on a local level, seem painfully slow and that individual contributions, in a global context, appear to be a mere drop in the ocean can easily lead to disappointment. Such disappointment threatens inactivity and explains the indecision of Harm and Dörte as to whether or not to have a child of their own. This gives Grass an opportunity to state his well-known attitude towards progress. Taking up the snail image from *Aus dem Tagebuch einer Schnecke* he has his narrator reject any undue hope in progress:

[I made a mistake in banking on the snail. Ten and more years ago I said: Progress is a snail. The people who shouted at the time, "Too slow! Too slow for us!" may recognize (as I do) that the snail has slipped away from us, has hurried ahead of us. (141 / 121)]

All the same the *Autoren-Ich* insists on setting a cautious optimism against the resigned attitude of his fictional characters and emerges from the dialogue as the more positive force who gives some encouragement to the Peters's generation. Grass's narrator reflects the author's view[8] that however painful and slow real progress may seem, it is worth working for:

[I am not chucking it. Every time I try, I (only seemingly elsewhere) slip back into my old commitments from a different direction. My down-at-heel escape shoes. To be present again, I often have to take a running start from remote centuries. There once was: there once is. There will have been once again. I'm curious about the eighties: a meddling contemporary. (152 / 131)]

Grass frequently uses the *Autoren-Ich* to express the belief of the *Bürger* Grass in the necessity of slow change. The narrator's memory stretches back further; he has experienced National Socialism. A good deal of sympathy has gone into the portrayal of the characters, even when the narrator mocks them. They have a genuine sense of responsibility, are forthright in their attitudes, and show a growing awareness of global conflict. Whenever the *Autoren-Ich* comments on the couple a productive friction develops, and occasionally he modifies their attitudes by bringing his knowledge of the past to bear on them. Harm Peters comments on the candidature of Franz Josef Strauss in the federal elections:

[We were born after that shit. We're guilty of entirely different shit. But wherever we go they ask us if there are Nazis in Germany again. As if the whole world wished there were. No! We have other worries. Not that everlasting prehistoric stuff. But what's going to happen tomorrow. How we're going to get through the eighties. Even without Strauss. That one's another relic of the day before yesterday. Still trying to hold Stalingrad. (84 / 69–70)]

Grass's narrator counters:

> [On the other hand, I have succeeded in persuading Harm Peters and
> Dörte as well, using examples from my days as a member of the Hitler
> Youth, to keep the candidate out of the lexical field "fascism, fascistoid,
> latently fascist," and both of them have accepted my line of argument
> that Strauss has achieved too little to be Chancellor even if one counted
> his various affairs as achievements. (172 / ed. trans.)]

Different though their arguments may be, the narrator stresses the
common ground between himself and the younger generation — the rejection of Strauss, the concern about nuclear energy programmes, and the
problems of the Third World.

Grass incorporates a great wealth of material in *Kopfgeburten* and
attempts to synchronize diverging narrative strands: hence the threat of
"chaos." Frequently, the narrator abandons the story of Harm and Dörte
Peters to take up a variety of issues that occupy the mind of the *Autoren-
Ich* at the time of the writing. He is compelled to speak on a multiplicity of
issues, always as "ich," following Grass's decision to simulate "simultaneity." In this context, his preoccupation with the medium of the film is
revealing, as this medium has a much greater synchronizing potential than
narrative prose.

> [The *verbal* artwork, in its epic form, is fixed in one dimension by the
> typographic medium and its linear sequence of grammatical elements
> following each other digitally or syntagmatically. . . . The *film* as
> artwork . . . employs a multidimensional medium capable of portray-
> ing not only temporal sequence and spatial juxtaposition but also
> movement, sound, and, finally, the simultaneity of synchronous actions.
> (Bisanz, 198)]

Grass's attempts to incorporate film techniques in his narrative prose reach
back to *Die Blechtrommel*, where the fictive narrator experiences and
describes a past episode as film and projects a fantasy on a wall. In *örtlich
betäubt* the dentist's television screen fulfils a similar function for the
development of the fictive narrator's fantasies. The cinematographic
aspect of Grass's narrative technique in *örtlich betäubt* has already been
analysed in some detail.[9] In *Kopfgeburten* the *Autoren-Ich* operates with
similar devices and, moreover, explicitly envisages as film the whole
narrative strand of Harm and Dörte Peters while he is narrating it. Grass
has his narrator discuss a joint project with Volker Schlöndorff, with
whom he collaborated on the filming of *Die Blechtrommel*:

> [Which explains why I said to Volker Schlöndorff, whom we met with
> Margarethe von Trotta in Djakarta and later in Cairo, 'If we do this
> picture, we should shoot it in India or in Java or — now that I've been
> there — in China, if they let us.

> The idea is for our teacher couple to take a trip, the way Ute and I,
> Volker and Margarethe take trips. (13 / 8)]

The ["interruptive narrative style"] (Gerstenberg, p. 118) which results from the attempt to simulate simultaneity by narrative means presents a continuation of the narrative experiment of *örtlich betäubt*. In *Kopfgeburten* there is often neither a transition nor an obvious link between the diverging levels. Facets of authorial reflection on the one hand and the fictive journey on the other are interspersed with references to the narrative process itself. Is it true, as Grass claims in the passage quoted at the outset of this article, that order emerges from chaos? Does he manage to overcome the threat of disintegration posed by his decision to allow the simultaneity of thought processes to dictate the narrative flow?

The narrative strands seem to diverge most seriously when Grass introduces material purely on the level of authorial reflection from which the fictional characters are barred. While the atomic power plant in Brokdorf, Strauss's candidature, and the plight of the Third World population can be "discussed" both by authorial narrator and by fictional characters, a passage like the account of the slow death of Grass's friend and fellow-author, Nicolas Born, appears to be an abrupt interjection. But in the following chapter there is news of another death — Rudi Dutschke's — and cause for another lament; this time the Peters's generation is more immediately affected. In the evolving dialectic structure of the narrative, Dutschke briefly becomes a counterpart to Strauss, while his death is juxtaposed to that of Nicolas Born.

The account of clandestine meetings of East and West German writers in East Berlin some years ago, and numerous comments on the situation of writers in the two German states, document a literary involvement in which the fictional characters have no part ["Harm and Dörte, for example. For them literature is at most a diversion" (178 / ed. trans.)]. But even such a resigned statement, which calls into doubt the communicative potential of literature — particularly if we assume that the generation of Harm and Dörte Peters are envisaged as the principal recipients in the communicative structure of *Kopfgeburten* — underlines the dialectic of the narrative.

More closely integrated with the fictive level is that part of Grass's *Vergegenkunft* ["paspresenture"] which deals with the future. The fact of a Chinese population of 950 million prompts the narrator to speculate ironically about the possibility of the same number of Germans populating the earth. The somewhat frightening vision of a *Volk ohne Raum* is immediately complemented by its antithesis ["living space without people" (7 / 13)] based on the actual fall in the birthrate in both German states. A connected theme on the fictive level is the couple's indecision about whether to have a child of their own. In theory they would both like a child, but the prospects of a nuclear future and Germany with Franz Josef Strauss as Chancellor are discouraging and lead to indecision:

["What sort of future are you going to let a child loose in? What prospects will it have? Anyway, there are enough children already, too many. In India, Mexico, Egypt, China. Look at the statistics." (12 / 7)]

Describing the eighties as "Orwell's decade" (85 / 71), the *Autoren-Ich* imagines what he would do if he became dictator in Germany for one year. His fantasy is complemented by that of Harm Peters on the fictive level. While there are differences of opinion, the common ground between the generations prevails. Not all elements of fantasy and speculation are used to link the narrative levels in such a direct manner. Grass's fantasy of Franz Josef Strauss as a fellow-author instead of a politician is addressed to his colleagues: ["Yes, yes, I know, dear colleagues: he is dangerous" (173 / ed. trans.)]. Although obviously a counterpart to the thoughts of Harm and Dörte on the subject of Strauss, this fantasy remains confined to the authorial level.

Kopfgeburten has a much stricter formal structure than the narrator's comments suggest. The nine chapters of the book clearly provide a frame which corresponds to nine months of pregnancy, a pattern first employed in *Der Butt*. While it is true that Harm and Dörte Peters are in the end no closer to having their own child, the author's efforts have been more fruitful. He has finished his book and even feels justified in having his narrator use the disparaging term ["wind egg" (136 / 117)] to describe the child — as a counterpart to his own *Kopfgeburten*. Much of the narrative is concerned with its own genesis, which the reader witnesses from the conception of an idea to the finished product in front of him.[10] ["The title of the film or book or both might be *Headbirths*, harking back to the god Zeus, from whose head the goddess Athene was born: a paradox that has impregnated male minds to this day" (8 / 4)]. The narrator's integrating role is an essential unifying factor in the book. The differences between the wide-ranging authorial perception and the perception of the fictional characters are considerable. The narrator persists in bridging the gulf in what often appears to be a negotiating process. Grass has endowed him with a role that is both provocative and at the same time conciliatory, as he opens up a dialogue between the representatives of the younger generation and authorial positions, in the course of which much common ground is discovered. The threat of chaos is overcome by a careful juxtaposition of views.

Finally, as in all of the author's narrative works, the title provides a central image which is carefully worked into the narrative strands and exercises an integrating influence. The image of the human head as bearer of ideas seems to have occupied Grass for some time. It is first used in the essay "Wettlauf mit den Utopien" ["Competing with Utopias,"] written in 1978:

[The human head sees itself as larger and more comprehensive than the terrestrial globe. It can think up and think around itself and us from distances no longer subject to terrestrial gravity. It writes itself in one way, reads itself in another. The human head is monstrous.

Hence this immoderation, the reason we can do something that no animal (not even birds) can do: we point beyond ourselves. This is why headborn progress can surpass us. We sniff out the way, beyond ourselves, towards our happiness and stray with tiny hearts through the huge systems of the head. (*Aufsätze zur Literatur*, 122)]

Grass explains in this essay how he derived the image from Döblin's *Berge, Meere und Giganten* (1924), a utopian novel about a world without toil and hunger, in which man had degenerated into a physically inactive and listless creature of slight build and massive head.

The term *Kopfgeburten* is applied repeatedly to the author's fictional characters and to his phantasies and speculations, such as his dream of a national cultural institution:[11]

[Because Harm and Dörte are my headbirths, I put things into their cradle that concern me — for instance, the continuation of the Brokdorf trial on Monday, November 26, 1979, in Schleswig. (133 / 114)]

[Such a National Endowment would have room for many things. The Prussian cultural heritage, cantankerously claimed by both states, would find its place. The chaotically dispersed cultural vestiges of our lost Eastern provinces could, if assembled there, help us to learn why those provinces were lost. There would be room for the contradictory trends in the arts of today. . . . Admitted. It's a wide-awake daydream. (Another headbirth.) (155–56 / 134–35)]

Notes

1. [Ed. note: Page references are given in the text in parentheses and in double form. Numbers before the slash refer to *Kopfgeburten oder Die Deutschen sterben aus* (Neuwied: Lucterhand, 1980); numbers after the slash refer to *Headbirths or The Germans Are Dying Out*, trans. Ralph Manheim (New York: Fawcett Crest, 1983).]

2. See Adam J. Bisanz, "Linearität versus Simultaneität im narrativen Zeit-Raum-Gefüge," *Zeitschrift für Literaturwissenschaft und Linguistik, Beiheft Erzählforschung, I* (1976), p. 199. . . .

3. Günter Grass, " 'Rede von der Gewöhnung' anläßich einer Israel-Reise in Tel Aviv und Jerusalem," *Frankfurter Allgemeine Zeitung*, 20 March 1967, reprinted in *Über das Selbstverständliche* (Munich, 1969).

4. Hanspeter Brode, "Von Danzig zur Bundesrepublik," in *text + kritik* I/Ia (Munich, 1978), p. 85.

5. Heinz Ludwig Arnold, "Gespräche mit Günter Grass," in *text + kritik* I/Ia, p. 28.

6. [See] Volker Neuhaus, . . . *Günter Grass* (Stuttgart, 1979), pp. 10–11.

7. See Grass, *Aufsätze zur Literatur* (Darmstadt and Neuwied, 1980), pp. 122–49 ("Im Wettlauf mit den Utopien"), an essay written in 1978 which anticipates many of the Third World themes of *Kopfgeburten*.

8. See *Aufsätze zur Literatur* p. 144 . . .

9. See Renate Gerstenberg, *Zur Erzähltechnik von Günter Grass* (Dissertation, Heidelberg, 1980), p. 109. . . .

10. All of Grass's narrative works incorporate references to a fictive or authorial narrative process on the level of ["narrative time"].

11. He [Grass] renewed his proposal that East and West Germany agree to set up a joint national culture foundation, based in Berlin, to preserve their common heritage. The art and archaeological collection of the former Prussian state, at present divided between East and West Berlin, could form its nucleus, he said" (*The Times*, 29 October 1981: "Günter Grass calls unity an 'illusion' ").

The Federal Republic in the Eighties: On German Representation
Elisabeth Finne and Wes Blomster*

They finally want to know who they are. . . . Who are we? Where do we come from? What causes us to be Germans? And what the hell is that: Germany?

Günter Grass, Kopfgeburten

"I'm curious about the 80's," comments Günter Grass in his latest book.[1] His curiosity is shared by the readers of Grass and of his creative countrymen who currently populate the German literary scene. One aspect of this curiosity regards the role which Grass himself will play within German literature in the decade which has just opened. The observations which follow concern the problem of representation in contemporary German writing: to what degree can a present-day writer represent his nation, and, if the question is of possible validity, who among German writers might serve this representational function in the present decade? Despite the evidence which negates the writer as the representative of a pluralistic society, it is not unreasonable to claim this status for Günter Grass.

The concept of "German representation" is brought to mind by Peter de Mendelssohn's essay on the role played by Gerhart Hauptmann and Thomas Mann in the Weimar Republic.[2] Although it is easier to discuss such matters when they lie in the past, speculation upon a literary representative in the German Federal Republic in coming years focuses attention upon major problems of the writer within the context of modern society. Present-day Germany offers no parallel to Mann and Hauptmann — both middle-aged writers at that time — in the nation's earlier democracy; this, however, should not lead to the facile conclusion that

*Reprinted from *World Literature Today* 55 (1981): 560–64, by permission of *World Literature Today* and the authors. © 1981 by the University of Oklahoma Press.

representation is no longer possible within modern literary activity. It is perhaps, rather, necessary to redefine this concept for the eighties.

Many aspects of contemporary German life seem to invalidate the concept of a representative writer. The centrality of the printed word has eroded in Germany just as it has in other modern societies; the primacy of great literary culture is challenged everywhere — and with numerical and economic success — by the alternate, the sub- and countercultures which mark the modern age: drugs, rock music, stadium concerts, gurus, portable cassette players, along with founders and leaders of pseudo-mystic collectives, have contributed to shorter lines at — if not the closing of — the neighborhood bookstore. The book trade itself has been disrupted by anti-fairs and mini-presses. Indeed, the frequency with which talk of "body language" is encountered would seem sufficient to stop the presses set in motion by Gutenberg five centuries ago.

It has been suggested that the cinema has become the art form of Germany within which representation must be sought in the 1980s. On the international scene, the reputation of Werner Herzog, Rainer Werner Fassbinder, Margarethe von Trotta and Volker Schlöndorff is perhaps greater than that of their writing contemporaries. Within Germany itself, however, the popular appeal of Hollywood's *Star Wars* caused domestic production to assume an anemic pall. German films draw an informed audience to the art cinemas of the world; at home, however, they are the concern of limited circles. The masses remain home with television. Nonetheless, Germany remains a land of tremendous literary activity in terms of creative effort, publication and translation from other literatures. It is reasonable to assume that the nation's interest in the printed word will diminish little during the present decade.

The quest for a representative writer involves, of course, not merely his identification, but the far more difficult issue regarding that which he represents and for whom he does so. The pluralism of contemporary West Germany — in contrast to the one-dimensional socialist orientation of its sister state — is an established fact. Gone, therefore, is the day when Mann or Hauptmann — illusory as this function might seem in retrospect — could stand with dignity at the center of the cultural stage in command of the respect of the total literate population.

A brief look at — or perhaps even for — Heinrich Böll, the first writer to gain wide popularity in Germany after the second war, is informative. Böll, now in his mid-sixties and possessor of the Nobel Prize for a decade, is the senior member of today's literary establishment; yet it is clear that he is in no way a figure of monumental magnetism in Germany at present. He will write further bestsellers in the 1980s, and he will continue to take a controversial stand on controversial issues. The voice of widely respected spiritual authority, however, is not his; he speaks neither for minions of literati nor for wide circles of the general population — to mention the two foremost factors in literary representation.[3]

The very quality of contemporary German writing is problematic. One might well ask whether Siegfried Lenz will equal his achievement in *Die Deutschstunde* (*The German Lesson*; 1968); indeed, will Grass rise again to the literary quality of *Die Blechtrommel* (*The Tin Drum*; 1959)? Will Böll write another novel as good as *Billard um halb zehn* (*Billiards at Half Past Nine*; 1959)? Will there be works of lesser quality distinguished by the impassioned concern of Gerd Gaiser in *Schlußball* (Final Ball; 1958) or by the energetic narrative impulse through which Hans Scholz brought literary grace to high trivia in *Am grünen Strand der Spree* (On the Green Banks of the Spree; 1955)?

Germans today speak frequently of a midlife crisis in their literature. New, exciting and promising names either are lacking, or they are obscured by an understandable but uncomfortable specialization in production, which — carried to an extreme — could result in painful provincialism: women's literature, leftist and rightist literature and alternative literature. The younger German of today, still involved in university studies but destined to seek integration into the society of this decade, is disquieted by the thought of a representative writer. He looks back with doubt and suspicion upon Hauptmann and Mann in the 1920s; he does not share the enthusiasm with which his elders recall the furious cultural productivity of the Weimar years. The near-Goethean grandeur of Hauptmann does not overshadow the human weakness manifested by the earlier Nobel laureate in critical hours of German history.

One example underscores the young German's discomfort. In December 1917 Ernst Toller wrote in his diary: "Everyone is silent. Who will finally speak?" Toller wrote to Hauptmann: "Your work obligates you; we young people are waiting for the word of a spiritual leader in whom we believe." Toller received no answer from the author, busy then with war hymns and soldier songs. Hauptmann's silence, although never an act of totally false consciousness, nonetheless enabled him to live in uneasy detente with National Socialism, while Toller committed suicide in New York in 1939.[4]

The effusive affirmation with which de Mendelssohn treats representation illuminates the rejection of the concept by young Germans today. In a paragraph laced with quotations, de Mendelssohn discusses Hauptmann's positive stand on the Weimar Republic; he stresses that "nothing was more distant from Hauptmann than to affirm with words that which was going on around him." De Mendelssohn luxuriates in the flood of Dionysian emotion through which Hauptmann supposedly upheld the Republic: "He beheld the whole thing, he loved and affirmed it; he saw elementary events and forces of nature at work in the German nation. He felt growth, development, change and formation" (*R*, 192). De Mendelssohn overlooks the fact that those who hoisted the banner imprinted "Germany, awake!" a decade later knew parallel feelings; yet he concludes with an insight central to any discussion of literary representation in the eighties: "Spiritual representation without spiritual authority in the web of the state was a useless and shameful affair" (R, 222).

For this reason, in the ears of today's younger German the concept of representation in literature rings unpleasantly with the swollen pathos of the nation's past; the term is not a component of his intellectual vocabulary, but rather a painful anachronism. For him the German literary industry — *Literaturbetrieb* — with its innumerable awards and prizes, stipends, talk shows, readings and autograph parties proves the absence of a representative writer today. Indeed, the entire scene seems an act of self-deception staged by those most directly involved.[5] In the sense of the 1920s, therefore, it is necessary to conclude that the representative writer as a creative artist with whom both the individual and the collective can identify is an antiquated concept.

Despite these many factors which speak against the assignment of a representative role to any German writer in the 1980s, it is clear that one man will continue in a position of central importance to German society during this decade. Even if his position requires redefinition of representation, Günter Grass seems destined by work and character to be present actively at every intersection of art and politics in his country.

A review of major turning points in Grass's career emphasizes the changing nature of representation. Grass will probably never again know the solidarity with any generation of Germans manifested in his march down Berlin's Kurfürstendamm in January 1967, arms locked with students chanting "Ho-Ho-Ho-Chi-Minh." This liaison ended with the police's killing of the student Benno Ohnesorg before the West Berlin Opera in June of that year. (That demonstration, it is recalled, protested the presence of the late Shah of Iran in Berlin.) This began, in turn, the series of macabre and tragic events which continues in Germany today. Terrorism and violence — forces of which Grass disapproved totally — brought to the headlines the names of Rudi Dutschke, Andreas Baader and Ulrike Meinhof. Today Grass lives largely in isolation. His alienation from such organized political forces as the New Left, however, does not contradict his position as a representative writer.

In another sense, Grass is today the victim of his own early popularity. "To become a classic in our time . . . may involve being condemned to ineffectuality," Michael Hollington has observed. While Grass, at a previous point in his career, "represented to the intelligentsia . . . the 'active conscience of Germany,' " he is now "widely mistrusted as a treacherous establishment liberal." One scholar has concluded that "he is no longer of contemporary relevance."[6] His representative position is consequently denied.

Hollington defines two reasons for widespread lack of interest in Grass within Germany. The guilt of the Nazi period, to which Grass devoted so much energy, is a dead issue for a generation of readers totally postwar in orientation. "Liberal democracy has for them no value in itself, as it had for Grass and his generation, brought up in the Nazi period." A more general reason involves "a very widespread deterioration . . . of the vitality of the liberal humanist tradition." Consequently, Hollington concludes, "Grass, with his vigorous and consistent adherence to the ideals of the Enlightenment and their fragmentary continuation in the Weimar Republic, begins to look distinctly old-fashioned in the late seventies, its intellectual climate dominated by Marxism and structuralism."

The analysis is correct; yet it underscores the necessity that Grass be seen as the representative writer of Germany today. Precisely for the reasons stated above, Grass grows increasingly important as the mediator between Germany past and present. Current lack of concern for these two issues — the Nazi past and the humanist tradition — does not make them unimportant. The current upsurge in neo-Nazi activity in the country, combined with beginning economic troubles, will reaffirm the centrality of these problems and — if there are eyes to read — will focus renewed attention upon Grass's endeavor. Grass is beyond doubt literary Germany's most significant link between past traditions and modernity; he is simultaneously both the roots and foliage of that creative continuity upon which the spiritual well-being of the nation depends.

Grass himself manifests continuing awareness of these problems. In his latest prose work he looks back over the postwar epoch.

> In 1945 the defeat of Germany was not only military. Not only its cities and industrial facilities were destroyed. Still greater damage lay before us: the ideology of National Socialism had betrayed the German language of its meaning; it had corrupted the language and laid waste to it in the entire mammoth region of words. In this wounded language, dragging behind itself all these marks of damage, writers began more to stammer than to write. The measure of their helplessness they found in Thomas Mann, Brecht, the giants of emigration literature. Against such classic greatness, stuttering was the only form of expression which could exist. (K, 9–10)

Grass will remain a controversial figure; the Right will see him as dangerously leftist, and the Left will view him as an impotent intellectual liberal. It is precisely this position, however, which qualifies him as the representative writer of a society torn by contradictions and lacking that common denominator which seemingly validated the representative function of writers in previous epochs.

Ernst Toller once defined the political poet as "a human being who feels responsible for himself and for each of his brothers within the human community."[7] Grass will never become the leader of a revolutionary government as Toller did in Munich at the end of the first war, nor will he speak quite so headily as Toller did. In more sober language he refers to himself as "a contemporary who gets involved in things" (K, 152). This involvement will continue — to the chagrin of many and to the pleasure of a relative few.

In the discomfort which he causes, Grass is something of an heir of Heine. For him there are neither taboos nor sacred cows; he permits himself detours around nothing. Indeed, there are some in the troubled Germany of today—haunted by the black myth of professional persecution or *Berufsverbot*—who assert that open admiration of Grass would involve the risk of unemployment. This suggests that Grass is the representative of an intellectual underground within his own nation; a significant truth might be contained in this assertion.

Two final perspectives demand consideration. Today Grass commands more attention in the rest of the world than any other living German writer. Even if the pluralistic society within which he works is unable to view him as its representative, he certainly is this in the eyes of the world. Looking also at divided Germany, Grass has recently advanced the thesis that modern Germany involves indeed two states; they compose, however, one cultural nation.

Ever since Grimmelshausen took stock of Germany in the Thirty Years' war in his *Simplicissimus*, the picaresque novel has been a narrative vehicle of special importance to Germans in time of crisis. A trio of such novels produced in the third quarter of this century offer a conclusion to the thoughts recorded here. In 1955, the last of his eighty years, Thomas Mann affirmed the Olympian elevation of his effort through the completion of the would-be first volume of *Felix Krull*. Within the account of his early life, Krull speaks of later periods spent in prison; the details of such incarceration would have been learned only in a second volume. Grass began his career with *The Tin Drum* in 1959. In it Oskar Matzerath tells the story of his life from his bed within a penal hospital. The picaro in the shadow of criminality takes on new shades of realism in the younger author Peter-Paul Zahl, who produced *Die Glücklichen* (The Happy Ones), his picaresque account of a family of modern Robin Hoods in Berlin-Kreuzberg, while imprisoned for a Düsseldorf shoot-out in 1972.

While it is obvious that no direct blood line runs from Mann through Grass to Zahl, the growing obscurity between fiction and the facts of life in the modern German picaro evokes unsettling visions of the future. Although Zahl is allowed to leave prison for public readings and for such occasions as the award to him of the Bremen Literary Prize, it is obvious that he will never be accepted as a representative writer within his country. Zahl commented recently: "I don't think that happy people write; whoever writes, expresses some lack. The monk in his medieval cell, in prison, Robinson Crusoe, Genet, Papillon. . . . Only a picaro, fool or criminal can tell the truth."[8] Grass expresses parallel sentiments on a certain hollowness which he detects within Germany today, noting that "our lack is neither material nor social, but rather a matter of spiritual emergency" (*K*, 157).

Today's representative writer necessarily stands in isolation from all blocs of tangible power, for only in this way can he retain clear critical vision. He will support those causes which he finds worthy — as Grass has repeatedly done in election campaigns — and he will criticize the man whom he has helped win the election when this is appropriate — as Grass did in expressing to Willy Brandt his doubts about the Great Coalition in an open letter of 1966. He will at times even travel with the man in power when so important a matter as Brandt's Warsaw trip of 1970 is involved. He will, however, never surrender the objectivity of detachment, nor will he ever shroud himself in the silence to which Hauptmann subjected Ernst Toller.

De Mendelssohn's anxiety regarding "spiritual representation without spiritual authority in the web of the state" remains of relevance in Germany in the 1980s. On 8 March 1981 German television brought a special on "Spirit without Power: Intellectuals and Politics." There is today, however, no illusion of such power in the hands of artists and intellectuals. The fundamental formulation of the contemporary writer's position was given by Grass at Princeton University in 1966 when he spoke "On Writers as Court Jesters and on Non-Existent Courts." His plea then as now was for people who "busy themselves with the trivia of democracy."

Günter Grass's entire mature life has been a translation into reality of the metaphor of the two beer mats — his creative effort and his political involvement — offered late in *Aus dem Tagebuch einer Schnecke* (*From the Diary of a Snail*; 1972). Grass will continue to juxtapose opposite truths; impossibility will continue to confront impossibility in congenial coexistence. He will weave further personal experience, speculation and the reality of contemporary Germany into an often rough but coherent tapestry out of which the turbulent history of the twentieth century can be read. To saddle him with the designation "representative writer" might well be as unwelcome to him as the concept of the writer as the conscience of the nation once was. Nonetheless, Grass is there; he is beyond doubt the most representative writer of Germany today, and there is reason to assume that he will continue his effort undaunted throughout the eighties. Indeed, it has been suggested that Grass might well be viewed as the Sisyphus of this decade; Grass himself affirms: "I'm not going to quit" (*K*, 152).[9]

Notes

1. Günter Grass, *Kopfgeburten oder Die Deutschen sterben aus*, Darmstadt, Luchterhand, 1980, p. 152. Subsequent references are indicated by the abbreviation *K*. Translations are our own unless otherwise indicated.

2. Peter de Mendelssohn, *Von deutscher Repräsentanz*, Munich, Prestel, 1972. The essay on Hauptmann and Mann gives the volume its title. Subsequent references are indicated by the abbreviation *R*.

3. It must be recalled, of course, that when Thomas Mann was Böll's age he was packing his bags for the move from Switzerland to Princeton; henceforth his representational role would be played only among Germans in exile.

4. Quoted in Jürgen Serke, *Die verbrannten Dichter*, Weinheim, Beltz & Gelberg, 1977, p. 8.

5. Consider the following excerpt from a letter to me (Blomster) by a German student: "Spare me the literature star Grass with his DM 15,000 per reading. With all his talk about his Group 47 and his political statements, he doesn't represent anything at all to me (any more). Bienek's Silesian stories and Kempowski's family saga are of only peripheral interest, and Handke's collected sensitivities cause me to grow increasingly weary."

6. Michael Hollington, *Günter Grass: The Writer in a Pluralist Society*, London, Boyars, 1980, foreword. J. P. Stern, "Günter Grass's Uniqueness," *London Review of Books*, 5–18 February 1981, is a recommended study which supports the assessment of Grass offered here.

7. Quoted in Albert Soergel and Curt Hohoff, *Dichtung und Dichter der Zeit*, vol. 2, Düsseldorf, Bagel, 1963, p. 291.

8. Quoted in "Eulenspiegel und Kämpfer," *Die Zeit* (Hamburg), 20 February 1981.

9. The opinions of many individuals found their way into this essay; of particular value were the perceptive comments of Rainer Querfurth (Frankfurt) and Steven Uppendahl (Regensburg). . . .

POSTSCRIPT

Grass's Doomsday Book:
Die Rättin
Patrick O'Neill*

In November 1982, in Rome, Günter Grass delivered an address on the occasion of his being awarded the Antonio Feltrinelli Prize. The address was entitled "The Destruction of Mankind Has Begun" and struck a decidedly unfestive note:

> Honors of this kind not only acknowledge work done, but are also encouragements to remain active in the future. Optimism is expressed at all award ceremonies, as though one could take it for granted that life will go on as it is. Up until now this attitude and pose have supported our concept of progress, for somehow life has gone on.
>   My message of thanks obtrudes doubt into traditional expectations. Our present makes the future questionable and in many respects unthinkable, for our present produces — since we have learned above all to produce — poverty, hunger, polluted air, polluted bodies of water, forests destroyed by acid rain or deforestation, arsenals that seem to pile up of their own accord and are capable of destroying mankind many times over.[1]

A little more than three years later, in early 1986, this doomsday scenario found literary expression in a 500-page narrative with the unlikely title — unlikely for any writer other than Grass, at any rate — *Die Rättin* (The Rat). The same three years saw the publication of two volumes of graphic work, a collection of the poems from *Der Butt* (*The Flounder*) with further graphics, a volume of political speeches, and Grass's election as President of the Berlin Academy of Arts.[2] *Die Rättin*, preceded by lengthy extracts in major newspapers, was an instant best-seller and remained so for several months; even before it appeared on the market, its existence was greeted by the publication of a parodic counterversion, allegedly the work of one Günter Ratte ("rat"), and entitled *Der Grass*.[3] As of early August 1986, according to newspaper reports, translations of *Die Rättin* were being prepared in twenty different languages.

"I asked for a rat for Christmas" (7),[4] begins the narrator of *Die*

---

*This contribution was written expressly for the present collection, which had already gone to press when *Die Rättin* appeared.

213

Rättin, and thereby hangs a tale — or rather a whole collection of them, for *Die Rättin* is less a "novel" in any traditional sense than a collection of latter-day grim fairy tales. Very much latter-day, in fact, for in his latest work Grass focuses on no less final a scenario than the nuclear Big Bang that obliterates all trace of human life on earth. No one is quite sure who finally pushes the button or why, but somehow, à la *Dr. Strangelove*, it happens anyway, as if by the sheer weight of inertia. Humanity perishes, a victim of its own hubris, and disappears as completely as the dinosaurs once did. But even though humankind fails to survive, there *are* survivors, and they are legion: the rats. So, at least, the narrator is informed, as he tells us, for the basic narrative structure of the book establishes itself very quickly: the gift rat under the Christmas tree metamorphoses into a voice of doom inexorably relating the imminent, inevitable, and apocalyptic end of human affairs, while the narrator, once again a Scheherazade,[5] desperately spins and juggles tale after tale in the hope of fending off disaster, postponing if not preventing the inevitable.

If the talking flatfish of *The Flounder* embodied the spirit of Hegelian optimism in history, the rat, as voluble as the flounder ever was, incorporates the spirit of Spenglerian pessimism in a West caught up in the last throes of ultimate decline. Her tale (for she is a female rat) is a straightforward one, and its point is a simple one: ultimate disaster is inevitable, ultimate disaster, indeed, *was* inevitable, for, as far as the rat's narrative is concerned, the whole affair is not a matter of the future but of the past. Humanity *has* ceased to exist. As far as the narrator is concerned, the nightmare scenario is at worst in the perhaps postponable future, or, even better, in a purely hypothetical world — humanity *might* cease to exist — whose validity can be challenged and relativized by the construction of other, different, multifarious counterworlds, whose competing reality may cause the reality of the rat's world to fade and grow dim. The plot, in other words, is couched in the form of a narrative duel, a contest of stories, worlds, realities. The opponents in this single combat adopt different strategies, the rat's monolithic and linear No held uneasily at bay by the narrator's feinting, shifting, and not altogether successful efforts at saying Yes.

The narrator has a whole collection of narratives, and they are related not one after the other in a linear sequence, but all together, interweaving in a complex, flickering narrative statement. There is, first of all, the story of the five women who set out to forestall disaster in the Baltic, for the life of the Baltic as an ecosystem is endangered not merely by anything as mundane as industrial effluents or acid rain, but by a population explosion of jellyfish. The five women, one of them a marine biologist, undertake a research trip in an old converted freighter to measure the extent of the damage. Their voyage turns out to be a continuation of *The Flounder*; indeed, at one point their captain, Damroka (a church organist who has outlived eleven clerical husbands), consults with the mythical flounder himself, cross-eyed as ever and still espousing the feminist cause.[6] The narrator (known only as *"ich"*) is in love with Damroka and, Edek-like, has had relations of one kind or another with each of the others as well, though now each of them in turn has written him out of her life. The boat is called the *New Ilsebill*, and no men need apply. All five of the women (except one, the cook) are impassioned knitters, "as if they never wanted the yarn to break off" (39). But if the yarn is the story of feminism, the narrator implies, it has already broken off, for in the Germany of the eighties feminism has come to nothing, all the real power is still firmly in the hands of men, the flounder's promises were lies, and "nothing has changed" (65). The optimism of the seventies is a thing of the past, and the future holds only the threat of nuclear holocaust. The research trip is redirected by Damroka into the search for a promised land in the form of the legendary sunken city of Vineta, a feminist Utopia, an Atlantis beyond the reach of men and their perverted lust for self-destruction. The women are miraculously guided to the site of Vineta both by the flounder and by a supernatural chorus of jellyfish, only to find, as they gaze down on the towers and steeples of the city, that it has already been recolonized: the streets are swarming with rats. The women's realization that "there is no escape, anywhere, any more" (324) coincides with the moment of the first nuclear strike against nearby Danzig that vaporizes them instantaneously, terminating both their quest and their story.

The narrator's tale of the women who try to escape turns, whether he wants it to or not, into a demonstration of the impossibility of escape, even into a world of fiction, a dream world. The women's attempt to take cover, to go under in a sunken city of the mind, may well remind the reader of Mahlke's attempt to dive to safety in the sunken mine-sweeper of *Cat and Mouse* or Oskar's attempts to emulate his grandfather and disappear under his grandmother's skirts. And that is exactly where we find Oskar at the moment the five women are vaporized, for both Oskar and Anna Koljaiczek reappear as characters in *Die Rättin*, thirty years older than when their careers were temporarily suspended at the end of *The Tin Drum*. Anna Koljaiczek is now no less than 107 years old, and it is to celebrate her birthday that Oskar returns to Danzig in 1984 in a chauffeur-driven Mercedes, the chauffeur none other than his old keeper, Bruno. Oskar himself is approaching sixty and has grown prosperous and respected as the director of a film company called Post-Futurum Productions. After making his fortune in pornographic movies, Oskar has moved with the market into educational videos, under the proud slogan "We Produce the Future." The narrator and he are on cautiously friendly terms, and Oskar is interested in producing one or two of the narrator's scripts in due course, and even collaborates with him on the plot, since he suspects the narrator of being totally out of touch with marketing trends. Oskar has considerable reservations about making the trip back to Danzig — or rather Gdańsk, for that, as Oskar sees it, is just the problem. There can be no real going back, and to attempt to do so, he feels uneasily, may be to court disaster. He is, of course, more right than he can imagine, for his trip to Danzig is simultaneously a voyage into both a fictive past and a hypothetical future, and the dangers of both are unknown. At the height of the birthday celebrations the world ends, and Oskar ends with it, vainly fleeing in his last seconds to curl up as of old in the finally ineffectual shelter of his grandmother's skirts.

Or, at any rate, that is one version of what happens, for in another version Oskar remains blissfully ignorant of his own demise and travels back through Poland and East Germany tormented not by regret for his own untimely passing but by an acute prostate problem. Oskar, unaware that he *has* been written out of the script, will later accuse the narrator of trying to write him out of the script by having him die prematurely as a result of his prostate condition—a fate averted, as Oskar somewhat bitterly notes, only by quick thinking on the part of Bruno in getting him to a hospital as quickly as possible. Dead or not, Oskar in due course celebrates his sixtieth birthday, the occasion marred only by a telegram announcing the death of Anna Koljaiczek, who also chooses to ignore her previous death of radiation poisoning and obstinately dies of natural causes. The narrator is an invited guest at Oskar's party, but is treated with some coolness; on the other hand, Oskar seems favorably disposed towards the narrator's striking companion, Damroka, who, no longer dead either, has returned home safe and sound from her research trip. She is glad the trip is over, sick of canned food and counting jellyfish, eager to get back to her music, and has not mentioned a word about Vineta (463).

The world of *Die Rättin* is the world of *Märchen*, the world of the fairy tale, where all reality is relative, where Little Red Riding Hood will be found safe and sound inside the wolf, none the worse for having been devoured. In Grass's version of the Grimms' story, indeed, the threshold between disaster and escape is modernized and mechanized: the wolf comes equipped with a zipper to facilitate escape, and Red Riding Hood courts disaster for amusement when she is bored. For *Die Rättin* reanimates the world of the Grimms as well as that of *The Flounder* and *The Tin Drum*, and among the dramatis personae we find not only Little Red Riding Hood and the wolf, but also her grandmother, who reads aloud to the wolf from the thirty-two volumes of the Grimms' other masterpiece, their monumental dictionary of the German language. We have Snow White, suffering scandalous and repeated abuse at the hands of her seven lascivious dwarfs, we have Briar Rose and her Prince, who has developed a compulsive addiction to kissing, we have Rumpelstiltskin, Rapunzel, the Frog Prince, Hansel and Gretel and their Witch, whose embonpoint is of decidedly greater interest to Hansel than the gingerbread house ever was. For good measure we also have the brothers Grimm themselves, metamorphosed into the ministry of the environment in the federal cabinet.

There is need of them there, for the woods of Germany are dying, and with them the *Märchen*. Desperate measures are necessary, and they are invoked by Hansel and Gretel — who in reality, in another reality, are not Hansel and Gretal at all but Johannes and Margarete, the runaway children of the Federal Chancellor himself. The children run away into the deep woods in search not of gingerbread houses but of an alternative to the inevitable creeping devastation of the natural environment. Hansel and Gretel succeed in radicalizing the fairy-tale world they find still intact there to the point where a protest march on Bonn is planned — "as if salvation could be found in Bonn" (183) — followed by the abduction of the government and the seizure of power. Success seems momentarily assured when the brothers Grimm are declared leaders of the revolutionary government and the world of *Märchen* guaranteed a voice in all future government decisions. Ultimately, however, their demands — clean air and water, uncontaminated fruit and vegetables — are so outrageously unrealistic that they provoke a counterrevolution, and the world of the Grimms, the world of metamorphosis, transformation, and the possibility of changing direction, is crushed out of existence by the combined forces of church, capital, army, and riot police. The only survivors are Hansel and Gretel. Once again they flee into the deep woods, "as if fairy tales still existed" (467), the dead forest this time bursting into life around them as they run. At a crossroads a carriage with four white horses is waiting, and the children join its occupants, the brothers Grimm, as it moves slowly, pulling the white horses behind it, into the shelter of the past, into a time when woods were still woods and magic was magic. The ending is Oskar's contribution — for the whole story of the dying forests is a scenario by the narrator for one of Oskar's educational videos. "Somebody has to escape. Nobody wants to be completely without fairy tales" (466), for without them, "Where is there hope any more?" (469).

The past is the abode of *Märchen* in more ways than one, for while changing what will happen in the future seems to be beyond the powers of human imagination, changing what happened in the past is within the reach of all. Oskar, that master himself in the art of creative reinterpretation, is less interested in the story of Hansel and Gretel than in the career of his contemporary, the East Prussian painter and master forger Lothar Malskat. Lübeck was the site of Malskat's rise and fall, for when the rubble had been cleared away after the British bombing of the cathedral there, and while masons were discreetly removing the swastika chiseled above the high altar on the orders of a Party-minded bishop, Malskat, to the surprise and delight of the chapter and art experts alike, was able to uncover mural after mural that clearly dated back to the heyday of Gothic art. When Malskat tires of the game, and of the fact that nobody wanted to see the initials he carefully included in each of his creations, nobody wishes to acknowledge that what was so convenient as truth could be anything but truth. Only when Malskat retains a lawyer and proves beyond all doubt that he is indeed guilty of forgery are the sanctions of law and order belatedly invoked.

Appearances are deceptive, however, the narrator observes. Malskat was no forger. His paintings were genuine Gothic; what was a forgery was the times in which he was forced to paint them. Other forgers, however, the narrator goes on, *were* at work in those days, the early fifties, and everybody knew they were forgers — but, happily, since they, unlike Malskat, never chose to draw attention to the fact themselves, nobody else had to either. The master forgers were Adenauer and Ulbricht, "The Great Pretenders" (473), who chiseled away the swastikas so cleanly in their respective states that no one ever had to remember ever again that the nightmare of Nazism once did really happen. Forgery has become the norm; Malskat's originals, however, are whitewashed over, leaving ugly stains as reminders on the walls, as much casualties of a forged reality as were the devastated woods and the devastated world of the *Märchen*.

History is not a record of what really happened, it is a narrative of what may have or what might have happened; for facts die without fictions to perpetuate their reality, and fictions can be contested by other fictions perpetuating other realities. Nineteen eighty-four is not just Orwell's year and the year of Oskar's sixtieth birthday; it is also the 700th anniversary of the Pied Piper's seduction in 1284 of all the rats of Hamelin, "a thousand or more" (43), lured to their death in the river Weser by the sweet sounds of the flute. According to another version of the legend, however, it was not only rats that were lured to destruction, but children also — 130, to be precise, in the narrator's version of the story. For the narrator is able to give us the "sad truth" (439) of what really happened in Hamelin, even though civic authorities nowadays are understandably reluctant to have too much attention focused on the event. The year 1284, like 1984, had its punks too, High Gothic punks, dropouts and protesters like their future counterparts, complete with chains and safety-pins and pet rats dyed violet or pink or green to match multicolored counterculture hairstyles. In Hamelin, it turns out, things got a little out of hand when first the mayor's daughter and later other young ladies too allowed their pet rats increasing liberties, and a crisis point was reached when Gret, the mayor's daughter, gave birth after an unusually short pregnancy to triplets, three tiny perfectly formed infants whose only peculiarity was their tiny little rats' heads. The other 129 Gothic punks of Hamelin are delighted with this miraculous conception and delivery, but the common people, as yet unfamiliar with the notion of genetic engineering (441), and disturbed by the unsettling intrusion of fairy-tale happenings into the solidity of their everyday world, seem in imminent danger of beginning to wonder at just how solid that solid everyday world might be. With civil disturbances, strikes, even riots rumored, the authorities must move quickly to contain the situation. A piper is engaged, for a certain number of pieces of silver, to entrap the punks in their own love of dancing and carousing. Hans and Gret (for the rat's name is Hans) and their three infants (who have been duly baptized Kaspar, Melchior, and Balthazar) have fled for safety to a cave in the hillside called the Kalvarienburg, or Mount Calvary, and there they are joined, on the feast of St. John, in June 1284, by the remaining 129 Gothic punks and their 129 pet rats, led by the piper. The night passes in a delirium of dancing and other activities, until at dawn the piper slips unnoticed away. Thereupon, the cavemouth, according to plan, is quickly walled up by skilled masons, hidden under loads of sand, sprinkled with holy water—and everything returns to normal.

All of the narrator's tales, individually and in their interrelationship, explore the possibility of escape: escape from the future, escape from the present, escape from (and to) the past, and in each case the possibility is exploded. The rat as counternarrator, on the other hand, tells a single relentless tale of the impossibility of escape—and can do so only because she and her fellow rats have always escaped, always managed to survive. Their abilities as escape artists have been honestly come by over the course of eons, for always, the rat complains, they have been hunted down and exterminated, feared and loathed as carriers of disease, plague, and death, held to be responsible for all ills: "The rats and the Jews, the Jews and the rats are to blame" (138). The injustice goes back to earliest times, for even Noah, according to the rat, disobeyed the express command of the Lord and refused rats alone entry to the Ark—but that did not prevent them from surviving the Flood. Then as later they were able to dig in and wait out the storm, for a key factor in their survival mechanism is to be able to spot a sinking ship in good time, to recognize disaster when they see it coming, an ability humankind has never managed to emulate. The signs of humankind's final death throes were far too obvious to be missed towards the end: hunger, warfare, overpopulation, and massive unemployment worldwide; seas, rivers, woods, fields, and air poisoned and dying; humankind choking on its own garbage—and irresistibly itching for the delicious ultimate release of self-obliteration. Warnings were sounded, the rat observes, if only for the reason that man makes garbage and rats live on garbage: just before the end hundreds of thousands of rats marched in formation on the White House, Red Square, Trafalgar Square, the Champs Elysées, but their well-meant warnings met only with rat poison and flame-throwers. When it was clear that there was no further hope, they washed their hands of humankind and began to dig in again, deeper and deeper. Which side finally pushed the button is no longer of any interest—maybe it was even the rats themselves who eventually gnawed their way into the central computer systems, tired of having their warnings ignored.

After the decades of firestorms and duststorms, radiation poisoning and the general inconvenience of nuclear winter, the rats, unchanged except for their new bright green coats, venture forth again and establish their own civilization in the Danzig area. After initial genocidal religious strife among warring sects, harmony is established and agriculture flourishes under a fertility goddess and the divine infant discovered by the rats under her skirts — for the deity and her assumed offspring are none other than the shrunken and mummified remains of Anna Koljaiczek and Oskar, while other liturgical impedimenta include several of the 130 smurfs Oskar had brought to his grandmother's party as gifts for the local Kashubian children and a Solidarność badge contributed by one of the other guests. Rumors still circulate about a savior or a race of saviors still to come, however, and in due course a derelict hulk appears in the harbor, and from it, to the tolling of all the bells of Danzig (spared out of cultural considerations by the neutron bombs that obliterated all human life), the messiahs climb ashore. "First five of them, then seven, then twelve" (418), they are blonde, blue-eyed, the size of a three-year-old child, perfect little human beings with perfectly proportioned little rats' heads. The hulk is the remains of the *New Ilsebill*, whose five feminists (previously planned, says the narrator, as being seven in number, reduced from an original twelve) had returned from a brief shore leave unwittingly accompanied by some escaped laboratory rats on whom Swedish scientists had been conducting gene-splicing experiments. The desired result is Ratman, a synthesis of human rationality, smurflike industry, and the rat's ability to survive, a postmodern centaur, a neogothic grotesque à la Malskat — one of whose more inaccessible miniatures, as it happens (and if fuzzy photographs can be trusted), contains a map showing the site of Vineta, while nearby another shows three small ratmen playing flutes over a legend referring to Sts. John and Paul's day in Hamelin (446). The experiment is a failure, however, for the quickly multiplying ratmen have all too little of the rat's ability to survive and all too much of the human thirst for military expansion, carried out to shouted commands of "Quicksmurfmarch! Smurf two three four!" (430). Having lived through human history before, and with no desire to repeat it, the rats, under the now sacred sign of Solidarność, rebel and wipe them out. The last five survivors of the ratmen make a vain attempt to escape on the *New Ilsebill*, still lying in the harbor, but are eaten alive by the victorious rats, whose coloring has now reverted from green back to black. The last of them to die is the one in whom the narrator claims to recognize his Damroka.

The relationship between the narrator and the also narrating rat is the driving force of *Die Rättin*, and the relationship hinges on the possibility of escape. For the rat's voice, like that of Death or the Devil in a medieval morality play, drones the inescapable gnawing truth that escape is impossible. For the narrator, the narrating *ich*, there *must* be a possibility of flight, whether in "his" Damroka's flowing hair (177), in the fairy-tale forests of more innocent days, or in whatever other "games with alternative realities" (486) he can construct to hide behind, like Briar Rose behind her hedge of impenetrable thorns. Like Oskar and the talking flounder, indeed, the narrator can be said to have been "borrowed" from another text, for the narrating *ich* of *Die Rättin* is the same *ich* we are familiar with from *The Flounder*: cowed, defeated, helpless, ineffectual. It would, of course, be simplistic to identify this *ich* with the writer Günter Grass; but we also need to be careful in calling this *ich*, without further qualification, the narrator, as we have been doing so far for simplicity's sake. Behind or beside the narrator who calls himself *ich* there is another voice whom we might distinguish by a capital as the Narrator and whose role is previously the *balancing* and juxtaposition of the two narrative voices, that of the narrating *ich* and that of the rat, one against the other. The narrator continually refers to the rat as "the rat I dream about," but who is dreaming whom?

> I dreamed about a man, / said the rat I dream about. / I talked him into believing / he was dreaming me and said in his dream: the rat / I dream about believes she is dreaming me; / we read each other in mirrors / interrogating each other. / / Could it be that both / the rat and I / are being dreamed and are dreams / of a third order? (423)

To be dreamed is to be without responsibilities (478), as when the narrator visualizes himself orbiting the devastated earth in a space capsule, listening to the rat over the communications system, but unable to affect the situation in any way, for better or for worse. To be a member of society demands the acceptance of responsibilities, and it is the rat's voice rather then the narrator's we hear reiterating that demand throughout. The rat is a pedagogue, and her message is a simple one: Be afraid, forget dreams of immortality, acknowledge that you are indeed going to die, and, just possibly, you may live a little longer (168–69). The rat, to this extent, is precisely the "footnotes and commentary" (13) on human idealisms and ideologies, the shadow side of all human endeavor, "fear embodied" (167), "evil itself" (119), Mephisto's No to Faust's dreams of Yes. The rat, in a word, is Oskar's *bête noire*, the Black Witch, the boring truth the narrator refuses to face when he talks of his "worry, grown gray with me, that all lies and fictions could be exploded, leaving only the boredom of truth" (97). The Narrator (with a capital), however, whom we may regard either as the narrator's "better" self or, as narrative theorists would put it, as the "implied" (rather than the real, empirical) author, knows better: "Children, we play at running away / and find ourselves much too soon" (178). And, knowing better as he does, he goes on playing anyway, for if the narrator deals in narrative escape, the Narrator deals in narrative play.

The answers to impending destruction that one can glean from *Die Rättin* are powerless platitudes: Love thy neighbor, abandon arrogance, learn from our mistakes, be reasonable, tolerant, and kind—the standard maxims of eighteenth-century Enlightenment thinking, perfectly sound advice, and perfectly useless. But the point of *Die Rättin* is hardly to offer us a hitherto unsuspected path to salvation. The narrator is well aware, for example, that his film on the death of the woods, even if Oskar produces it, will be quite powerless to save the forest, or anything else either, for that matter. The point of art is not to provide us with real-life solutions to real-life problems, but to provide us with new ways of envisaging the reality we inhabit. We may, if we wish, take the rat's warning at face value, but we must not forget that the warning is constructed as a *Märchen*, not a treatise; we may deduce a moral, if we wish, but we need to be constantly aware of the element of play, of parody involved as well. The pseudonymous Günter Ratte's parody of *Die Rättin* is ultimately unreadable, for instance, because it unsuccessfully attempts that most difficult literary feat, the parody of what is already a parody. From the opening sentence, with its ironic allusion to other earlier and fruitless attempts such as Lessing's at educating humankind—"I asked for a rat for Christmas, hoping for provocative words for a poem to deal with the education of the human race" (7)—Grass implicitly pokes ironic fun at his own pedagogical ambitions and efforts over the years.[7] More than that, the very notion that art *can* educate, *can* achieve change, is parodied, and the parody is strengthened throughout by the obstreperous inappropriateness, even for Grass, of the chosen vehicle for the ostensible message. *Die Rättin* is very far from being the sort of cultural Third Program that the narrator listens to on the radio, where a troublesome world is tidily packaged into neat explanatory commentaries, interspersed with baroque music (219). The element of parody, self-parody, has been strongly present in Grass's work from its very beginnings: in *Die Rättin* it becomes the paramount consideration. For Grass's latest narrative parodies not only the pedagogical aspirations of a Brechtian concept of writing, but also writing itself; not only the processes of constructing historical fictions, but also the subsequent inability to break away from those fictions; not only the practice and process of searching for conclusive answers in life as in literature, but also the very idea that there may be any final answers to look for in the first place.

This kind of all-encompassing parody has, of course, an element of satire in it, but the relationship is a distant one. Traditionally the satirist has written authoritatively, from a position of knowledge: he knows what is right and castigates, with a greater or lesser degree of mercilessness, any deviations from that unassailable norm. There are episodes in *Die Rättin* that are still satiric in this sense (the Malskat narrative is an obvious example), where an implicitly corrective attack is launched on a relatively sharply focused target. When the focus becomes so diffuse as to encompass human impotence itself, there is little point in calling it satire any more, for the satirist's optimistic trust in the power of corrective medicine is exposed as itself a fraud and a fiction. It is possible to read a number of Grass's earlier books as belonging to this latter category, *Local Anaesthetic*, for example, or *From the Diary of a Snail*; it is difficult to read *Die Rättin* as anything else. Humanity disappeared, says the rat, because it was incapable of change (360). *Die Rättin* is a book filled to bursting point with changes, transformations, and metamorphoses, but in the end nothing changes either. Just as Oskar's film of his grandmother's birthday eventually turns into the film of itself (317), so the end of *Die Rättin* runs into its beginning in a vicious circle, the discussion marking time rather than developing, rat and narrator frozen in a narrative stasis.

Rats have long been a part of Grass's highly personal and idiosyncratic iconography. We find them as early as 1957 in the play *Flood*, where two rats comment from the roof on the desultory efforts of the house's inhabitants, as flood waters rise dangerously, to come to grips with the impending catastrophe. These efforts are hopelessly misdirected, but the flood waters eventually fall anyway, and the two rats, knowing that a return to normality will also mean a return to rattraps, decide to leave well enough alone and head for the rat-friendly town of Hamelin. We find rats again swarming over the mound of bones outside Stutthof concentration camp in *Dog Years*, while Störtebeker rationalizes their presence in terms not of monstrous barbarity and human suffering but of pseudo-Heideggerean doubletalk. We find the rat again in the poem "Racine Changes His Coat of Arms" in *Gleisdreieck* (Triangle of Tracks, 1960); the playwright Racine deletes the rat from his coat of arms, which had formerly contained both a swan and a rat, but in the absence of the latter has nothing more to say and can only relapse into silence. In one sense *Die Rättin* is an extrapolation of Racine's coat of arms: swan and rat, light and shadow, Apollo and Dionysus, Goethe and Rasputin, hope for survival and fear of extinction. Each is a necessary function of the other, and without a constant awareness of the rat the swan has no future: "It is by affirming the rat in ourselves that we become truly human" (480).

In Grass's latest headbirth not just the Germans are dying out, everybody is. The Danzig trilogy, in J. P. Stern's phrase, matched an unbelievable past with unbelievable metaphors;[8] *Die Rättin* performs the same task for an unbelievable future. If Oskar can escape his predestined end, can we? Is it possible that common sense, peace, brotherhood, and all the other similarly outmoded virtues could still save us in the end, against all the odds? " 'A beautiful dream,' said the rat, before she faded out" (505). Whether the dream will become reality may still, we hope, be up to us. *Die Rättin* trades in dreams and realities, shows how fluidly each can metamorphose into the other, just as future and past can reverse their roles, shows how order inevitably disintegrates and that entropy may yet still be reversible. The Baroque poets of *The Meeting at Telgte*, we remember, eventually produce an exquisitely carefully worded manifesto against barbarism, only to have it go up in flames with the tavern in which it was written: "And so, what would in any case not have been heard, remained unsaid."[9] *Die Rättin* may not be enough to save the world, but it will not have remained unsaid.

Notes

1. Günther Grass, *On Writing and Politics 1967–1983*, trans. Ralph Manheim (New York: Harcourt Brace, 1985), 137.

2. *Zeichnen und Schreiben* (Drawing and Writing) appeared (vol. 1) in 1982 and (vol. 2) 1984; *Ach Butt, dein Märchen geht böse aus* (Alas, Flounder, Your Tale Will Have a bad ending) appeared in 1983; *Widerstand lernen* (Learning Resistance) appeared in 1984.

3. Frankfurt am Main: Eichborn, 1986.

4. Parenthetical page references are to *Die Rättin* (Neuwied: Luchterhand, 1986); translations are my own.

5. Cf. Patrick O'Neill, "'The Scheherazade Syndrome: Günter Grass's Meganovel *Der Butt*," in *Adventures of a Flounder: Critical Essays on Günter Grass' "Der Butt*," ed. Gertrud Bauer Pickar (Munich: Fink, 1982), 1–15.

6. *Die Rättin* is dedicated to another organist: Ute, Grass's second wife, whom he married in 1979, after his divorce in 1978 from Anna Grass.

7. Gotthold Ephraim Lessing, *Die Erziehung des Menschengeschlechts* (1780; The Education of the Human Race).

8. See p. 82 above.

9. *The Meeting at Telgte*, trans Ralph Manheim (New York: Harcourt Brace, 1981), 131.

BIBLIOGRAPHY

I. Works by Günter Grass

FICTION

Die Blechtrommel. Neuwied: Luchterhand, 1959. Trans. Ralph Manheim as *The Tin Drum*. London: Secker & Warburg, 1961. New York: Pantheon, 1962.

Katz und Maus. Neuwied: Luchterhand, 1961. Trans. Ralph Manheim as *Cat and Mouse*. New York: Harcourt Brace; London: Secker & Warburg, 1963.

Hundejahre. Neuwied: Luchterhand, 1963. Trans. Ralph Manheim as *Dog Years*. New York: Harcourt Brace; London: Secker & Warburg, 1965.

Örtlich betäubt. Neuwied: Luchterhand, 1969. Trans. Ralph Manheim as *Local Anaesthetic*. New York: Harcourt Brace, 1969. London: Secker & Warburg, 1970.

Aus dem Tagebuch einer Schnecke. Neuwied: Luchterhand, 1972. Trans. Ralph Manheim as *From the Diary of a Snail*. New York: Harcourt Brace, 1973. London: Secker & Warburg, 1974.

Der Butt. Neuwied: Luchterhand, 1977. Trans. Ralph Manheim as *The Flounder*. New York: Harcourt Brace; London: Secker & Warburg, 1978.

Das Treffen in Telgte. Neuwied: Luchterhand, 1979. Trans. Ralph Manheim as *The Meeting at Telgte*. New York: Harcourt Brace; London: Secker & Warburg, 1981.

Kopfgeburten oder Die Deutschen sterben aus. Neuwied: Luchterhand, 1980. Trans. Ralph Manheim as *Headbirths, or The Germans Are Dying Out*. New York: Harcourt Brace; London: Secker & Warburg, 1982.

Die Rättin (The Rat). Neuwied: Luchterhand, 1986.

Poetry

Die Vorzüge der Windhühner (The Merits of Windfowl). Neuwied: Luchterhand, 1956.

Gleisdreieck (Triangle of Tracks). Neuwied: Luchterhand, 1960.

Selected Poems. German text with trans. by Michael Hamburger and Ralph Manheim. New York: Harcourt Brace; London: Secker & Warburg, 1966.

Ausgefragt (Interrogated). Neuwied: Luchterhand, 1967.

New Poems. German text with trans. by Michael Hamburger. New York: Harcourt Brace, 1968.

Gesammelte Gedichte (Collected Poems). Neuwied: Luchterhand, 1971.

Mariazuehren. Munich: Bruckmann, 1973. Trans. Christopher Middleton as *Inmarypraise*. New York: Harcourt Brace, 1974.

Liebe geprüft. Bremen: Schünemann, 1974. Trans. Michael Hamburger as *Love Tested*. New York: Harcourt Brace, 1975.

In the Egg and Other Poems. Trans. Michael Hamburger and Christopher Middleton. New York: Harcourt Brace, 1977.

Plays

Hochwasser (Flood). Frankfurt: Suhrkamp, 1963.

Onkel, Onkel (Mister, Mister). Berlin: Wagenbach, 1965.

Die Plebejer proben den Aufstand. Neuwied: Luchterhand, 1966. Trans. Ralph Manheim as *The Plebeians Rehearse the Uprising*. New York: Harcourt Brace, 1966. London: Secker & Warburg, 1967.

Four Plays: Flood, Mister, Mister, Only Ten Minutes to Buffalo, The Wicked Cooks. Trans. Ralph Manheim and A. Leslie Willson. New York: Harcourt Brace, 1967. London: Secker & Warburg, 1968.

Theaterspiele (Collected Plays). Neuwied: Luchterhand, 1970.

Max: A Play (Davor). Trans. A. Leslie Willson and Ralph Manheim. New York: Harcourt Brace, 1972.

Critical and Political Writings

Speak Out! Speeches, Open Letters, Commentaries. Trans. Ralph Manheim. New York: Harcourt Brace; London: Secker & Warburg, 1969.

On Writing and Politics 1967–1983. Trans. Ralph Manheim. New York: Harcourt Brace, 1985.

Graphic Work

Zeichnen und Schreiben. Bd. I: Zeichnungen und Texte 1954–1977. Ed. Anselm Dreher. Neuwied: Luchterhand, 1982.

Zeichnen und Schreiben. Bd. II: Radierungen und Texte 1972–1982. Ed Anselm Dreher. Neuwied: Luchterhand, 1984.

II. Works About Günter Grass

Cunliffe, W.G. *Günter Grass*. New York: Twayne, 1969.

Hayman, Ronald. *Günter Grass*. London, New York: Methuen, 1985.

Hollington, Michael. *Günter Grass: The Writer in a Pluralist Society*. London: Marion Boyars, 1980.

Lawson, Richard H. *Günter Grass*. New York: Ungar, 1985.

Leonard, Irène. *Günter Grass*. Edinburgh: Oliver & Boyd, 1974.

Mason, Ann L. *The Skeptical Muse: A Study of Günter Grass' Conception of the Artist*. Bern: Lang, 1974.

Mews, Siegfried, ed. *"The Fisherman and His Wife": Günter Grass's 'The Flounder' in Critical Perspective*. New York: AMS Press, 1983.

Miles, Keith. *Günter Grass*. London: Vision; New York: Barnes and Noble, 1975.

Pickar, Gertrud Bauer, ed. *Adventures of a Flounder: Critical Essays on Günter Grass' 'Der Butt'*. Munich: Fink, 1982.

Reddick, John. *The "Danzig Trilogy" of Günter Grass*. London: Secker & Warburg; New York: Harcourt Brace, 1975.

Willson, A. Leslie, ed. *A Günter Grass Symposium*. Austin: University of Texas Press, 1971.

III. Bibliographies

Görtz, Franz Josef. "Kommentierte Auswahl-Bibliographie." *Text + Kritik* (Munich), nos. 1/1a (fifth series, 1978), pp. 175–99.

O'Neill, Patrick. *Günter Grass: A Bibliography, 1955–1975*. Toronto: University of Toronto Press, 1976.

INDEX

229